MW016E1042

THE CERTIFICATION SERIES

Basic Keelboat

The National Standard for Quality Sailing Instruction

Copyright © 2024
Fifth Edition
ISBN 978-1-938915-54-3

The United States Sailing Association

Printed in the United States of America.

Published by the United States Sailing Association
1 Roger Williams University Way, Bristol, RI 02809

www.ussailing.org
www.sailingcertification.com

Acknowledgments

Ray Wichmann Author

At 30 years of age, with six years of college, no degree, and living on the beach in Hawai'i, Ray became a sailor. His first experience was crewing on a sail and snorkel boat in Kona, on the Big Island. This was followed by 10 years as an inter-island charter skipper. When he returned to the mainland, he accepted an instructor position at OCSC Sailing on San Francisco Bay and has been teaching there for 30+ years. He has sailed in Mexico, the Caribbean, and the Mediterranean, on boats ranging from eight to 150 feet, with one, two, and three hulls. He is a US Sailing Master Instructor Trainer, and a member of US Sailing's National Faculty.

Margaret Pommert Co-Author

Seattle-based Margaret Pommert learned to sail as a teenager and became an avid sailboat racer and cruiser. She enjoys co-leading annual flotillas of recreational boats up the Inside Passage from Washington to Alaska. As a US Sailing/US Powerboating instructor, instructor trainer, and member of the National Faculty, she has worked with a wide range of US Sailing schools and students, and enjoys being part of a team teaching new keelboat instructors for the US Naval Academy in Annapolis during the summer. In 2020 Margaret was recognized with the National Women's Sailing Association/Boat U.S. National Leadership in Women's Sailing Award.

Karen Prioleau Contributor

Karen Prioleau directs the Professional Mariners Program at Orange Coast College in Newport Beach, CA. A lifelong sailor and professional captain, she has cruised all over the world, including a four-year voyage through Mexico, French Polynesia, and New Zealand, as well as offshore voyages to Easter Island, Hawai'i, and Alaska. Currently, she is a Master Instructor Trainer for both US Powerboating and US Sailing, and chairs the US Sailing Keelboat National Faculty curriculum committee that develops training materials for US Sailing.

Additional Thanks

This book has been created by our talented team of designers, illustrators, photographers, and writers. Bradley Schoch designed the page layouts. Management of this project was provided by Jessica Yorke. Content and standards overview was performed by Bonnie Braddock, Janel Martin. Photography provided by Peter Lyons Photography, Lexi Pline, and Karen Davidson. Photo shoot location and boats provided by Conanicut Yacht Club. Invaluable input and advice were provided by sailing schools, charter companies, and volunteers, and there are a number of prior contributors to this book who deserve special recognition: Tim Broderick, Timmy Larr, Mark Smith, Monk Henry, Kim Downing, Rob Eckhardt, James Chen, David Norton.

Introduction to US Sailing

Since its founding in 1897, the United States Sailing Association (US Sailing) has provided educational opportunities for sailors at all levels of abilities—in all kinds of sailboats. The primary objective of US Sailing's education programs is to provide a national standard of high quality instruction for all people learning to sail. The US Sailing Keelboat Certification System includes a program of student certifications, a series of books, and an extensive educational and training program for instructors. It is one of the most highly developed and effective national training systems for both students and instructors and is recognized nationally and internationally.

US Sailing is a nonprofit organization and is recognized by the U.S. Congress as the National Governing Body for the sport of Sailing in the Ted Stevens Amateur Sports Act. It has national training programs for sailors in dinghies, multihulls, and keelboats. It is also the official representative of the United States to World Sailing, the International Governing Body for Sailing.

The US Sailing Keelboat Certification System is designed to develop safe, responsible, and confident sailors who meet specific performance and knowledge standards.

The program begins with the Basic Keelboat certification level and progresses through Basic Cruising, Bareboat Cruising, Coastal Navigation, and on to Coastal Passage Making, Celestial Navigation, and Offshore Passage Making.

With your US Sailing certifications and experience documented in the *Official Logbook*, you will have a passport to cruising and chartering boats both locally and nationally. Many graduates go on to confidently charter boats internationally.

Basic Keelboat is intended to give you the foundation in your sailing education. It was created to help you accelerate your learning curve and clarify your understanding of the concepts and techniques of sailing.

What Makes Sailing Special?

Sailing is open to people of all ages, incomes, and abilities. Sailing offers virtually limitless choices of boats, each with its own unique characteristics, and the opportunity to explore a nearby cove or an exotic tropical location.

Most sailors will acquire entry-level skills quite rapidly. Mastering those skills is an experience that will be rewarding, exciting, and pleasurable for a lifetime.

As you continue to sail, you will find that sailing is more than simply being pushed and pulled by the wind. For most people, sailing is meeting new friends, enjoying nature's beauty, challenges, and sharing a unique fellowship with all boaters. A tremendous camaraderie exists among sailors, particularly on the water, which makes sailing—and the people who do it—very special.

Table of CONTENTS

Italicized words and terms in the text are included in the glossary.

Chapter 1

Introduction to Keelboat Sailing

In many endeavors, preparation is a major key to success, and this is certainly true of sailing. Preparation will include choosing what to wear, informing those ashore of your plans, and understanding local wind patterns, currents, and the marine environment you will encounter. Being prepared for the sailing environment and having necessary safety requirements at hand are just the beginning and are essential for your voyage. This introductory chapter will acquaint you with the standard procedures, personal preparation, and safety checklists used by successful sailors. For your first sail, many of these pre-departure items may already be taken care of if the sailor is with an instructor, but ultimately, this responsibility is yours to ensure a safe and enjoyable sailing experience.

THE SAILING ENVIRONMENT

Welcome to the world and lifestyle of keelboat sailing. Each day on the water you will learn a vast amount of knowledge about the mechanics of how the boat moves through the water and how you can control or adjust the movement of the boat. People learn to sail keelboats for many reasons. What brought you here?

EXPLORATION

You will be confident exploring harbors, rivers, lakes, bays, and even oceans in a small keelboat. For the most part as a beginning keelboat sailor, you will be sailing on your local waters. You will be able to see land and even identify some objects on land while you sail. For many sailors, exploring their local home by water can be a completely new perspective. The world looks and feels different when you are on the water.

TYPE OF SAILING AREA

Learning to sail happens all over the United States. Some may be learning to sail on a small inland lake or a nearby large river. Others are taking their first lessons on a much larger body of water like the Great Lakes, a coastal bay, or an ocean. In all instances, as you begin sailing on your home waters, you will learn about local wind patterns, *current*, and the marine environment. Understanding how these factors affect your sailing will make your time on the water safer.

Local Wind Patterns

Currents

Marine Environment

PERSONAL PREPARATION & SAFETY

When planning for your day out on the water, there are a lot of choices to make about your clothing, shoes, and safety equipment for yourself and the sailboat. By preparing all of these aspects prior to leaving the *dock*, you will be able to mitigate emergency situations and enjoy your time on the water.

SKILL EVALUATION

☐ **Prepare** - Wear protective clothing, sunscreen & hat.

☐ **Shoes** - Wear closed-toe shoes.

☐ **Life Jacket** - Wear U.S. Coast Guard approved life jacket properly buckled or zipped and have a whistle attached for safety.

☐ **Emergency** - Outline steps to take in case of an emergency on land or on the water.

WARM-WEATHER DRESSING

To enjoy sailing, you need to be comfortable. Preparation is the key, so put together a sailing *gear* bag with clothing that will protect you and make you feel at ease in all weather conditions. Whether it's cloudy or sunny, protect yourself with sunscreen and a hat. While sailing, you can get sunburned even on a cloudy day. The sun's rays are intensified because they reflect off both the boat and the water.

Sunglasses
cut down the glare from the water and ease eye strain. Attach "keepers" (a cord around your neck) to your sunglasses to keep from losing them overboard.

Synthetic shirt
that is light-colored, will keep you cool and protect your neck and upper arms from sunburn. Consider wearing a rash guard for extra protection.

Watches
tend to take a beating on a boat. Leave a fine timepiece at home and wear an affordable, water-resistant model on the water.

Sailing gloves (with cutaway finger tips) protect your hands from injuries caused by line handling.

Shoes
should be comfortable, with good grip, and have non-marking soles to keep the deck clean. There are sailing specific shoes one can buy that are quick-dry or waterproof, but you can also wear an old pair of sneakers.

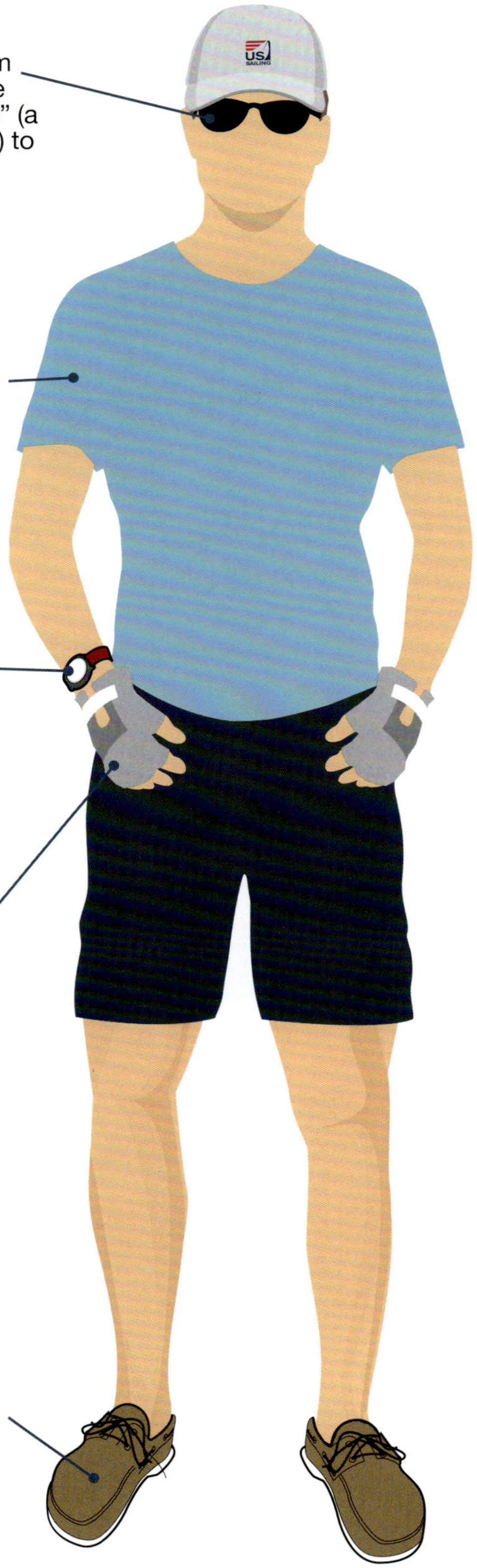

Life jackets are essential.

US Sailing recommends they be worn by each crew member at all times, on the dock, pier or on deck.

COOL-WEATHER DRESSING

Cold, wet weather offers more challenges to staying comfortable. Remember, just because a day is dry and warm in the morning doesn't mean it's going to stay that way. Also, since the air temperature out sailing is influenced by the temperature of the water, conditions can be cooler on the water than on land. Be prepared for a change in the weather by using a layered approach. Wearing long underwear, thermal shirts, and fleece are some examples. Top your base layers with a foul-weather gear jacket and pants. Keeping your hands, feet, and head warm with gloves, thick socks, and a hat is essential for comfort.

Knit ski cap
10% of body heat escapes from the top of the head. A weather-proof hat will help keep you dry. Tie it on so it doesn't get lost overboard. The combination of a knit ski cap under the hood of your foul-weather jacket will keep you both warm and dry.

Nylon-fleece jacket
with a tall collar will keep you warm and protect your neck from wind and spray. When worn over a turtleneck and sweater, you will be warm enough for most sailing situations.

Full-fingered sailing gloves
make it easier to hold onto *lines* (ropes) and *tiller* on a chilly day.

Loose-fitting long pants
over long underwear is usually enough to keep most people's legs warm. If you're still cold, you can wear your foul-weather gear pants on top. Loose pants also allow easier movement.

The protection provided by the foul-weather gear keeps sailing pleasurable even in wet conditions. Two-piece *foul-weather gear* (pants and a jacket) is more versatile than a one-piece jump-suit. There are often weather conditions in which you will want to wear only the jacket or only the pants.

In selecting colder-weather gear to layer, make sure it:
▶ Fits comfortably with enough room for movement and for extra clothes underneath
▶ Has flaps covering zippers and pockets
▶ Has Velcro or elastic closures at the ankles and wrists
▶ Has abundant pockets
▶ Has a hood

4

LIFE JACKETS

Selecting the appropriate *life jacket* requires careful consideration and adherence to certain requirements. It is essential to have a U.S. Coast Guard approved "*wearable*" life jacket on board for every individual on the boat. New life jackets might display a "*performance level icon*" on the inside label, indicating approval for use in both the U.S. and Canada. However, life jackets with the old labeling (**Type I, Type II, Type III, Type V**) remain approved.

When choosing the right life jacket, it should be worn consistently, fit properly with all straps and fasteners secured, and be appropriate for the water activity. Factors such as *buoyancy* level, indicated by a numeric measurement in newtons, is crucial in determining the life jacket's suitability. A lower numeric value provides more mobility and comfort for near shore activities, while higher values offer increased flotation and *stability* for *offshore* use, which allows more time for rescue.

Understanding your swimming ability is important, as weaker swimmers might require a higher level life jacket to stay upright and treading water. The typical novice basic keelboat sailor is recommended to wear a 70 N or Type III life jacket.

When selecting a wearable life jacket, consider an inflatable (Type V) on the left or inherently buoyant with built-in flotation (Type III) in the middle. And don't forget, your boat should always have a throwable device (Type IV) on the right.

New Life Jacket Label

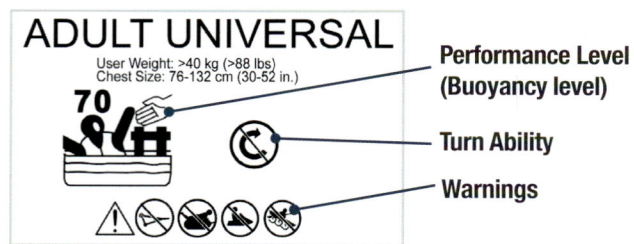

- Performance Level (Buoyancy level)
- Turn Ability
- Warnings

USCG Approved 160.064/XXXX/X
TC Approved XXXXXXX-X
ANSI/CAN/UL 12402-5

Model: XXXX   Style: XXXX
Lot No. XXXX

Certifying Lab Identification

USCG Approved Look for the USCG approval information.

Approval conditions state that this device must be worn to be counted as equipment required by vessels meeting Transport Canada or USCG regulations.

Performance Level

NEAR SHORE (CALM)   **OFFSHORE (WAVES)**

INCREASING TIME TO RESCUE

Warnings

 Water skiing

 Tubing

 Personal watercraft or wakeboarding

 White water paddling

Turn Ability

 Life jacket **will** turn an unconscious wearer face up—test before use.

 Life jacket will **not** turn an unconscious wearer face up.

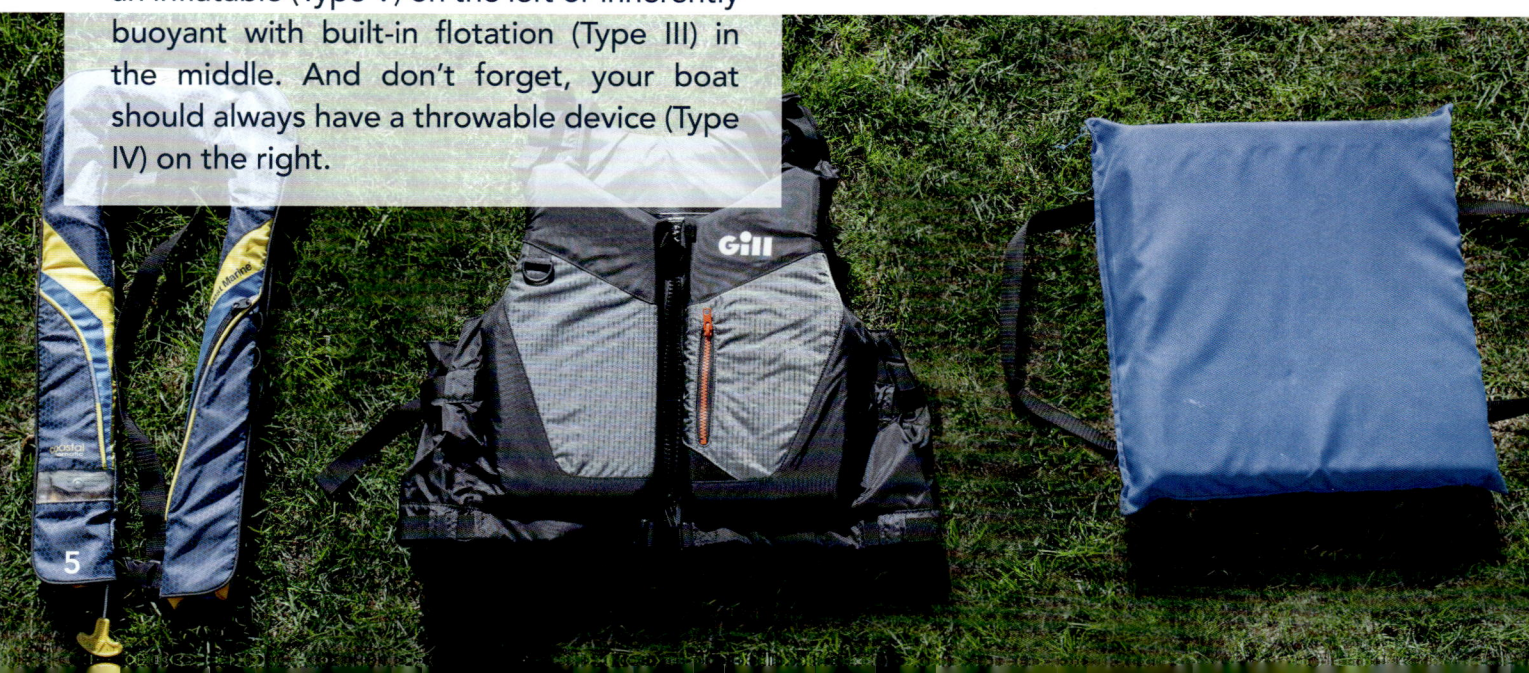

CHECKING YOUR LIFE JACKET

As a sailor, one of your primary responsibilities is safety. First, check that your personal life jacket is U.S. Coast Guard approved, fits properly, and is buckled or zipped.

Some tips from the National Safe Boating Council when conducting a life jacket check:

- ☐ Check the manufacturer's ratings for your size and weight.
- ☐ Make sure the life jacket is properly zipped and/or buckled.
- ☐ Check for fit by raising your arms above your head while wearing the life jacket and ask a friend to grasp the tops of the arm openings and gently pull up.
- ☐ Ensure your life jacket fits properly with no excess room above the openings and the life jacket does not ride up over your chin or face.
- ☐ Life jackets that are too big will cause the flotation device to push up around your face, which could be dangerous.
- ☐ Life jackets that are too small may not be able to keep you afloat.

SAFETY EQUIPMENT

There are a number of safety requirements specified by the U.S. Coast Guard for sailors operating boats on lakes, rivers, and the open ocean. Specific safety equipment information can be found by referencing the "Federal Requirements for Recreational Boating" - www.uscgboating.org

The U.S. Coast Guard requires recreational boats to carry safety equipment. This equipment list is a minimum and should be augmented by the boat owner. Recreational boats are bound by both federal, state, and municipal requirements. Any boating accidents must be reported to the nearest state authority per the federal requirements.

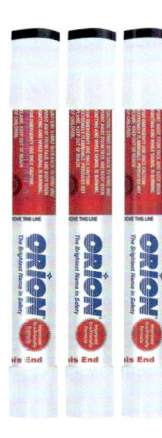

Safety Checklist

- ▶ All boats **must be registered in the state** of principal use and have a Certificate Number. This number must be displayed per state requirements. Any change in ownership, address, or boat status must be registered with the state within 15 days.
- ▶ **The USCG or any law enforcement officials may board the vessel when it is underway** and may terminate use of the vessel for negligent operation or violation of federal regulations.
- ▶ A USCG approved **fire extinguisher must be carried aboard all auxiliary powered vessels** (including sailboats with motors). Boats less than 26 feet must have one Type B-1.
- ▶ All vessels **must carry an efficient sound-producing device.**

- ▶ **USCG approved life jackets** are **required for each person** aboard the vessel **and one Type IV (throwable)** for vessels larger than 16 feet in length.
- ▶ USCG approved **visual distress signals must be carried aboard** vessels except: boats less than 16 feet in length, boats in organized events such as regattas, open sailboats less than 26 feet in length without auxiliary power, and manually propelled boats.
- ▶ Vessels operating or anchored between sunset and sunrise are required to display navigation lights.

A well-equipped first aid kit is a necessity on any boat.

Recommended Safety Equipment

▶ A VHF radio (for emergencies use Channel 16)
▶ *Navigation chart/* (printed or mobile app) and magnetic compass
▶ A manual bailing device such as a bucket or bilge pump
▶ An anchor and anchor line (*rode*)
▶ A tool kit, spare parts, and through-hull plugs
▶ Additional means of propulsion such as oars, paddle, or *auxiliary power*
▶ A basic first aid kit with instructions

PRE-SAIL CHECKLIST

When you arrive at the sailboat to go sailing for the day, spend a few minutes going through the boat. This is a good routine to develop. Take note of anything missing or damaged before loading the boat and heading out. At first, your instructor will do most of this, but throughout your course, everyone should get in the practice of checking out the boat and completing the pre-sail checklist. It helps to mitigate risk of equipment failure and will create a safer environment for the crew.

☐ **Safety Check** - Make sure you and all crew aboard are wearing properly fitting U.S.C.G. approved life jackets.

☐ **Boat Inspection** - Confirm safety equipment is aboard and current.

☐ **Rig Inspection** - Check that all sail controls, lines, and *rigging* are operational.

Example Pre-Sail Checklist:

☐ Weather forecast for duration
☐ Wind speed _____
☐ Wind direction _____
☐ Tide _____
☐ Identify shallow areas or other hazards on navigational charts
☐ Properly fitted life jackets for each person on board
☐ Boat inspection
☐ Rig inspection
☐ Lines ready for use
☐ Bilge check
☐ Battery status check
☐ Engine check
☐ Fuel status
☐ VHF radio charges and on Channel 16 for emergency notifications
☐ Sunscreen, sailing gloves, and other protective gear for the weather conditions
☐ Personal items stowed and hatches closed
☐ Float plan (see chapter 8)

PUTTING IT ALL TOGETHER

SUMMARY

- Your sailing environment and the sailing area you will encounter are important to understand before your sail. Understanding how local wind patterns, currents, and the marine environment affect your sailing experience will make your time on the water safer and more enjoyable.
- Protective clothing for hot or cool weather, hats, sunscreen, and proper shoes should be planned for before your trip.
- Safety equipment and a float plan should be in place before leaving the dock to mitigate emergency situations.

- U.S. Coast Guard approved "wearable" life jackets are essential and recommended to be worn by each crew member on dock, pier or on deck. When choosing a life jacket, swimming ability is important as weaker swimmers may require a higher-level life jacket. Check that your personal life jacket fits properly and is buckled or zipped.
- Be sure to perform your pre-sail checklist that includes a safety check, basic visual of the sailboat and a rig inspection.

KEY TERMS AND CONCEPTS

1. Understand the factors such as wind, current, and the marine environment that can affect your sailing safety and enjoyment.
2. The protection provided by protective **foul-weather** gear keeps sailing pleasurable even in wet conditions. You should wear a base layer underneath your foul-weather gear.
3. Newer life jackets may display a **"Performance level icon"** to indicate approval for use in both the US and Canada. Life jackets with the old labeling (Type I, Type II, Type III, Type V) also remain approved.
4. Create a **pre-sail checklist** to mitigate risk and create a safer sail.

CHECK YOUR UNDERSTANDING

1. When selecting gear for cool weather dressing, which of the following are suggested?

   ○ a. Wearing a one-piece tight-fitting jumpsuit
   ○ b. Jackets without a hood or pockets
   ○ c. Layered gear that allows room for movement
   ○ d. A large, billed hat

2. Which of the following statements is accurate regarding life jacket selection and use?

   ○ a. A life jacket should be worn at all times and fit properly
   ○ b. Any type of life jacket is acceptable for sailing
   ○ c. A life jacket should be able to ride up over your face
   ○ d. It should fit loosely, and under your clothing.

Chapter 2

Sailing Concepts & Terminology

Entering the nautical world is a very exciting endeavor. However, it can be a bit overwhelming at the same time. Not only are there entirely new concepts and ideas to absorb with new physical skills to master, but there is also a new language to learn. "Do sailors really talk like this?" The answer is yes, they do; and soon you will too! This chapter of sailing concepts and terminology will help you to become familiar with determining wind direction and understanding how a sail works. You will also learn a variety of nautical terminology and be able to identify the parts of a sailboat, *rig,* and sails along with being introduced to some key sailing concepts.

UNDERSTANDING WIND

Being able to understand wind, how it moves, its velocity, and patterns will help you harness the wind to move your boat forward. There are many indicators, both on land and water, that you can use to determine the velocity and direction the wind is coming from.

SKILL EVALUATION

☐ **Direction** - Identify the direction the wind is coming from.

☐ **Land Indicators** - Identify two wind indicators on land.

☐ **Water Indicators** - Identify two wind indicators on water.

WIND DIRECTION

Wind direction is described by the direction from which it comes. A *Westerly wind* is one that comes out of the west and blows toward the east. The wind on this compass rose is coming from a direction between north and west. It would be called a *Northwest wind* (or a *Northwester*).

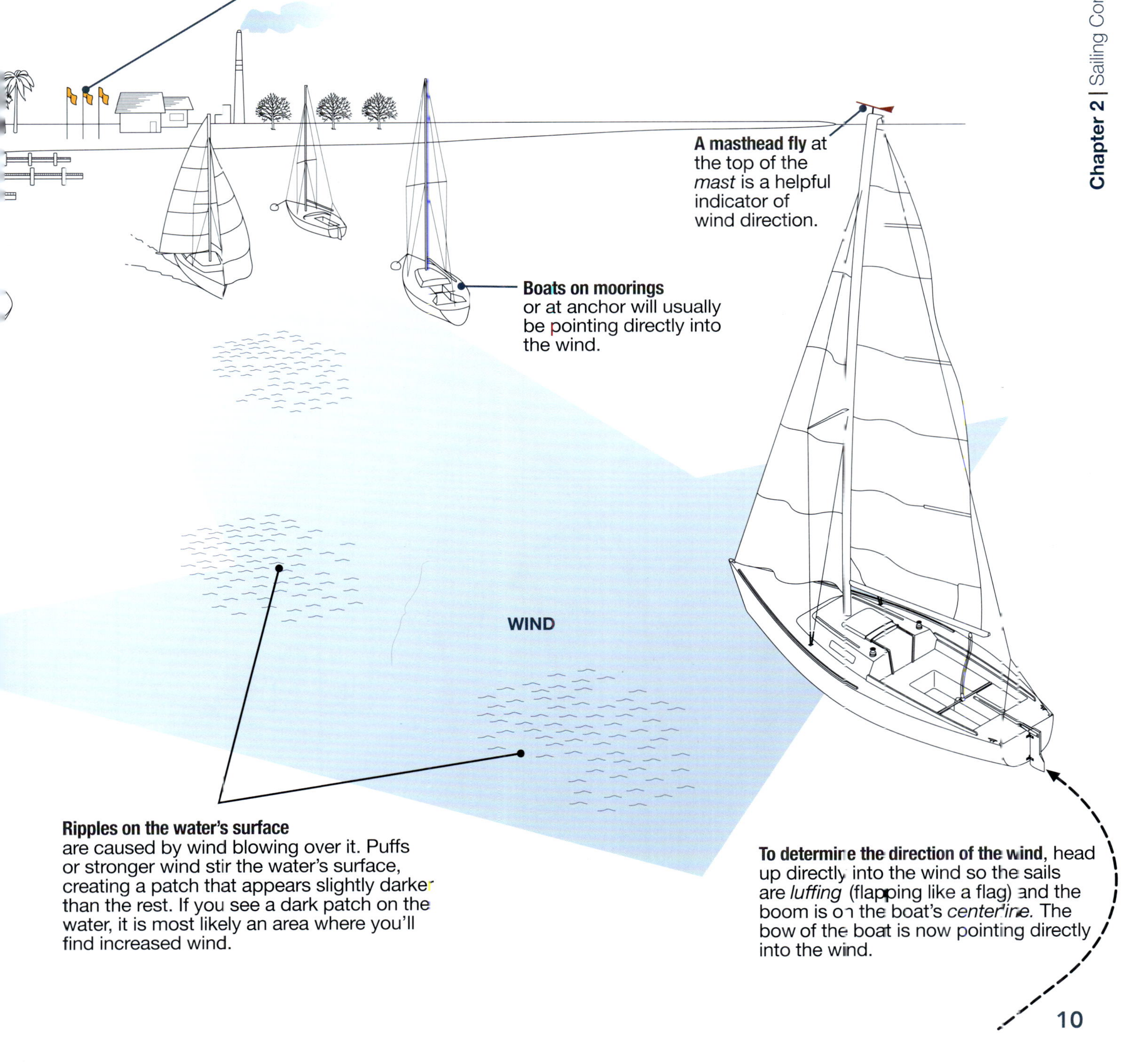

Look onshore for other wind indicators that may help. A flag or smoke from a stack are indicators of wind direction.

A masthead fly at the top of the *mast* is a helpful indicator of wind direction.

Boats on moorings or at anchor will usually be pointing directly into the wind.

WIND

Ripples on the water's surface are caused by wind blowing over it. Puffs or stronger wind stir the water's surface, creating a patch that appears slightly darker than the rest. If you see a dark patch on the water, it is most likely an area where you'll find increased wind.

To determine the direction of the wind, head up directly into the wind so the sails are *luffing* (flapping like a flag) and the boom is on the boat's *centerline*. The bow of the boat is now pointing directly into the wind.

HOW A SAIL WORKS

Sails are a sailboat's "engine", and they produce power in one of two ways. When the wind is coming from the side of the sailboat, it flows around both sides of the sail (like an airplane wing), creating *lift* which "pulls" the sailboat forward. When the wind is coming from behind the sailboat, it "pushes" against the sail and moves the sailboat forward.

PULL MODE

Your sail is much more efficient at using the wind than your hand. It is shaped to bend the wind as it flows by, creating higher pressure on the inside of the sail ➕ and lower pressure on the outside ➖, thus creating lift. The lift the sail creates tries to "pull" the sailboat forward and sideways. The sailboat's underwater surfaces (*hull, rudder,* and *keel*) resist sideways motion, and the sailboat moves forward through the water.

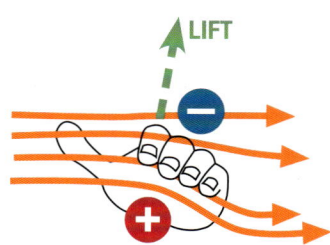

If you hold your hand out the window of a moving car, you can feel the force of the wind lifting your hand. This is the same force that "pulls" a sailboat forward when the wind comes over the side of the boat.

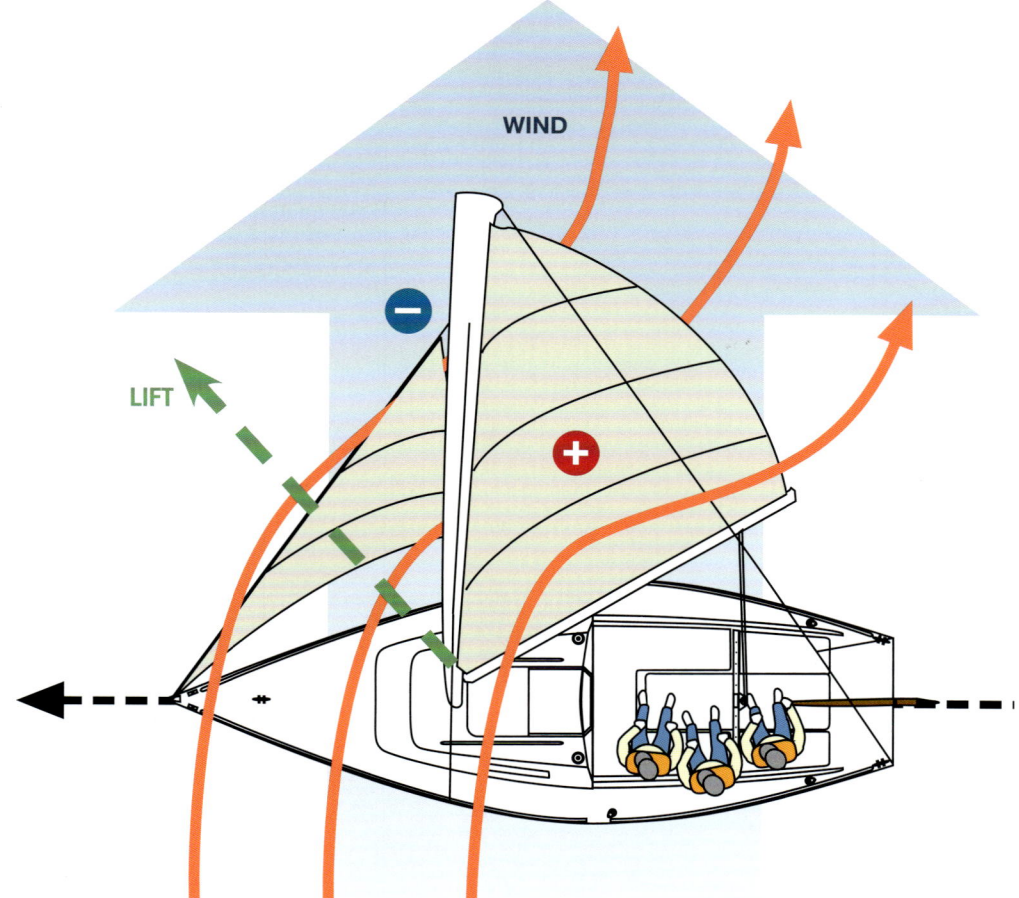

PUSH MODE

With the wind coming from behind, the sail (and boat) are simply pushed forward through the water.

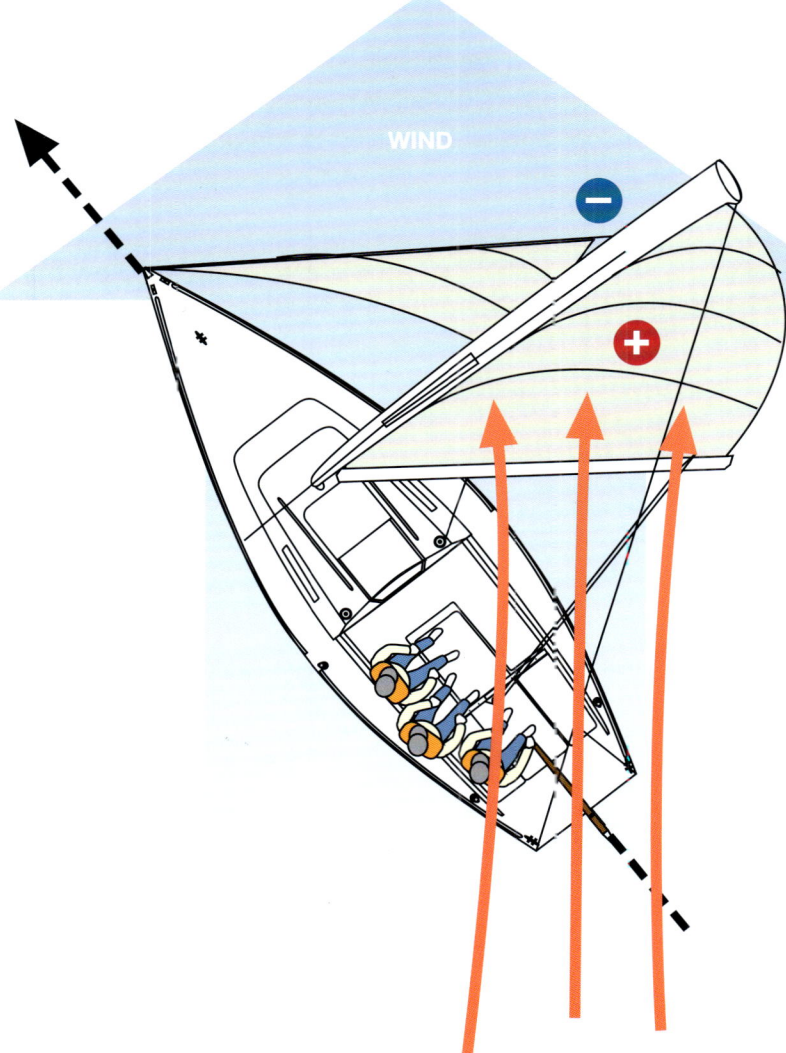

If you hold your hand out the window of a moving car with your palm facing the wind, you can feel the wind "push" your hand back. This is how a sail works when the wind is coming from behind.

NO-SAIL (NO-GO)

A sailboat cannot sail directly into the wind. You can try it, but your sails will only be luffing (flapping) and you'll be stopped in the water... or even start moving backward. Because there is no difference in wind pressure between one side of the sail and the other, the sail cannot generate "push" or "pull." No push...no pull...NO-SAIL (NO-GO)!

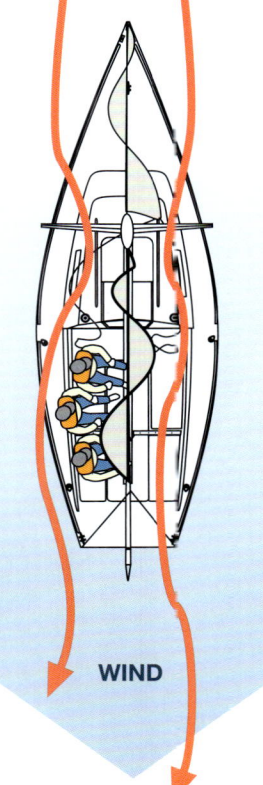

POINTS OF SAIL

Points of sail refer to specific angles of the sailboat in relation to the wind, encompassing various sailing directions such as *close-hauled*, *beam reach*, *broad reach*, and *run*. These points of sail dictate the positioning of the sails and the boat's maneuverability. Knowing your point of sail will help you in harnessing the wind efficiently for optimal boat speed.

Close-hauled (sailing as close to the wind as possible), beam reach (sailing at 90° to the wind direction), and running (sailing directly *downwind*) are quite specific points of sail. When sailing in the area between close-hauled and a beam reach, you are *close reaching,* and when sailing in the area between a beam reach and a run, you are broad reaching.

NOTE: For both diagrams, understanding the relation between the wind and the sails in the "No-Sail (No-Go) Zone" is crucial. Orient yourself to the sailboat within this zone and then explore how the wind interacts with the sails as you move around the circle, observing the variations in sail positions and wind angles at each point of sail.

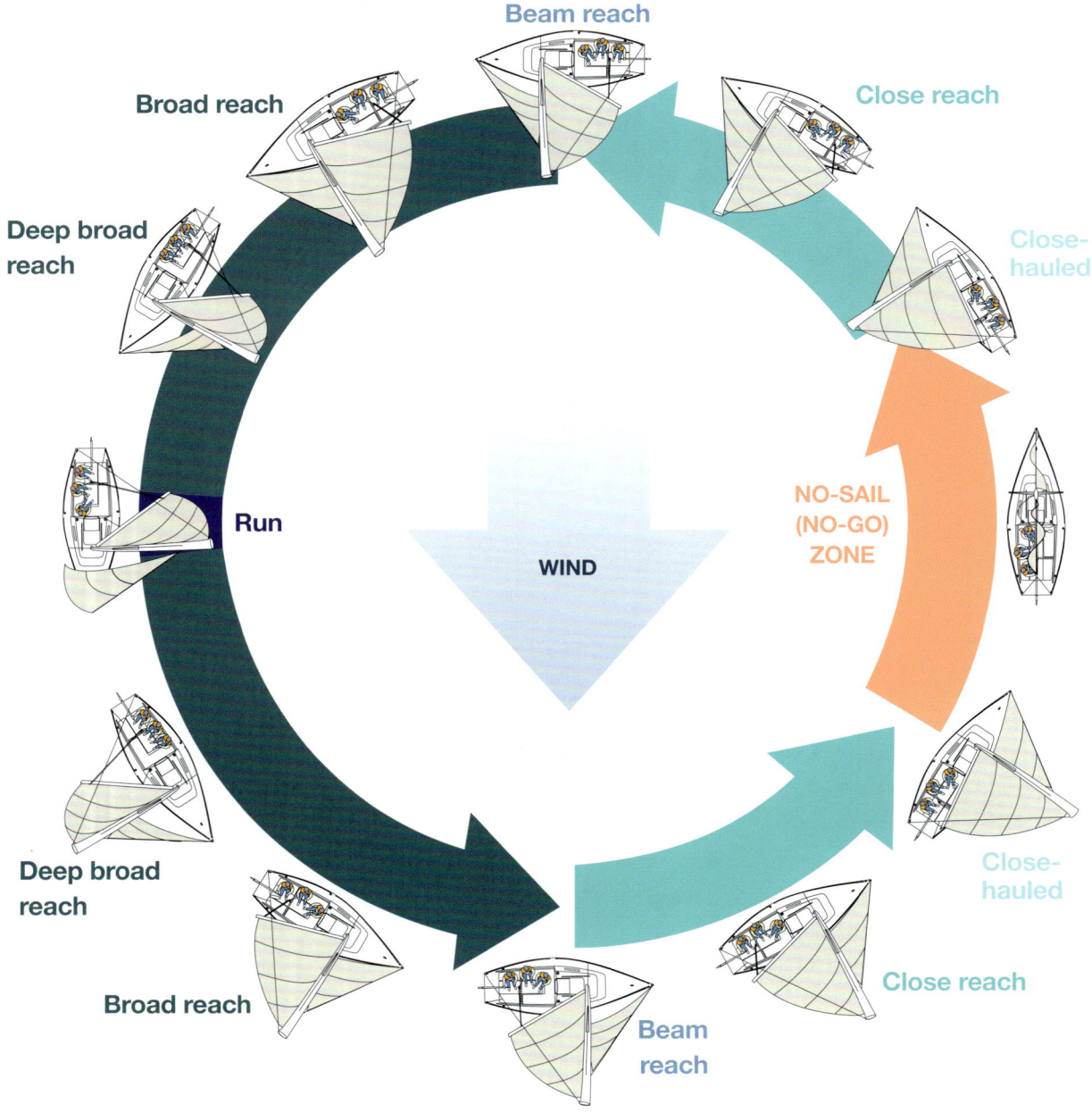

WHICH TACK ARE YOU ON?

When sailing you are on a course; this course is either on *port tack* or *starboard tack*. To figure out what *tack* you are sailing on look at the *mainsail*. The tack you are on will be the opposite of the postion of the mainsail. Usually your tack will be the same side of the sailboat the wind is coming over.

However, when running, the wind is coming over the *stern* of the sailboat, and your tack is still designated as the side opposite of the mainsail. The tack you are on is important in determining your rights and responsibilities under the International *Navigation Rules* (COLREGS).

SKILL EVALUATION

☐ **Points of Sail** - Identify the basic points of sail
  ▶ No Sail (No-Go) Zone
  ▶ Close-hauled
  ▶ Close reach
  ▶ Beam reach
  ▶ Broad reach
  ▶ Downwind (Run)

☐ **Demonstrate** - Adjust your *course* and sail *trim* to demonstrate the basic points of sail.

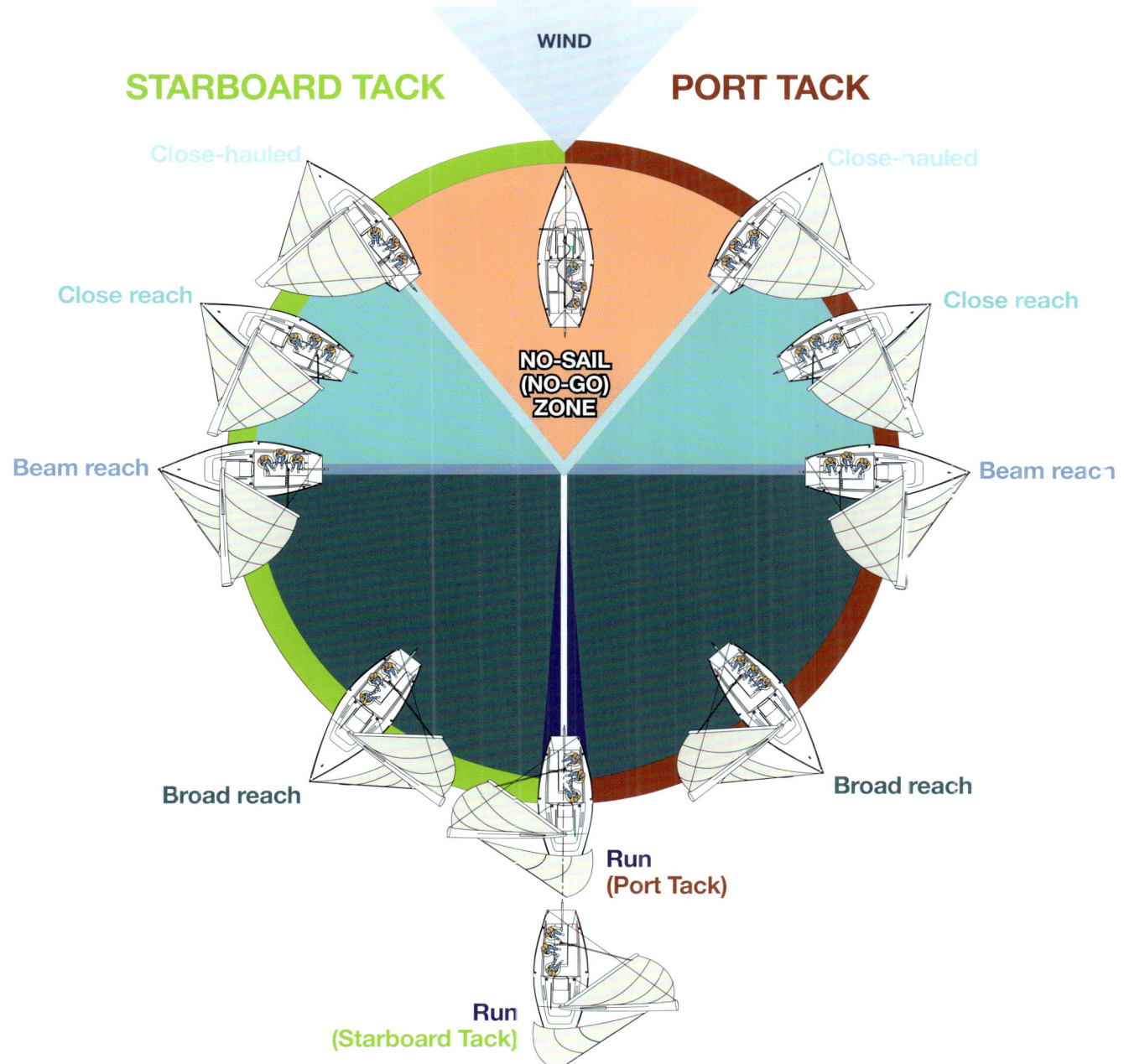

WIND

STARBOARD TACK   **PORT TACK**

Close-hauled   Close-hauled

NO-SAIL (NO-GO) ZONE

Close reach   Close reach

Beam reach   Beam reach

Broad reach   Broad reach

Run (Port Tack)

Run (Starboard Tack)

PARTS OF THE SAILBOAT

Let's begin by learning some of the important parts on a sailboat and their names. Knowing some of these sailing terms will allow you to communicate better when on board the sailboat. Here's a quick overview.

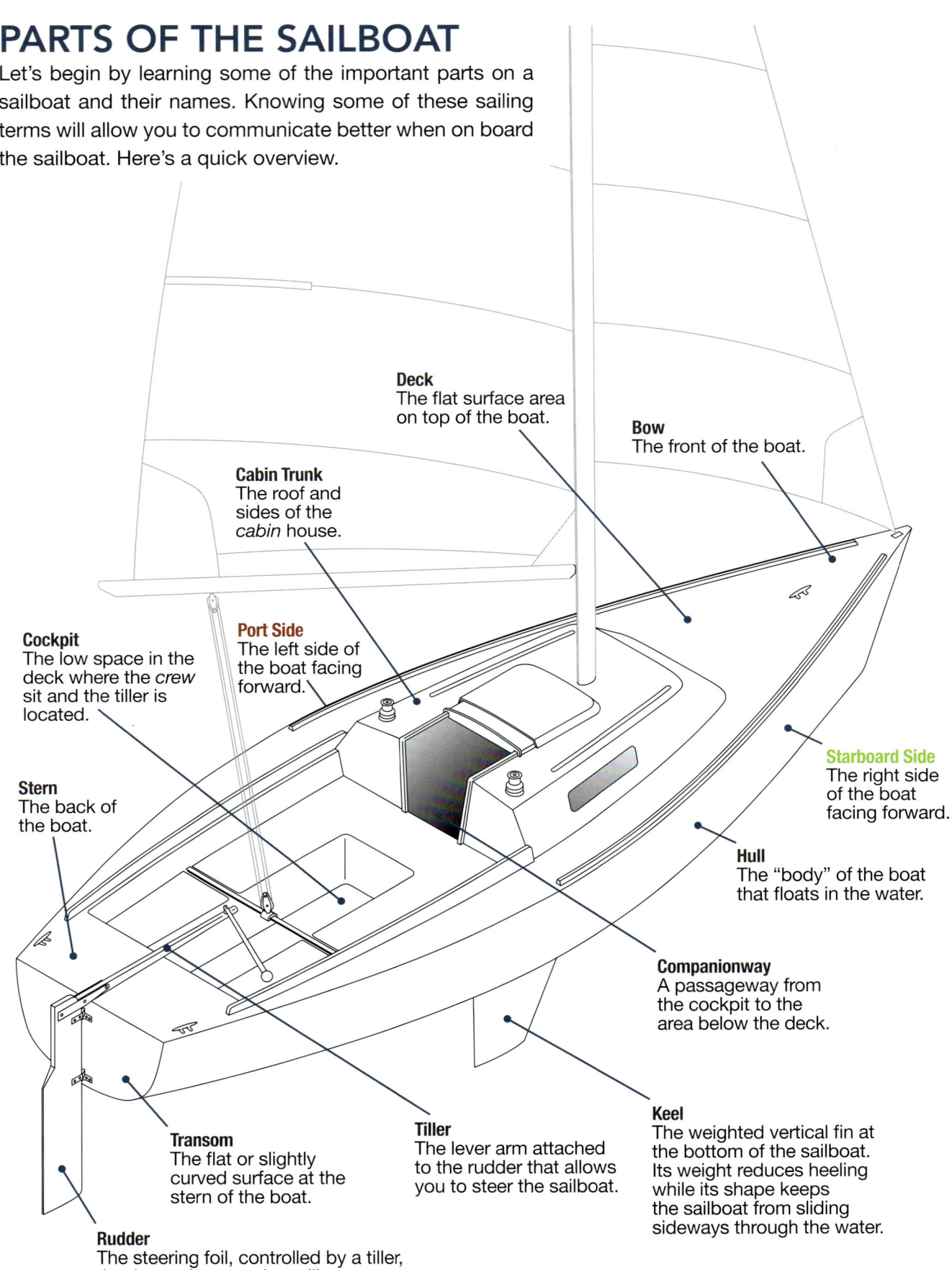

Deck
The flat surface area on top of the boat.

Bow
The front of the boat.

Cabin Trunk
The roof and sides of the *cabin* house.

Cockpit
The low space in the deck where the *crew* sit and the tiller is located.

Port Side
The left side of the boat facing forward.

Starboard Side
The right side of the boat facing forward.

Stern
The back of the boat.

Hull
The "body" of the boat that floats in the water.

Companionway
A passageway from the cockpit to the area below the deck.

Transom
The flat or slightly curved surface at the stern of the boat.

Tiller
The lever arm attached to the rudder that allows you to steer the sailboat.

Keel
The weighted vertical fin at the bottom of the sailboat. Its weight reduces heeling while its shape keeps the sailboat from sliding sideways through the water.

Rudder
The steering foil, controlled by a tiller, that is used to turn the sailboat.

PARTS OF THE RIG

The rig includes sails (mainsail and jib), spars (mast and boom), standing rigging (supporting wires).

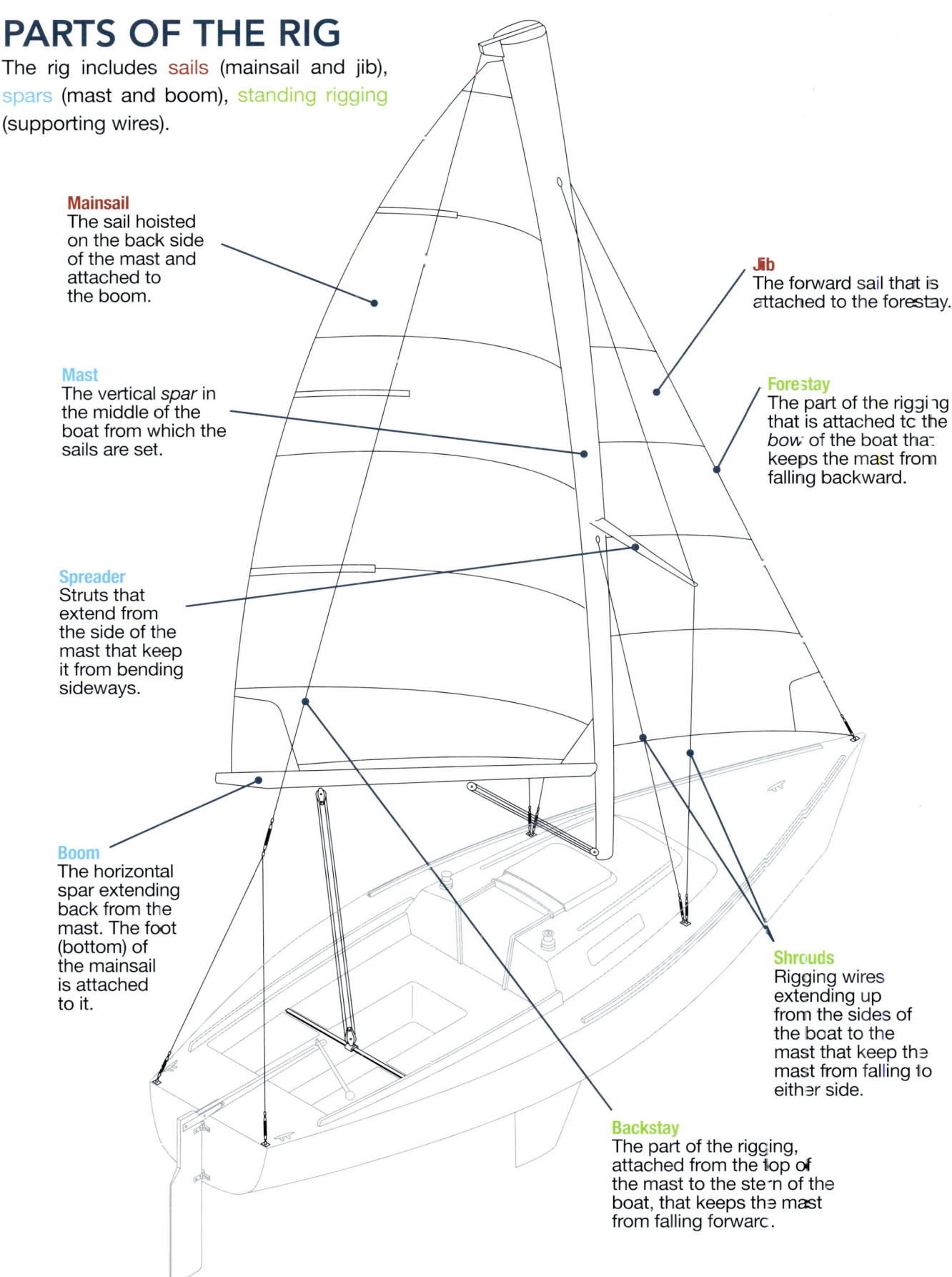

Mainsail
The sail hoisted on the back side of the mast and attached to the boom.

Mast
The vertical *spar* in the middle of the boat from which the sails are set.

Spreader
Struts that extend from the side of the mast that keep it from bending sideways.

Boom
The horizontal spar extending back from the mast. The foot (bottom) of the mainsail is attached to it.

Jib
The forward sail that is attached to the forestay.

Forestay
The part of the rigging that is attached to the *bow* of the boat that keeps the mast from falling backward.

Shrouds
Rigging wires extending up from the sides of the boat to the mast that keep the mast from falling to either side.

Backstay
The part of the rigging, attached from the top of the mast to the stern of the boat, that keeps the mast from falling forward.

PARTS OF A SAIL

Most sails have three corners and three edges. These all have specific names. Sails are raised by a line called a halyard attached to the head (top corner).

Edges of a Sail

▶ The forward edge of a sail is called the **luff**. On the jib the *luff* is attached to the forestay. The *luff* of the mainsail is attached to the mast.

▶ The aft (back) edge of each of the sails is called the **leech**. It is not attached to the rig, but has battens installed for support.

▶ The bottom edge of a sail is called the **foot**. The foot of a mainsail is attached to the *boom*, while the *foot* of a jib is unattached.

Telltales
Pieces of cloth, yarn, or tape that indicate wind flow over a sail.

Batten
A slat of fiberglass, plastic, or wood inserted into a pocket in the sail to help it hold its shape.

Halyards

Halyards are used to raise and lower the sails, and are often led inside the mast.

▶ The **jib halyard** runs over an internal *sheave* (pulley) in the front of the mast.

▶ The **main halyard** runs over the *sheave* on the back side of the top of the mast.

Corners of a Sail

▶ The top corner of each of the sails is called the *head*, and is where the **halyard** is attached when rigging.

▶ Both jib and mainsail are attached to the rig at their lower *forward* corners. This corner of the sail is called the **tack**.

▶ The lower back corner of each sail is called the **clew**.

Telltales
Pieces of cloth, yarn, or tape that indicate wind flow over a sail.

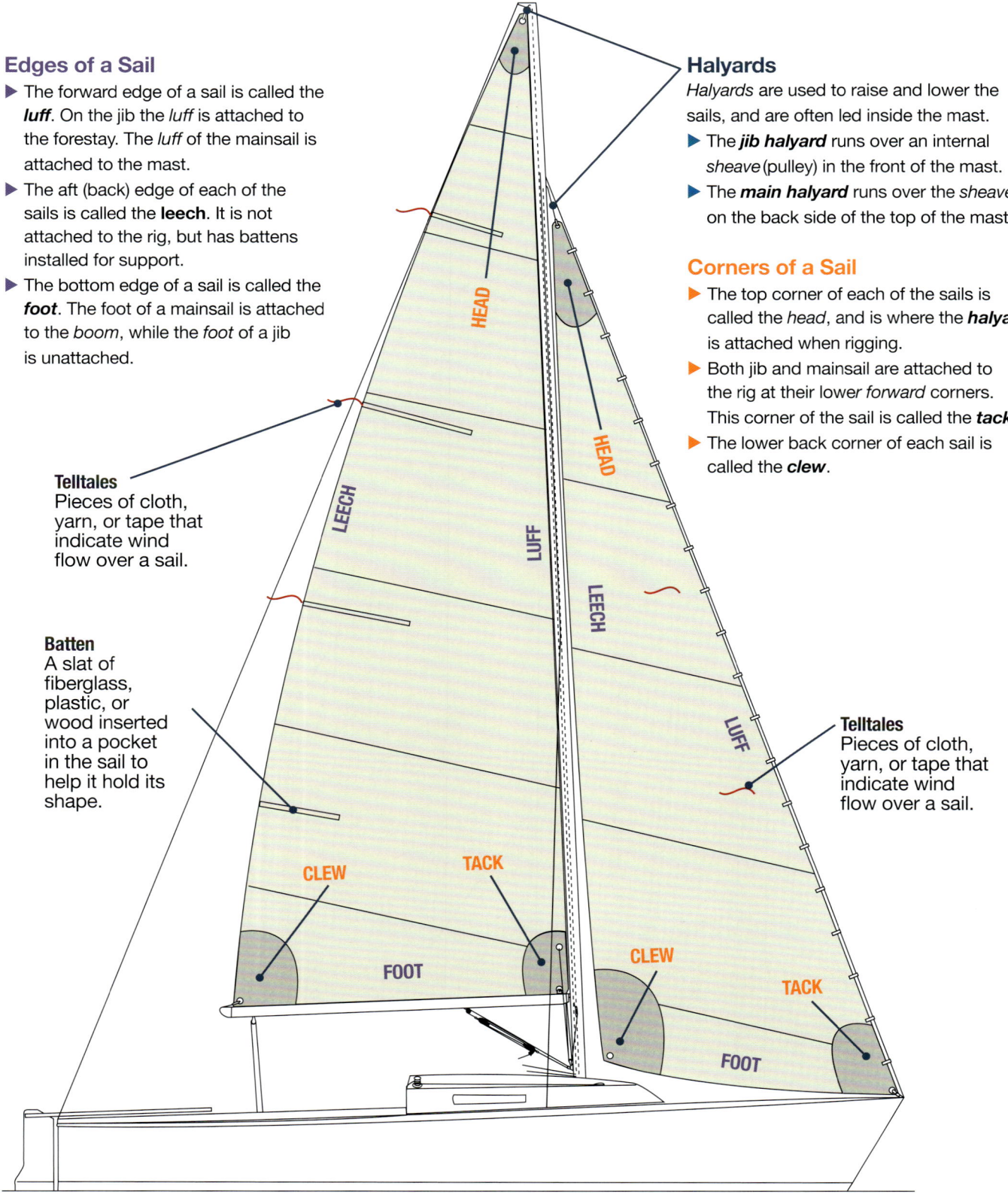

HEAD
HEAD
LEECH
LUFF
LEECH
LUFF
CLEW
TACK
FOOT
CLEW
TACK
FOOT

ATTACHING THE MAIN

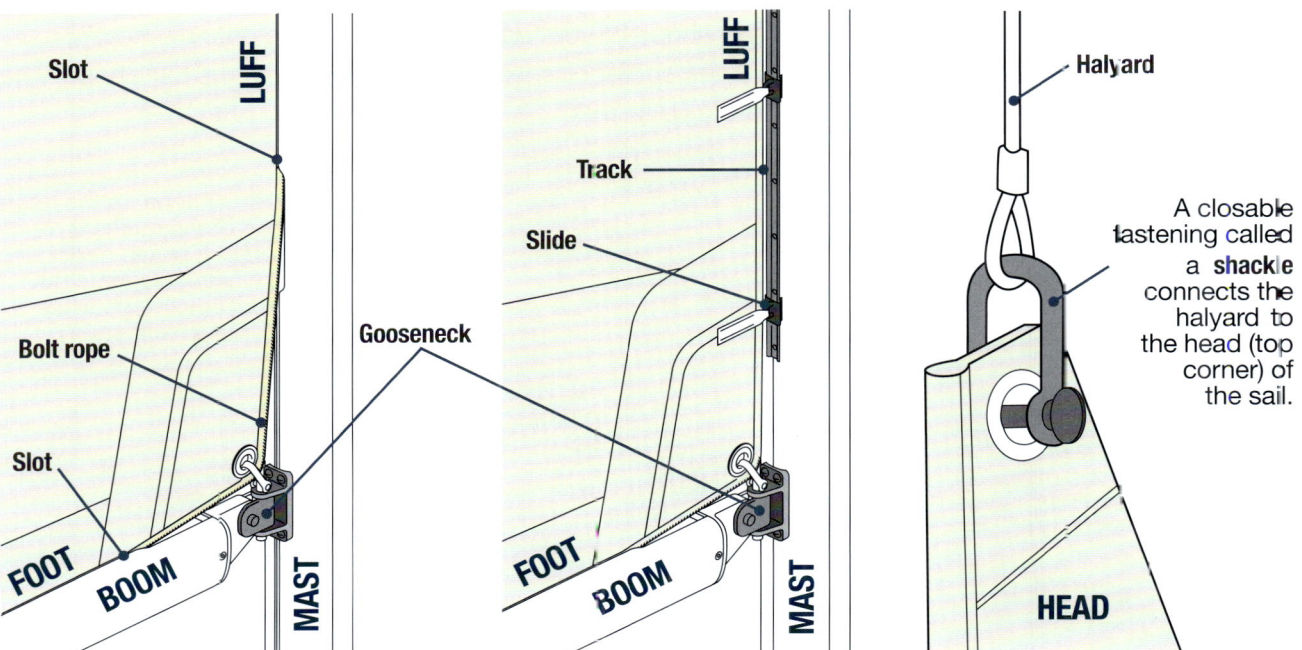

Slot
LUFF
Bolt rope
Slot
FOOT
BOOM
MAST
Gooseneck

Track
LUFF
Slide
FOOT
BOOM
MAST
Gooseneck

Halyard

A closable fastening called a **shackle** connects the halyard to the head (top corner) of the sail.

HEAD

GOOSENECK

Gooseneck is a fitting capable of pivoting in all directions that is used to connect the boom to the mast. This is where the *tack* of the mainsail is usually attached. The *luff* and *foot* of the mainsail are attached to the mast and boom by either a **slot** (left) or a **track** (mast on right). The sail is made with either a *bolt rope* or *plastic slugs* that fit into the slot, or metal fittings that slide on a track.

ATTACHING THE JIB

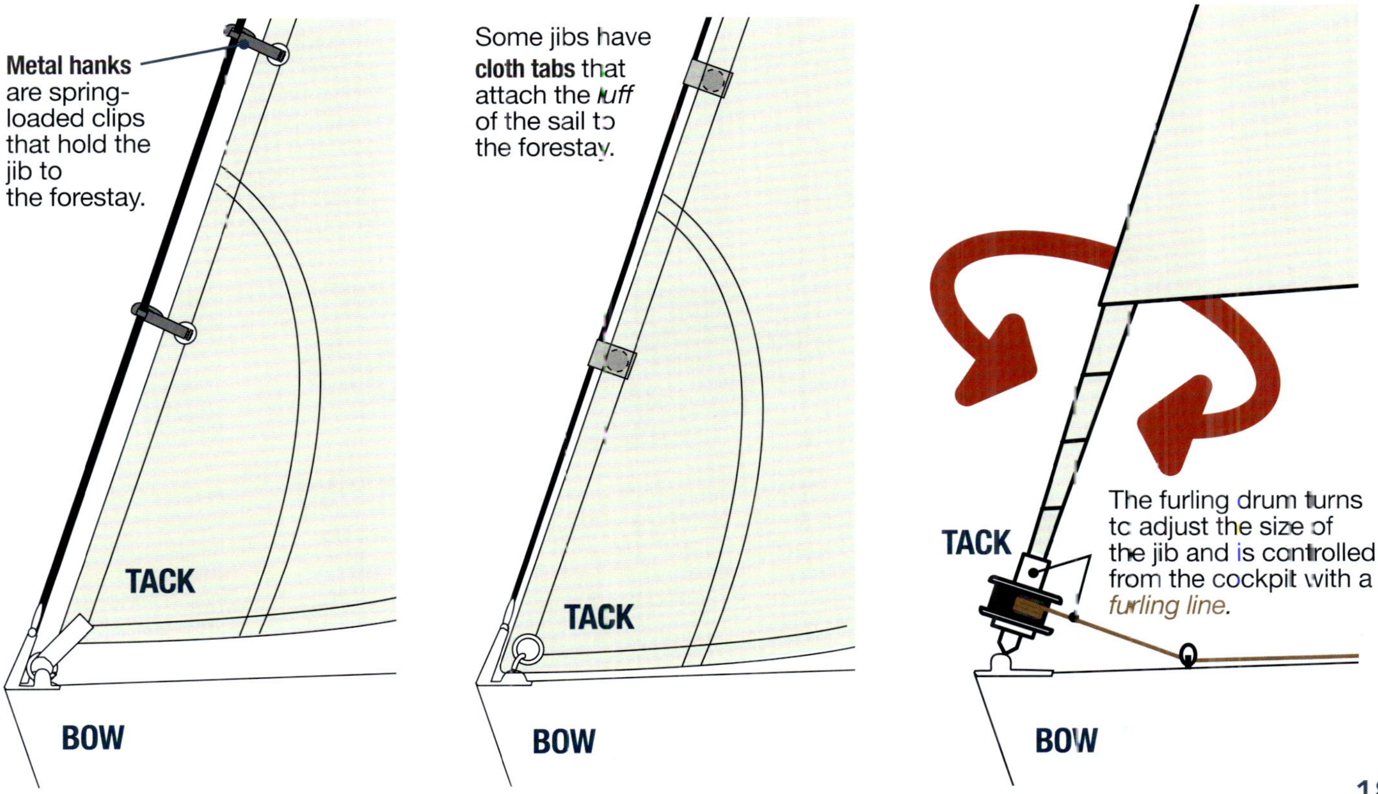

Metal hanks are spring-loaded clips that hold the jib to the forestay.

TACK

BOW

Some jibs have **cloth tabs** that attach the *luff* of the sail to the forestay.

TACK

BOW

TACK

The furling drum turns to adjust the size of the jib and is controlled from the cockpit with a *furling line*.

BOW

18

SAIL ADJUSTMENTS WITH CONTROL LINES

When sailing, you need to adjust the position and shape of your sails in response to a change in wind conditions or point of sail. Various sail controls (lines and equipment) are used to adjust the sail shape. The two primary sail controls are the *mainsheet* and the jib sheets.

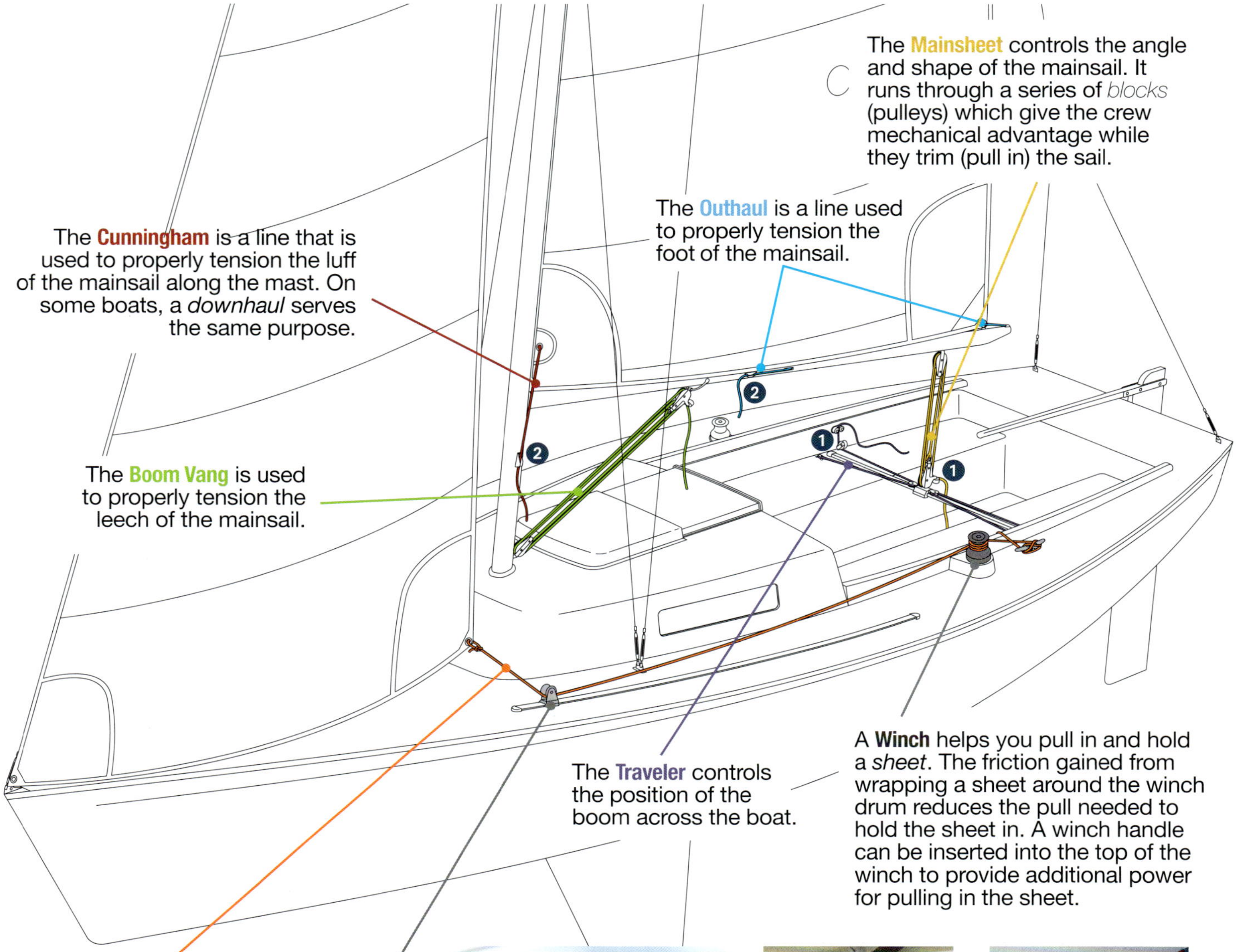

The **Mainsheet** controls the angle and shape of the mainsail. It runs through a series of *blocks* (pulleys) which give the crew mechanical advantage while they trim (pull in) the sail.

The **Outhaul** is a line used to properly tension the foot of the mainsail.

The **Cunningham** is a line that is used to properly tension the luff of the mainsail along the mast. On some boats, a *downhaul* serves the same purpose.

The **Boom Vang** is used to properly tension the leech of the mainsail.

The **Traveler** controls the position of the boom across the boat.

A **Winch** helps you pull in and hold a *sheet*. The friction gained from wrapping a sheet around the winch drum reduces the pull needed to hold the sheet in. A winch handle can be inserted into the top of the winch to provide additional power for pulling in the sheet.

Jib sheets control the jib. They run from the clew of the jib, back to the cockpit and are *trimmed* (pulled in) or *eased* (let out) to change the shape and position of the jib.

Jib sheets run through **Fairleads**. These *blocks* are usually attached to an adjustable track on the deck or to a rail on the side of the deck. The jib *fairlead* is moved forward and backward on the track to accommodate different sized jibs and trimming angles.

A **Clutch Cleat,** also known as a rope clutch, is used to hold the line in place. It can be opened to release the line or closed to lock it in place.

A **Cam Cleat ❶** has jaws with "teeth" that are spring loaded so they press and grip a line snugly. To release the line, pull and lift. Cam cleats can be difficult to release under heavy load.

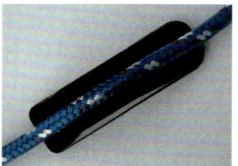

A **Clam Cleat ❷** is very easy to use... simply pull the line through it and let go. To release the line, pull and lift it out. This can be a difficult task under heavy load.

PUTTING IT ALL TOGETHER

SUMMARY

- Harnessing the wind is essential to move your sailboat. Using wind indicators on land and water will help you to determine wind direction.
- Sails harness power from the wind. In "pul mode", lift is created, pulling the sailboat forward. In the "push mode", the wind comes from behind you and pushes the sailboat forward.
- The 5 points of sail are: close-hauled, close reach, beam reach, broad reach, run. Knowing them will help you adjust your sails and steer.
- When the wind is coming over the bow of the sailboat, you are in the No Sail (No-Go) Zone.

- The tack you are on, starboard or port, determines your rights and responsibilities when boats meet.
- Understanding the names of the parts of the sailboat, the rig, and the sails will allow you to clearly communicate with your crew.
- Sail adjustments are crucial for changing wind conditions. This involves adjusting sail control lines to optimize the sail shape and trim.
- The mainsheet and jib sheets are the primary controls for sail trim.

KEY TERMS AND CONCEPTS

1. In **No Sail (No-Go) Zone** the sailboat is pointing into the wind with sails luffing.
2. **Close-hauled** is sailing as close to the wind as possible on edge of No Sail (No-Go) Zone.
3. **Beam reach** is sailing at 90 degrees to the wind direction.
4. **Running** is sailing directly downwind.
5. When sailing in the area between close-hauled and a beam reach, you are **close reaching**.
6. When sailing in the area between a beam reach and a run, you are **broad reaching**.
7. The **Cunningham** adjusts luff tension.
8. **Boom vang** adjusts leech tension.

CHECK YOUR UNDERSTANDING

1. When the wind is coming from the stern (behind the sailboat), how does the sail work?

   ◯ a. It creates lift, pulling the sailboat forward.
   ◯ b. It pushes the sailboat forward.
   ◯ c. It has no effect on the sailboat's movement.
   ◯ d. It causes the sailboat to stall out.

2. Which part of the sailboat keeps it from sliding sideways through the water?

   ◯ a. Sail
   ◯ b. Transom
   ◯ c. Mast
   ◯ d. Keel

Chapter 3

Preparation to Sail

Before a sailboat is ready to depart the dock, it needs to be prepared. This is a process known as rigging. As each part of the boat is readied, we have an opportunity to ensure that everything is in proper working order. The process of rigging is surprisingly universal, but each boat has unique differences. Rigging gives us an opportunity to discover these distinctions before getting underway. There are also many important skills you will learn that are necessary for each crew member to know. Some of these include using and loading a winch, handling and heaving line, and tying a variety of useful knots that are also easy to untie. After sailing, we will reverse these preparations in a process called de-rigging the sailboat and make sure everything is stowed, secured, and shipshape before stepping away from the keelboat.

GETTING ON AND OFF THE SAILBOAT

Stepping aboard a boat for the first time can be an unnerving experience unless you know how to do it safely. At the dock or on the *mooring*, a small keelboat can be unstable and will react to your weight by tipping slightly as you step aboard.

SKILL EVALUATION

- ☐ **Prepare to board** - Look around, orient the sailboat into wind, look for boom, and identify handholds.

- ☐ **Board sailboat** - Board sailboat at *shrouds* and use 3 points of contact.

- ☐ **Prepare to get off sailboat** - Identify handholds and look for the boom.

- ☐ **Step off the boat** - Maintain *balance* and carefully climb off the boat, secure dock lines.

FOLLOW THESE TIPS FOR BOARDING

▶ Make sure the boat is pulled close to the dock to easily step and not jump on to the vessel.
▶ Pass gear and equipment onto the boat first.
▶ Board the boat one person at a time.
▶ Announce "Stepping On" before or as you are coming aboard.
▶ Come aboard at the widest part of the boat, the beam, which is just behind the shrouds.
▶ Use three points of contact: one hand on the shrouds, one foot on the deck, and one hand to reach toward identified handholds.
▶ Once on board, move back into the cockpit and sit down.
▶ Take notice of your head clearance of the boom when sitting.

STEPPING OFF THE BOAT

Once the boat has returned to the dock or mooring, prepare yourself and your belongings to get off the boat. As a crew member, it is your responsibility to make sure the boat is properly tied to the dock or attached to the mooring before departing. Hand off your gear and equipment first, then step off while holding onto a shroud. Remember to use three points of contact for stability.

CREW POSITION

A small keelboat is relatively light, so the positioning of a driver and crew is critical to how the sailboat handles. The crew will trim sails and help to balance the sailboat. The crew should be positioned on the *windward* (high) side of the sailboat. When the crew sits farther out on the side (rail), their combined weight helps counteract the keelboat's tendency to *heel* (lean) when the wind pushes against the sails. This is important because excessive heel slows the sailboat and makes it harder to steer. Many times in beginner keelboat sailing, there are three people sailing and one instructor. Let's use this example to describe positions in the sailboat.

SKILL EVALUATION

☐ **Crew 1 (Forward)** - Sits forward in the cockpit and is responsible for trimming the jib with jib sheets.

☐ **Crew 2 (Mid)** - Sits in the middle of the cockpit between Crew 1 and the driver and is responsible for trimming the mainsail using the mainsheet.

☐ **Crew 3 (Driver)** - Sits in the back of the cockpit on the windward side and is responsible for safely steering the boat using the tiller.

CREW RESPONSIBILITIES

Crew 1 is in charge of trimming and easing the jib sheet. Crew 2, in the middle position, trims the mainsheet. Both crew members are responsible for communicating potential obstacles, changes in the wind, or other necessary information to the *skipper*. The driver holds the tiller with the hand farthest aft, sitting just forward of the tiller, checking the trim of the sail, and communicating with the crew.

NOTE: On a two-person boat, the driver will trim the mainsheet and steer with the tiller simultaneously.

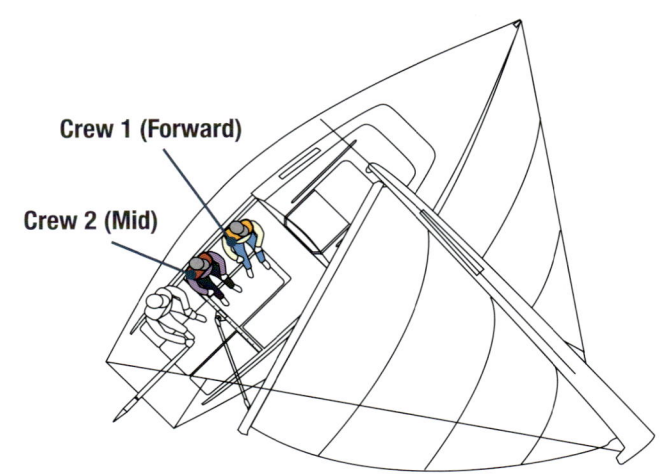

Crew 1 (Forward)

Crew 2 (Mid)

SKIPPER RESPONSIBILITIES

The skipper is responsible for the safety of the crew and vessel, directing the boat on course, avoiding collisions, and communicating with the crew in preparation for maneuvering the boat. The skipper may not always be the driver. If an instructor is onboard, they are the skipper.

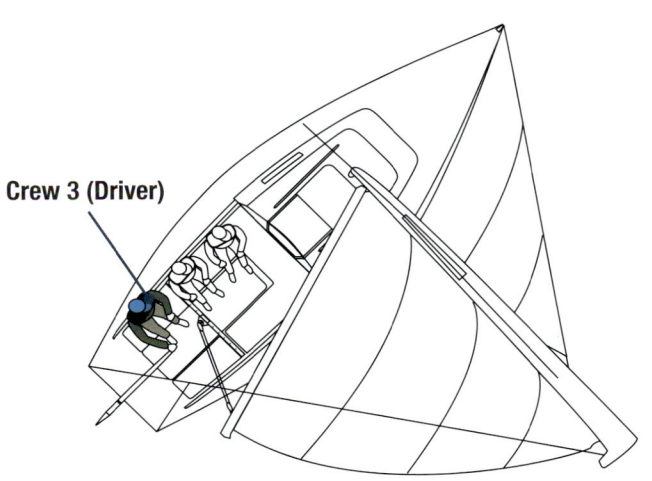

Crew 3 (Driver)

WORKING TOGETHER

During maneuvers, the boom often crosses over the cockpit. The driver and crew must first duck under the boom and cross over to the other side of the boat. Crew members are responsible for helping to balance the sailboat at all times, no matter where the wind is coming from.

HAKUNA MATATA

USING A WINCH

Winches are devices that assist you when adjusting the tension on a line. They are commonly used on halyards and jib sheets. The friction of the line wrapped around the barrel of the *winch* (ordinarily in a clockwise direction) reduces the load you feel when holding the line. The number of wraps needed will vary, depending on the size of the sail, the strength of the wind, and the crew's strength.

SKILL EVALUATION

☐ **Thumbs Towards You** - Grip line with thumbs towards you.

☐ **Prepare the Sheets** - Remove any slack in the sheet.

☐ **Load Winch** - Wrap the line clockwise from bottom to top around the winch.

☐ **Insert Winch Handle** - Grab the winch handle and insert it into the top of the winch.

☐ **Trim, Grind & Tail** - Tension the line by *grinding* and *tailing*.

☐ **Secure**- Secure line in cleat or self tailor and store the handle.

WINCH SAFETY TIP

The winch will be **under a heavy load,** and it's important to **avoid fingers getting trapped** between the line and the barrel when adding or removing wraps.

LOADING THE WINCH

Grasp the line with thumbs towards your body and lead it clockwise around the winch. While leading the line around the winch keep your hands at least a foot from the winch itself.

Grasp the line with you thumb towards your body. Take slack out of line and place it around the right side of the winch.

Make a clock-wise rotation around the winch to add a wrap. Your palm should twist up as you bring the line around, leaving your thumb pointed away from winch at all time.

Keep tension on the line as you finish your clock-wise rotation. Reset your hand to add another wrap if necessary.

GRINDING

The action of grinding and tailing must be performed when operating a winch. Grinding is the movement of the winch handle, sometimes in a complete circle and sometimes back and forth from the 1 o'clock to the 5 o'clock position. This movement rotates the barrel of the winch, also in a clockwise direction, and provides the mechanical advantage. When grinding the winch, tension must be kept on the line that is coming off the winch, known as tailing. Tailing ensures that the wraps have sufficient friction against the barrel of the winch. Some winches have an additional piece of hardware on top of the winch known as the self-tailer, which grips and tails the line without needing to hold the line for tension.

WINCH HANDLE

Some winch handles have a lock-in mechanism which must be activated before the handle can be inserted or removed from the winch. **A winch handle (even one with a lock-in mechanism) should not be left in the winch unattended.** Nor should it be placed on the cabin top or the cockpit seat and floor. Remove the wind handle from the winch and place it in the winch handle pocket each time after using a winch handle. **While there are a few winch handles that float, most do not!**

When using a self-tailing winch, the line must be led over the prefeeder before leading it into the self-tailing grooves.

TYPES OF LINE

Laid line consists of three large strands twisted around one another. Usually made of nylon, it is very strong but can be rough on the hands. Laid line stretches, which makes it excellent for anchor rode and dock lines. Braided line made from low-stretch materials is excellent for halyards and sheets, as it does not stretch as much as nylon. Braided line is relatively gentle on the hands. In addition to the above lines, there is an ever-changing assortment of new materials and construction methods designed for specific, higher-tech applications. Low-stretch and low-weight lines can be great additions on board to increase sailing performance.

Lines used on keelboats should be checked regularly for wear and damage. When you board, check lines for cuts, fraying, sun damage, and discoloration. These could be signs the lines need to be repaired or replaced.

Laid line

Braided line

LINE HANDLING

Line should not be simply left in a tangled pile, but should always be ready to use. Lines that are neatly organized and stowed are ready for immediate use. Make it a priority to tidy lines constantly.

COILING

When coiling a line, one hand makes long loops which is fed onto the other hand holding the loops previously coiled. With laid line, it helps to twist the line slightly as you coil to avoid kinks or twists in the line. Twisting braided line cause kinks and twists.

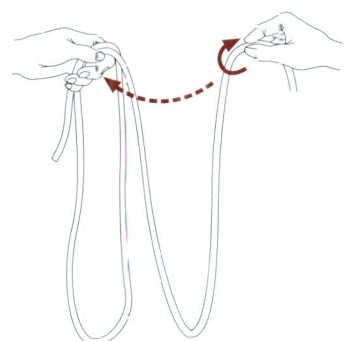

Coiling with a twist

CROWNING A COIL

Crowning is used to secure a *coil*. To *stow* a coiled line, wrap the end of the line around the coil two or three times. Make a loop with the end of a line and pass it through the loops of the coil. Pull the passed-through loop up and over the end of the coil and the tighten loop and wraps to compress and secure the coil.

HEAVING A LINE

When preparing to throw a line, make sure one end is secured. Hold half of the coil in your throwing hand and the other half in your other hand. Swing and throw the coil underhand, allowing the remainder of the line to run free from your other hand.

Secure *bitter* end and begin coiling by stretching out your arms.

Continue coiling by bringing your hands together.

Once all coils are gathered into one hand, separate out two coils into your throwing hand.

With your throwing hand swing and throw the coil underhand.

Allow the remainder of the line to run free from your non-throwing hand. Your non-throwing hand should placed with your palm upward and your fingers pointing at the target. Grasping the remaining coil with your non-throwing hand (as illustrated) will not allow the line to run free.

KNOTS

A good knot is one that is easy to tie, does the job, and is easy to untie. There are many knots used in sailing, but six basic, easy-to-tie knots will handle most, if not all, of your needs. Learn the knots well because an improperly tied knot is useless or worse.

☐ **Tie** - Tie the knot.

☐ **Undo** - Undo the knot.

☐ **Example** - Give one example where this is used in sailing.

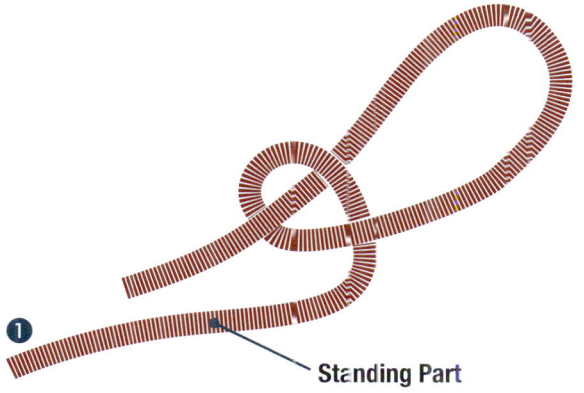

Standing Part

THE BOWLINE

The bowline (BOE-lin) puts a non-slipping loop at the end of a line. The knot becomes more secure under pressure, but remains easy to untie. It is a commonly used knot on sailboats. Among its many applications, the bowline maybe used to attach the jib sheets to the clew of the jib.

❶ To tie a bowline, put a small loop in the line where you want the knot to be. Make sure the end crosses on top of the standing part of the line. This small loop will end up as part of the knot.

❷ Run the end up through the loop you just made, down behind the standing part, back up over the edge of the loop, and down through the loop again.

❸ Snug the knot together, making sure the knot holds and the remaining loop does not slip.

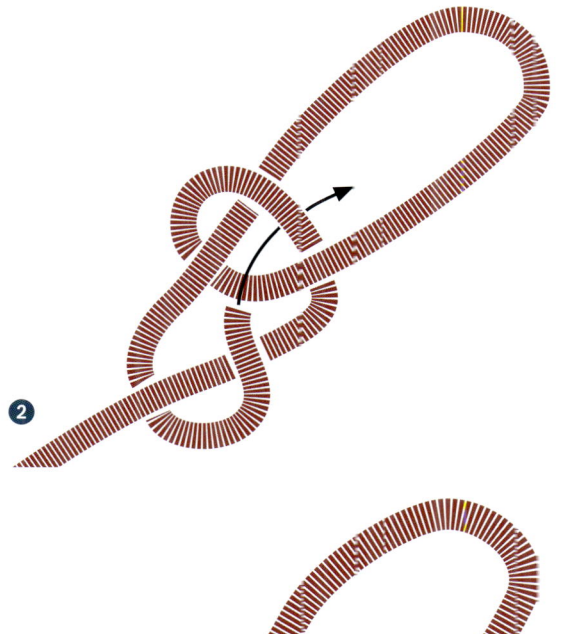

28

FIGURE-8 KNOT

The *figure-8 knot* looks like its name. It is the most common stopper knot, and is tied on the end of a line to keep the line from slipping through a fitting. Easy to untie, it is commonly used on the ends of the jib sheets in the cockpit.

❶ Pass the end over the standing part.

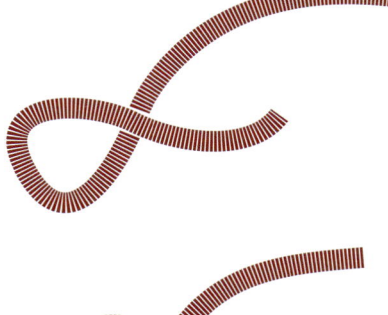

❷ Cross the end back under the standing part.

❸ Bring the end down through the loop. Tighten the knot.

SQUARE KNOT

The *square knot* is used only for sail lashings. It is not recommended for tying two lines together because it can be difficult to untie. It is a good knot for a sail tie.

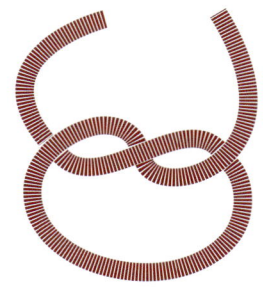

❶ Tie a simple overhand knot with the right end going over the left.

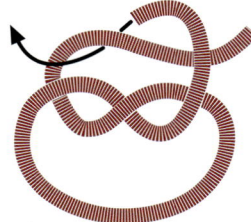

❷ Tie another simple overhand knot, this time crossing left end over right end.

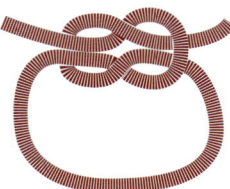

❸ As you tighten the line the knot should be symmetrical.

ROUND TURN AND TWO HALF HITCHES

This knot utilizes a loop to securely attach a line to an object. It's an excellent choice for fastening your fenders.

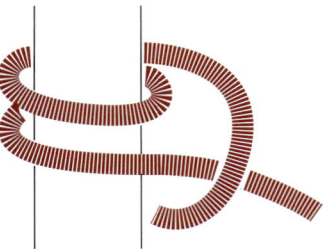

❶ Wrap the end of the line twice around the object.

❷ Cross the end over the outside of the standing part.

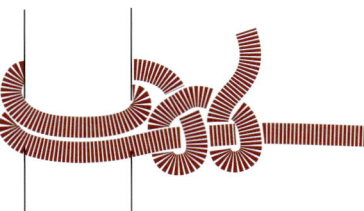

❸ Use the end to tie two half-hitches onto the standing part.

◄ CLEAT HITCH

A *cleat hitch* is the knot one will use to secure a line to a horn cleat. When properly tied, it is very secure but easy to untie. Commonly used to tie the boat to the dock or secure a halyard to the mast.

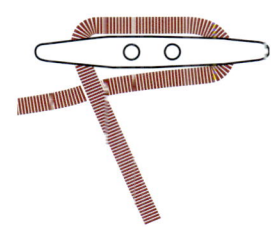

❶ Wrap a half loop around the horn of the cleat farthest from the line's origin (far horn).

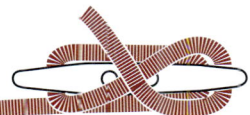

❷ Continue taking the line to the opposite horn (near horn) and wrap a half loop.

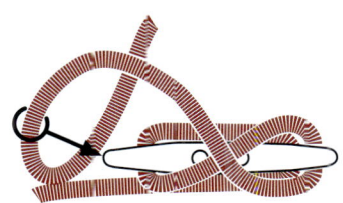

❸ Twist a half loop to complete the " figure 8" and wrap on around the far horn.

❹ Pull tight and make sure two parallel wraps are under the final twisted half loop.

Simply cutting through a line will cause the cut ends to fray. A line should be treated with an electric hot knife to cut and fuse the ends. Whipping a line by wrapping the end of it with thread will protect it from fraying and unraveling. It's best to *whip* the line before cutting it.

SLIP KNOT WITH A SAIL TIE

A slip knot is used to secure a sail tie or line quickly and can be pulled to release quickly. For example, you can use a slip knot with a sail tie to secure the mainsail to the boom when de-rigging the boat. Unfortunately, when this knot is put under pressure, it can be hard to release.

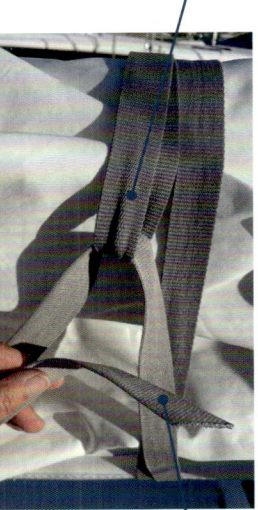

Sail Tie Loop

End of Sail Tie

Bight

End of Sail Tie

❶ Wrap the sail tie around the rolled or folded mainsail and thread the bitter end of the sail tie through loop on the other end of the sail tie.

❷ Pull slack out and make the sail tie snug around rolled mainsail.

❸ Pinch the sail tie loop with one hand to keep the wrapped sail tie tight around the rollled mainsail.

❹ While pinching, pass the end of the sail tie between the wrap and the sail, creating a loop on one side and the end of the sail tie on the other.

❺ Bend the end of the sail tie into a *bight* and pass the bight back through the loop. Pull tight.

❻ To Release: Pull firmly on the end of the sail tie to release to the knot.

PREPARE THE SAILBOAT: RIG AND RAISE SAILS

Before leaving the dock, the sails must be properly attached and raised. Sail controls such as an outhaul, *vang, downhaul*, or *Cunningham* may need to be adjusted before getting *underway*. Most boats are now fitted with a roller furler unit, a mechanical system to roll up a jib around the forestay. Roller-furled jibs are usually stored in the furled (rolled-up) position.

RIGGING THE JIB

SKILL EVALUATION

☐ **Rig** - Rig and raise sails properly and secure at all attachment points.

☐ **Boom** - Identify where *boom* swings when sails are raised.

☐ **Knots** - Demonstrate all knots needed for rigging.

☐ **Shipshape** - Demonstrate a shipshape boat while sailing.

RIGGING TIP

Make sure all halyard shackles are fastened securely. Jib sheets can be tied into the clew with bowline knots.

❶ Lay the jib on the *foredeck* with the tack of the jib nearest the *bow*. Fasten the tack of the jib to the proper fitting.

❷ Starting with the bottom fastener, attach the luff of the jib onto the forestay working sequentially from the bottom to the top.

❸ Attach the jib halyard shackle to the head of the jib. Check that the halyard is not twisted around the forestay, shrouds, or mast.

❹ Secure the jib sheets to the clew of the jib. Depending on the type of boat you are sailing, the jib sheets may pass inside or outside of the shrouds, then through the fairleads, and into the cockpit. Tie a figure-8 knot into the ends of the sheets in the cockpit.

RIGGING THE MAINSAIL

❶ Attach the entire *foot* to the boom by inserting the clew of the sail into the forward end of the boom slot, pulling it along the boom.

❷ Attach the tack of the sail to the gooseneck.

❸ Attach and tighten the outhaul to tension the foot of the main. Cleat the outhaul line.

❹ Connect the Cunningham but don't tighten. Attach the luff to the mast, making sure it's not twisted. If it is connected by metal or fiberglass slides, feed them onto the track, and make sure they are all attached. If it uses a *bolt rope,* slide the head into the slot on the mast.

❺ Find the main halyard, unclip it from the stowed position. Look up and make sure it is not tangled with other lines or the rig. Attach the main halyard shackle. Remove any slack to keep it from snagging a spreader and prevent the head of the mainsail from slipping out of the slot.

❻ If battens have been removed, insert them into their pockets before raising the sail. The end of the *batten* that is more flexible, thin, or tapered, should be inserted into the pocket first.

MAINSAIL RIGGING TIP

Before you hoist the mainsail, remove slack from the halyard to keep it from tangling in the rigging.

HOISTING THE SAILS

Before hoisting your sails, the boat should be pointed into the wind. The mainsail is usually hoisted first, as it will help keep the boat's bow into the wind until you are ready to *cast off.* If departing from the *windward side* of a dock, it may be preferable to hoist the jib first, sail away, and then hoist the mainsail once clear.

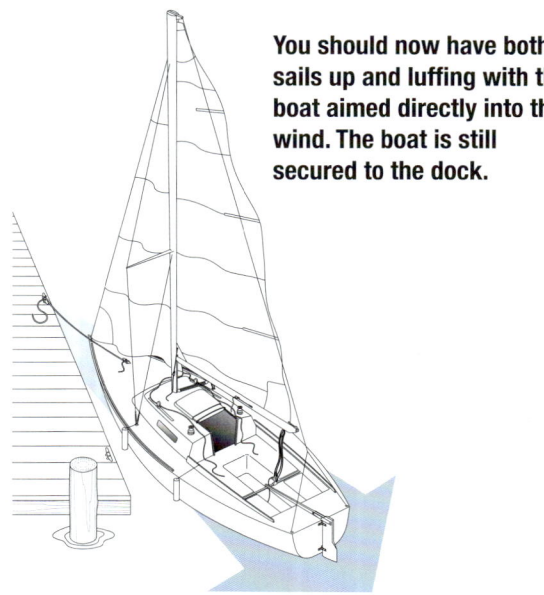

You should now have both sails up and luffing with the boat aimed directly into the wind. The boat is still secured to the dock.

SAILS UP AT THE DOCK TIP

Make sure the mainsheet and jib sheets are loose and free to run. This allows the sails to move freely in the wind so the boat doesn't start sailing at the dock!

STOW BOAT: DERIG & LOWER SAILS

Once you have completed your sail, you will need to derig and stow the equipment. The process will be in the opposite order as rigging. It is the crew's role to make sure everything is stowed, secured, and shipshape before leaving for the day.

HOISTING THE MAINSAIL

1. Loosen the Cunningham/downhaul and boom vang.
2. Center and tighten the traveler controls.
3. Loosen the *reefing* line and remove any sail ties from around the mainsail and boom.
4. Release the mainsheet.
5. Re-check the main halyard to make it is not twisted round the mast or shrouds.
6. Begin hoisting the mainsail with slow and steady pulls.
7. Look up the mast to check that the sail is going up smoothly and that the luff of the sail is staying attached to the mast.
8. Mainsail should be luffing so it will go up more easily.
9. Wrap the main halyard around a winch if it becomes difficult to hold and use the winch to tighten the main halyard for more luff tension.
10. Secure and coil the main halyard.

HOISTING THE MAINSAIL TIP

Feeding the mainsail luff into the slot of the mast as it is raised helps keep the sail from jamming in the slot.

HOISTING THE JIB

1. Everyone should clear the foredeck and move back to the mast or cockpit.
2. Make sure both the jib halyard and the jib sheets are clear and untangled.
3. Sheets should be *lead* to the cockpit and free to run.
4. Raise the sail with the jib halyard. Finish hoisting by using a winch and winch handle to properly tension the jib luff as necessary.
5. Secure and coil the jib halyard.

SKILL EVALUATION

☐ **Head to Wind** - Position boat upwind and raise or lower sails in the head to wind position.

☐ **Derig** - Lower and derig sails properly and detach all attachment points.

☐ **Stow Sails** - Flake, furl, or roll the sails when dry.

☐ **Shipshape** - Demonstrate stowing and securing all equipment, gear, and lines for boat to be left unattended.

☐ **Secure** - Double check that all lines securing the sailboat to the dock or mooring are the correct length and use the correct knot.

PUTTING IT ALL TOGETHER

SUMMARY

- When boarding or disembarking, be sure to follow proper procedures and always remember the three points of contact.
- Crew trims the jib and communicates with the driver. The driver, sitting forward of the tiller, steers with the hand farthest aft.
- To safely use a winch, grip the line with thumbs toward your body and wrap it clockwise around the winch. Keep hands at least a foot away from the winch to help prevent fingers from getting caught in the line.

- Coiling and crowning a line properly helps to avoid twists, kinks, and lines jamming.
- Neatly organize and stow coiled lines.
- Good knots are easy to tie and untie.
- Rig the sails before leaving the dock.
- Only hoist the mainsail when the sailboat is pointed directly to the wind.
- After completing your sail, derig and stow all equipment and ensure everything is shipshape before stepping away from the sailboat.

KEY TERMS AND CONCEPTS

1. Everyone must be aware that the boom crosses over the cockpit; they should stay seated and be ready to duck under the boom.
2. Crew weight is used to balance the sailboat.
3. It's important to avoid fingers getting trapped when adding or removing wraps from winch.
4. A winch handle should **not** be left in the winch unattended.
5. If you raise the sails at the dock, make sure the sheets are loose and free to run so the sailboat doesn't start sailing at the dock.
6. The crew must ensure the sailboat is stowed and secured properly at the end of the day.

CHECK YOUR UNDERSTANDING

1. When stepping aboard a sailboat for the first time, what precaution should be taken due to the sailboat's potential instability?

   ○ a. Jump onto the sailboat quickly to maintain balance
   ○ b. Move swiftly towards the far side of the sailboat
   ○ c. Avoiding holding onto anything for balance
   ○ d. Boarding at the shrouds and using three points of contact

2. What is the recommended sequence for hoisting sails when departing from the windward side of a dock?

   ○ a. Hoist the mainsail first, then hoist the jib
   ○ b. Raise both the mainsail and jib at the same time
   ○ c. Hoist the jib first, sail away, and then hoist the mainsail once clear
   ○ d. Hoist the jib halfway, then hoist the mainsail

Chapter 4

Your First Sail: Foundations of Sailing

Your first sail helps you see how preparation, rigging, new terms, and the wind create a delightful experience. In this chapter you will learn the concepts of how to steer, trim sails, control the sailboat's speed, and the art of balancing your heel. Learning these sailing skills will make you a more capable sailor.

STEERING WITH THE TILLER

Using a tiller to steer the boat is simple. A common rule of thumb when you begin sailing is to push or pull the tiller away from the direction you want to turn. If you want to turn left, push or pull the tiller right, and vice versa. After a short while, using a tiller will become instinctive.

SKILL EVALUATION

☐ **Prepare** - Properly adjust your body position, tiller hand, and mainsheet hand.

☐ **Steer** - Use the tiller or *tiller extension* to turn the boat to port and back to starboard.

☐ **Avoid Collisions** - Move the "Tiller Towards Trouble". Using just the tiller, you can steer away from trouble.

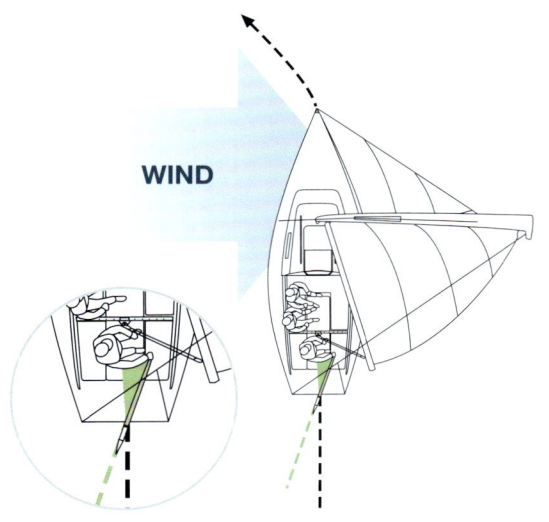

Turn to Port (Left)
When a boat sails forward through the water, moving the tiller to starboard turns the boat to *port*.

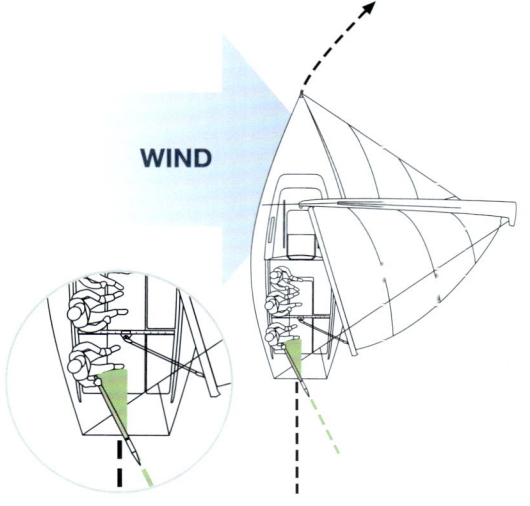

Turn to Starboard (Right)
When a boat sails forward through the water, moving the tiller to port turns the boat to *starboard*.

HEADING UP AND BEARING AWAY

Whenever a boat changes direction, it is also turning relative to the wind either *heading up* (toward) or bearing away (away) from the source of the wind.

HEADING UP

This boat is changing direction from sailing across the wind to sailing *upwind* by heading up.

▶ The driver pushes the tiller toward the boom.
▶ The crew trim in the sails all the way (close-hauled position).

Angle to wind gets smaller

WIND

STEERING TIP

The boat must be moving for you to steer. The *rudder* redirects the flow of water to create a steering force. **NO MOVEMENT... NO FLOW... NO STEERING!** Try to keep the steering motion firm, but smooth. Jerky tiller movements can disrupt water flow around the rudder and reduce its effectiveness.

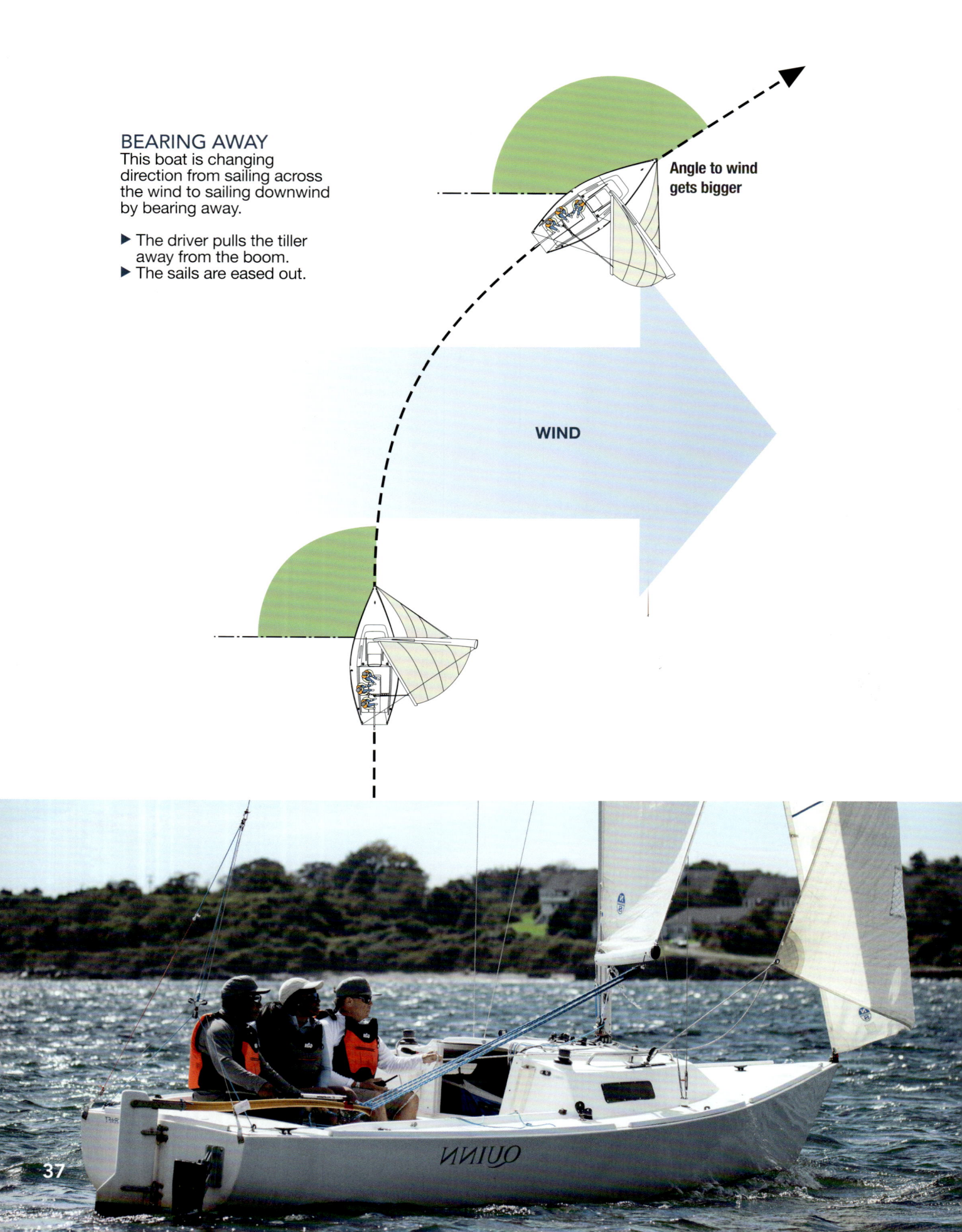

BEARING AWAY
This boat is changing direction from sailing across the wind to sailing downwind by bearing away.

▶ The driver pulls the tiller away from the boom.
▶ The sails are eased out.

Angle to wind gets bigger

WIND

PUTTING IT ALL TOGETHER STEERING A COURSE

(Follow sequence from bottom ❶ to top ❸)

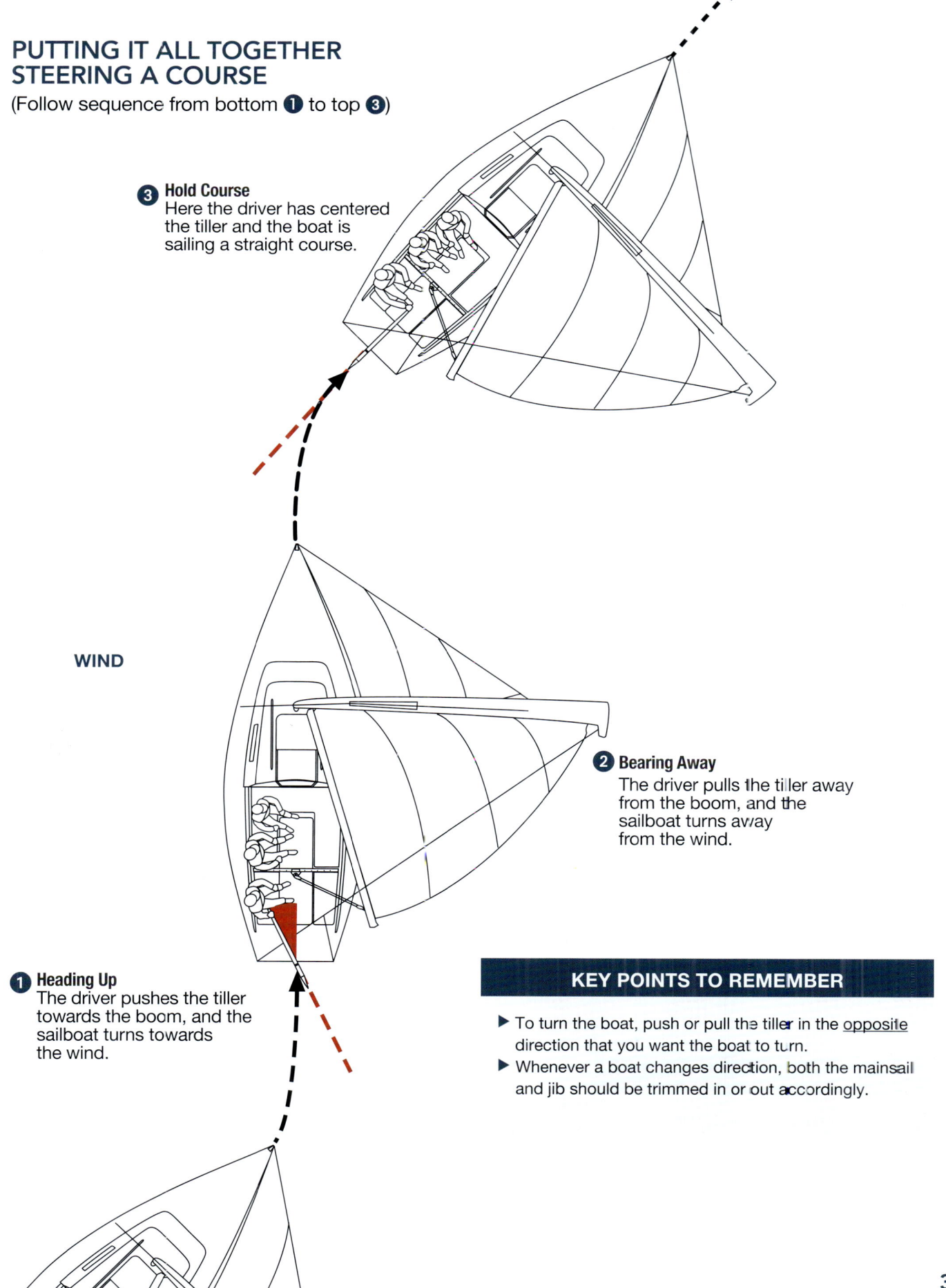

❸ **Hold Course**
Here the driver has centered the tiller and the boat is sailing a straight course.

WIND

❷ **Bearing Away**
The driver pulls the tiller away from the boom, and the sailboat turns away from the wind.

❶ **Heading Up**
The driver pushes the tiller towards the boom, and the sailboat turns towards the wind.

KEY POINTS TO REMEMBER

▶ To turn the boat, push or pull the tiller in the <u>opposite</u> direction that you want the boat to turn.

▶ Whenever a boat changes direction, both the mainsail and jib should be trimmed in or out accordingly.

SAILING ACROSS THE WIND (REACH)

Sailing across the wind, with the wind perpendicular to the side of the boat, is a fast and easy way to sail. In your first lesson, you will spend a lot of time sailing across the wind, learning how to steer and trim the sails.

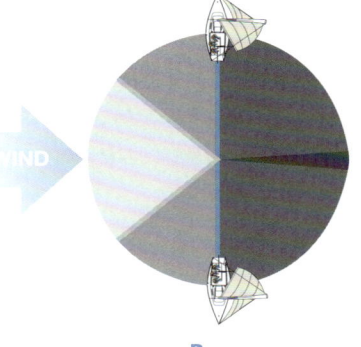

Beam reach

- ☐ **Heading** - Steer a steady, beam reach course, sailing directly across the wind.

- ☐ **Body Position** - All crew should balance boat to be flat and evenly balanced according to the wind. Skipper should sit forward and clear of the tiller.

- ☐ **Steering** - Adjusting steering with tiller and sail trim with sheets at the same time communicating between skipper & crew.

- ☐ **Sail Trim** - Adjust mainsail and jib trim to be about half way out.

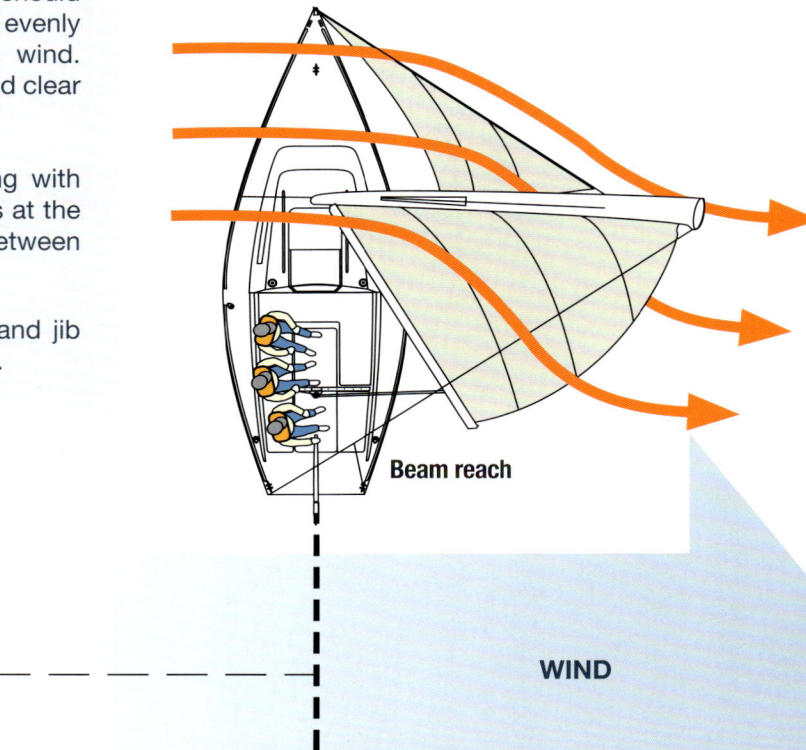

Beam reach

WIND

These boats are sailing perpendicular to the wind with the wind coming over the side of the boat. This is called a *beam* reach.

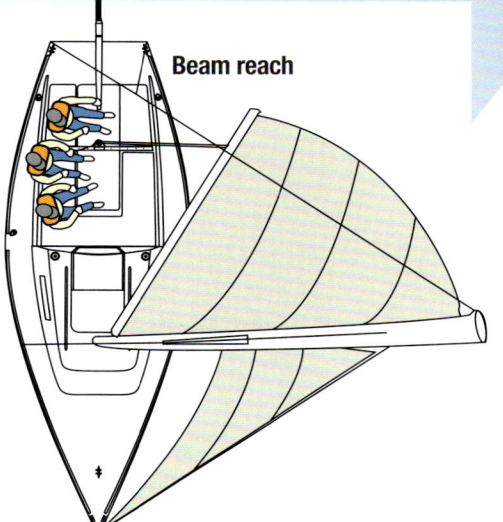

Beam reach

REACH CHECKLIST

- ▶ Feel the wind coming across the boat.
- ▶ Sheet the sails about halfway out.
- ▶ Steer toward an objective or landmark. Adjust the sails to changes in the boat's direction or changes in wind direction.

CONTROL SPEED

STARTING AND STOPPING

A sailboat can start and stop by using its sails, much like using the accelerator on a car. Sheeting-in a sail to proper trim is like stepping on the accelerator. Easing the sail out and letting it luff is like taking your foot off the gas. With the sails luffing, the boat will coast to a stop.

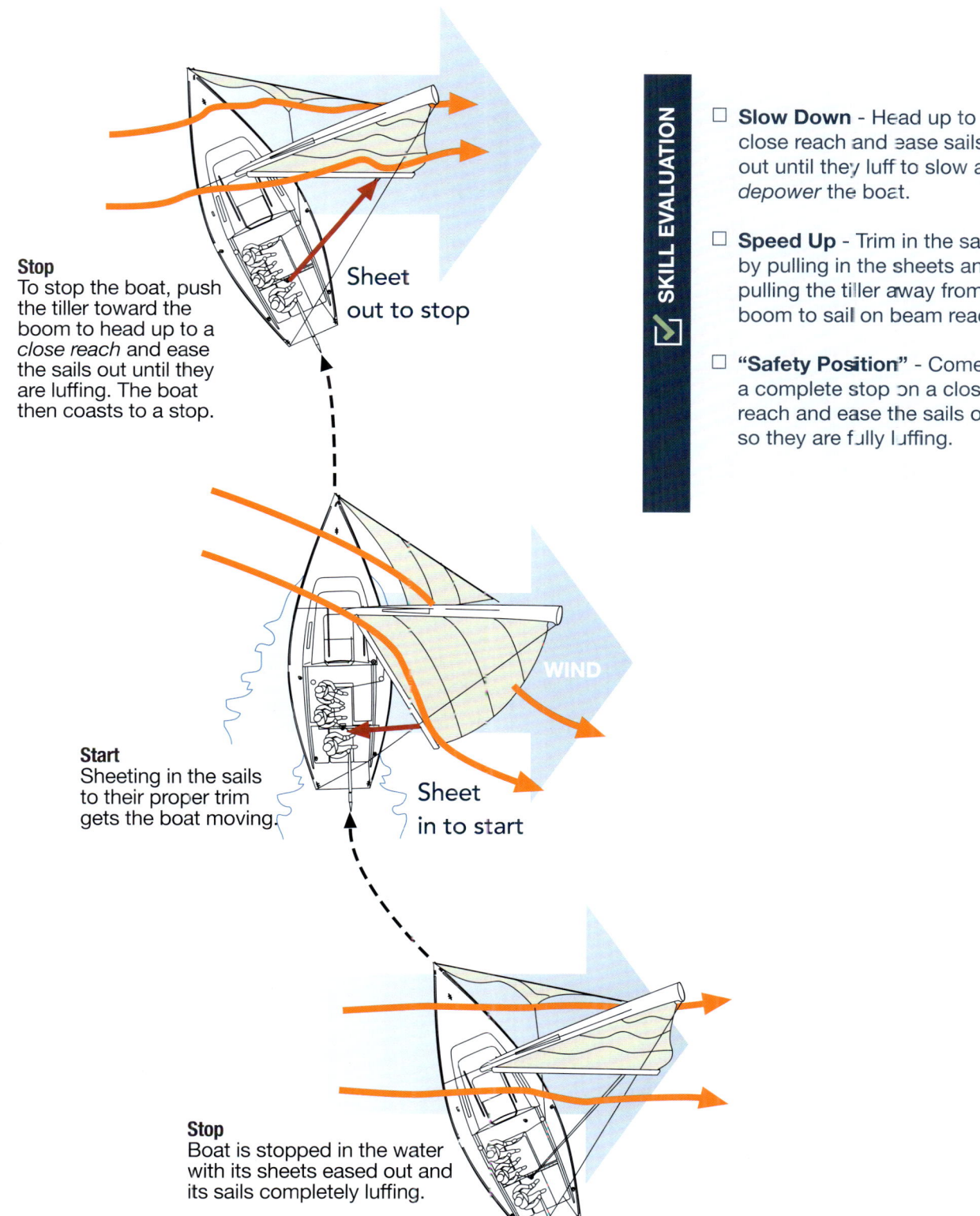

Stop
To stop the boat, push the tiller toward the boom to head up to a *close reach* and ease the sails out until they are luffing. The boat then coasts to a stop.

Sheet out to stop

Start
Sheeting in the sails to their proper trim gets the boat moving.

Sheet in to start

WIND

Stop
Boat is stopped in the water with its sheets eased out and its sails completely luffing.

SKILL EVALUATION

☐ **Slow Down** - Head up to close reach and ease sails out until they luff to slow and *depower* the boat.

☐ **Speed Up** - Trim in the sails by pulling in the sheets and pulling the tiller away from the boom to sail on beam reach.

☐ **"Safety Position"** - Come to a complete stop on a close reach and ease the sails out so they are fully luffing.

TACKING FROM REACH TO REACH

Tacking is a sailing maneuver where a boat changes direction by turning its bow through the wind. Any time you switch the wind from one side of the sailboat to the other by sailing through the No-Sail (No-Go) Zone, you are performing a tack. You may want to tack for a wide range of reasons; other boats, your destination, better wind or water conditions, etc.

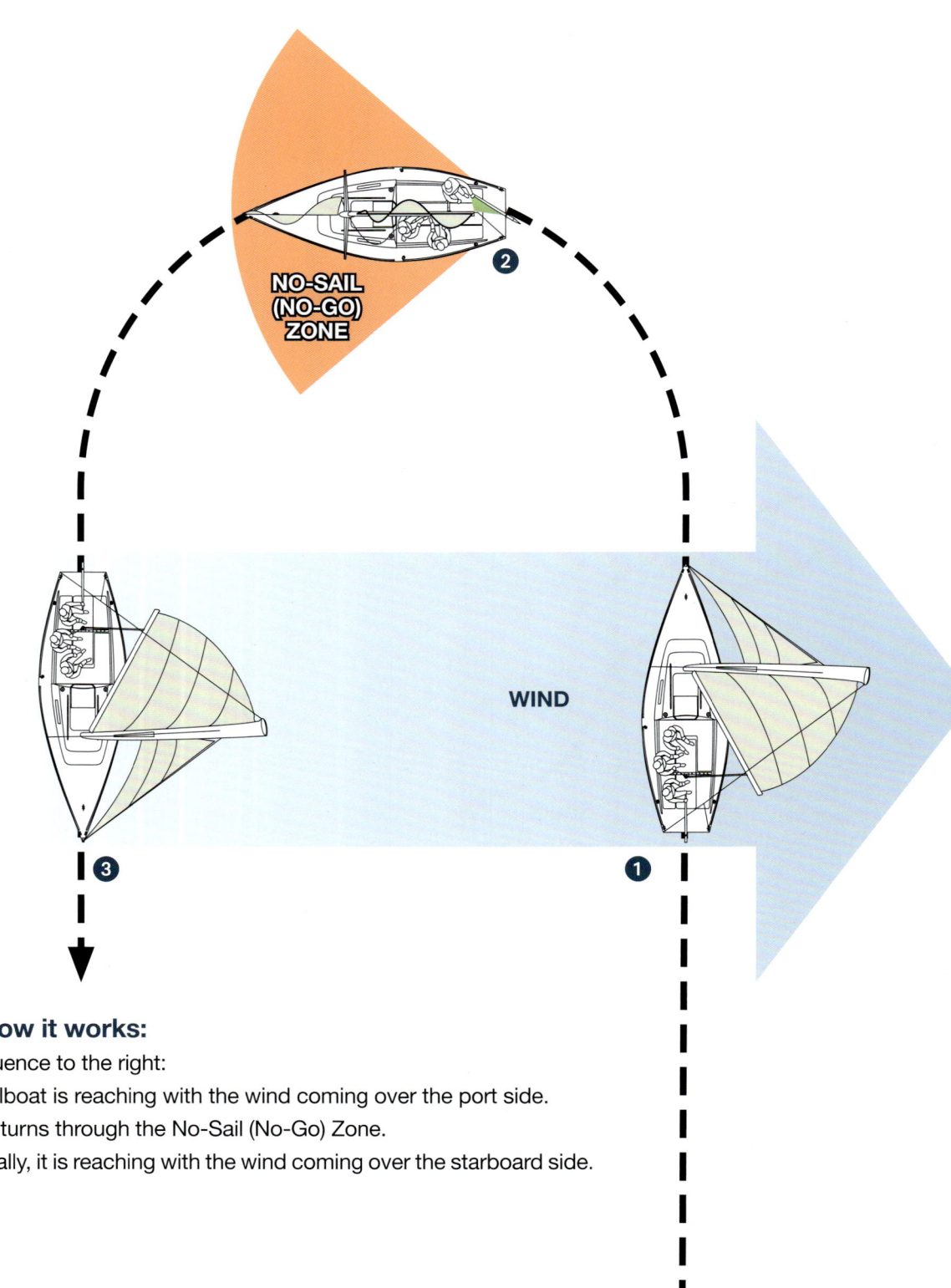

NO-SAIL (NO-GO) ZONE

WIND

Here's how it works:

In the sequence to the right:

1 The sailboat is reaching with the wind coming over the port side.

2 Then it turns through the No-Sail (No-Go) Zone.

3 And finally, it is reaching with the wind coming over the starboard side.

GETTING OUT OF IRONS

At some point while you are learning to sail, you will tack the boat too slowly through the wind and get stuck in the No-Sail (No-Go) Zone. You are now *in irons*. The sails are luffing, the boat slows to a stop, and the rudder no longer steers the boat. It's a helpless feeling, but easily correctable.

IN IRONS
The boat is pointed directly into the wind, both sails are luffing, the boat has come to a dead stop, and the rudder doesn't work since water has to be flowing past it to steer the boat.

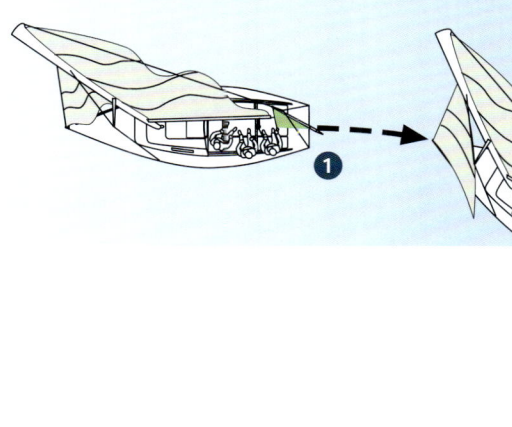

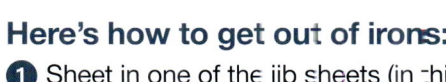

WIND

Here's how to get out of irons:

1 Sheet in one of the jib sheets (in this case the one on the port side) until the wind blowing over the bow makes the sail billow back toward you. This will push the boat backward and also push the bow off to one side. When the boat starts to move backward, move the tiller in the same direction that the bow is turning (in this case to the starboard) to help the boat turn more quickly.

2 When the wind is coming over the side of the boat, release the jib sheet and trim it in on the other side.

3 Then straighten the tiller sheet in the mainsail, and off you go!

42

TACKING STEP-BY-STEP

A tack or tacking is turning the bow of the sailboat through the source of the wind, from one side of the No-Sail (No-Go) Zone to the other. Whenever the bow turns through the wind, the sails will cross from one side to the other. When you need or want to tack, follow sequence from the bottom of the next page ❶ to bottom of this page ❹.

NO-SAIL (NO-GO) ZONE

WIND

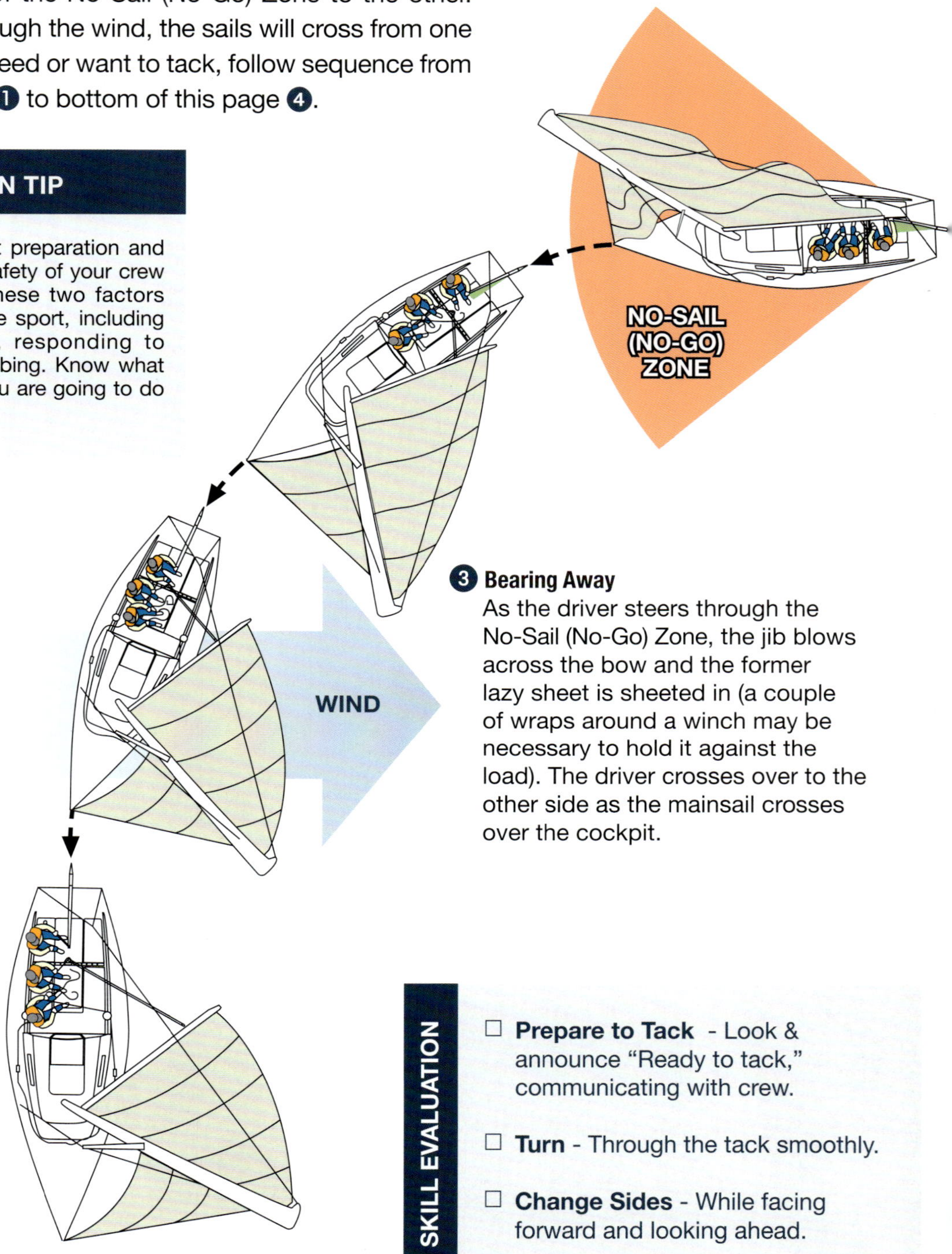

❸ **Bearing Away**

As the driver steers through the No-Sail (No-Go) Zone, the jib blows across the bow and the former lazy sheet is sheeted in (a couple of wraps around a winch may be necessary to hold it against the load). The driver crosses over to the other side as the mainsail crosses over the cockpit.

❹ **Tack Is Completed**

Once the sailboat is on the otherside of the No-Sail (No-Go) Zone, the tack is completed. The driver centers the tiller and steers for the reference point picked prior to beginning the tack. The crew adjust the mainsail and jib for the new course. The jib sheets are then coiled and readied for the next tack.

SKILL EVALUATION

- ☐ **Prepare to Tack** - Look & announce "Ready to tack," communicating with crew.

- ☐ **Turn** - Through the tack smoothly.

- ☐ **Change Sides** - While facing forward and looking ahead.

- ☐ **Finish** - Straighten course and adjust sail trim for your new course.

❷ Head Up

After the crew have announced they are ready, the driver calls out, "Tacking!" to announce the beginning of the tack. The driver then starts to turn the sailboat through the No-Sail (No-Go) Zone (tiller toward boom). As the sailboat turns into the wind, the sails begin to luff. When the forward edge of the jib is luffing, the crew releases the working jib sheet.

"Tacking!"

Forward edge luffing

Tiller toward boom

"Ready!"

"Ready!"

"Prepare to tack!"

❶ Preparing to Tack

The sailboat in this diagram is on a beam reach. The driver checks for anything that might be in the way, selects a reference point to steer for after completion of the tack, and then calls out, "Prepare to tack!" The crew checks to make sure the jib sheets are clear and ready to run out. Then the crew uncleats and holds the working jib sheet and gets ready to sheet in the lazy jib sheet before responding, "Ready!"

FINE-TUNING SAIL TRIM

Many sailors view a sailboat's mainsheet and jib sheet as they would the accelerator on a car...the sails are sheeted (pulled) in until they stop luffing to make the sailboat go. As previously described, a sail creates lift by redirecting wind flow. If the wind flows smoothly around the sails, maximum power is achieved, resulting in maximum boatspeed. If the sails are sheeted in or out too much, turbulent flow will result, reducing flow and slowing the boat. To fine-*tune* your sail trim, let the sails out until they luff and then sheet them in until the luffing stops.

Trimmed Just Right
▶ Smooth flow around sail
▶ Optimum power
▶ Optimum boat speed
▶ Easy steering
▶ Well-balanced

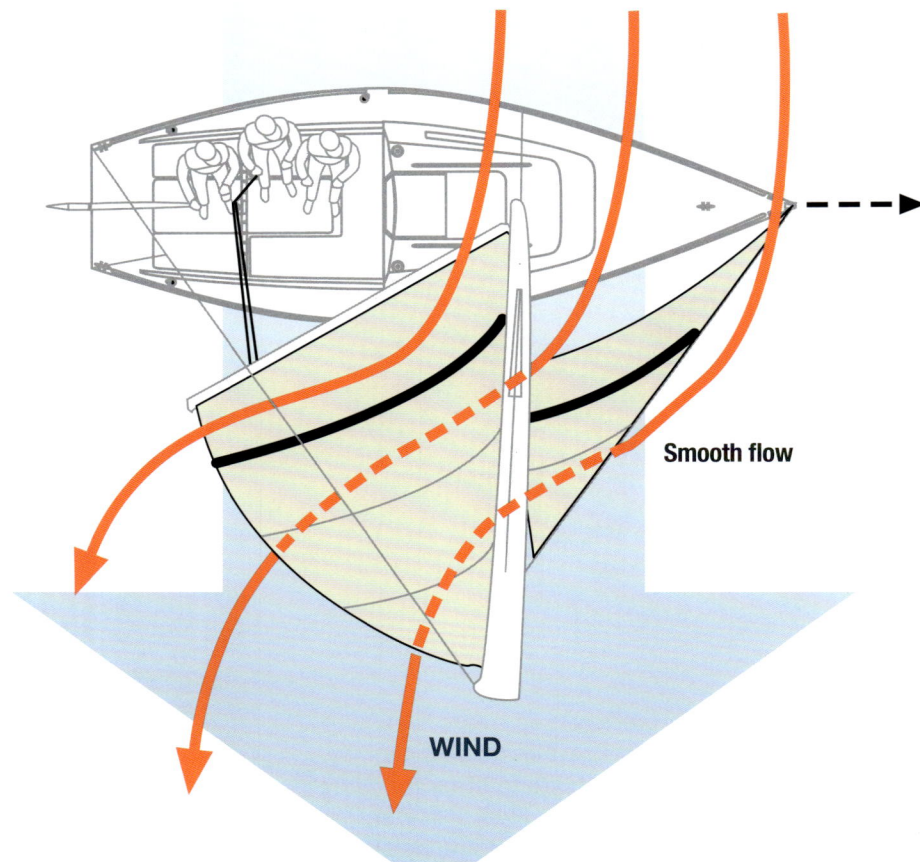

Smooth flow

WIND

KEY POINTS TO REMEMBER

▶ "When in doubt, let it out"

▶ "Out until it luffs, in until it stops luffing"

Trimmed Too Loose

▶ Turbulent flow around sail
▶ Minimum power
▶ Reduced boat speed
▶ Sails luffing and making noise

Sailing with your sails trimmed too far out is not necessarily bad. There are times when you will want to sail along slowly (at less than maximum speed) and will trim in your sails only part way.

Sheet in sails to the point where they stop luffing to trim them correctly.

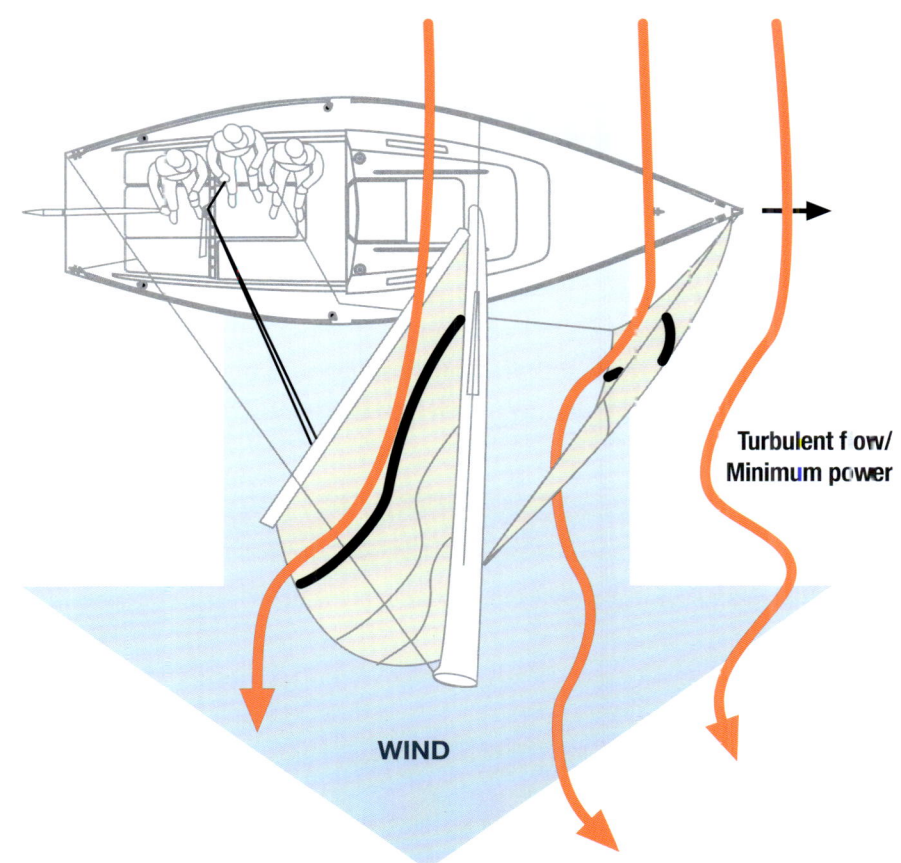

Turbulent flow/
Minimum power

WIND

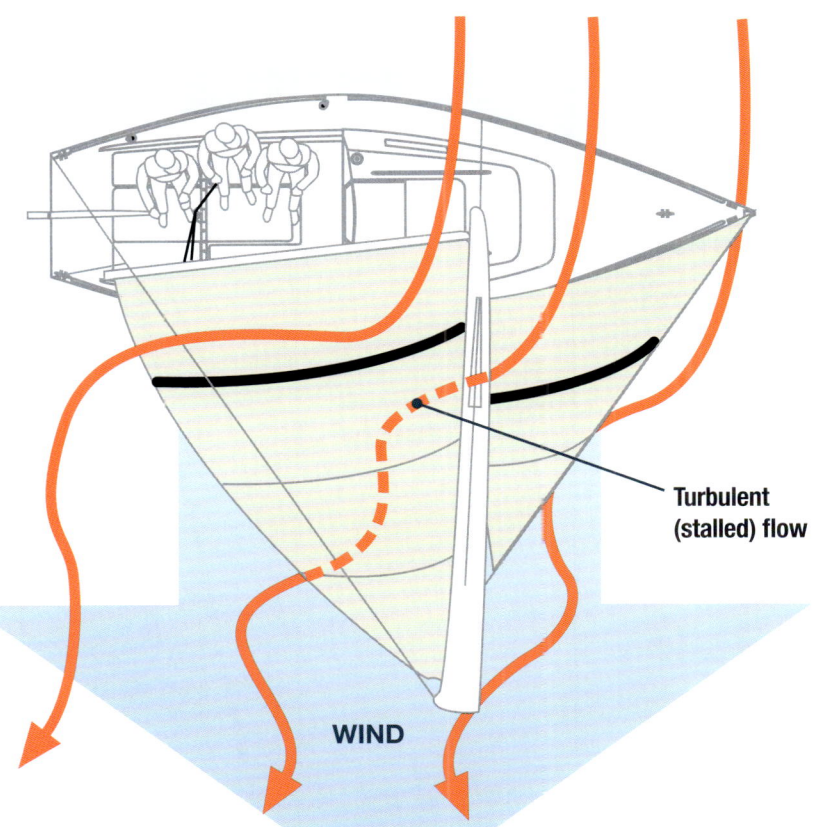

Turbulent
(stalled) flow

WIND

Trimmed Too Tight

▶ Sailboat slows down
▶ Turbulent flow around sail
▶ Difficult steering
▶ Excessive heeling

If you lose wind flow around your sails, your sailboat will begin to feel sluggish. To get a smooth flow going again, let out the sails until they luff. Then bring them back in until they stop luffing, and you feel the sailboat pick up speed.

BASIC HEEL CONTROL

The *heel* of the sailboat is the lean of the sailboat when pressure from the wind is applied to the sails. For example, when the pressure of the wind on the sails is significant, the sailboat will heel (lean) to leeward. Learning to control the heel of the sailboat is a skill in beginning sailing. Heel is controlled by two things: body weight and sail trim. When the sailboat heels to leeward, start by easing the sails and adjusting sail trim to keep the boat either flat or slightly heeled. The crew should shift their body weight within the cockpit, and if needed, move to the windward side of the cockpit.

KEY POINTS TO REMEMBER

▶ Body weight to the high side (windward side) of the boat.

SKILL EVALUATION

☐ **Ease out** - Adjust the sail trim by easing out to keep the sailboat flat.

☐ **Trim in** - Adjust the sail sail trim by trimming in to keep the sailboat flat.

☐ **Weight Balance** - Shift your body weight in and out to keep the sailboat flat.

Too Much Heel

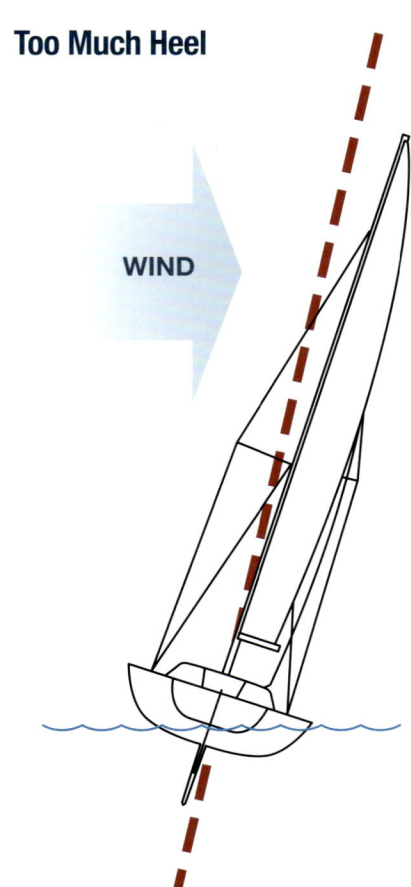

WIND

Slightly Heeled

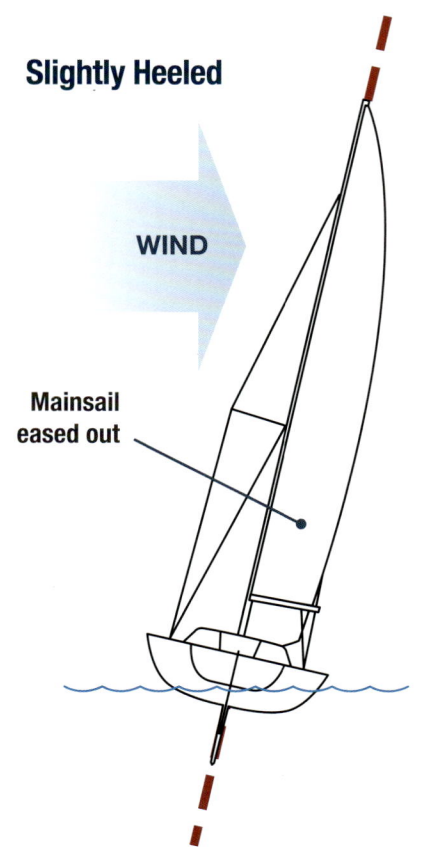

WIND

Mainsail eased out

DOCKLINES

Crew members should step off the boat onto the dock. **DO NOT JUMP!** Falling on the dock or between the dock and the boat can be painful. Nothing other than a *fender* should be put between the boat and the dock; do not use your hands or feet.

Care should be taken while getting on and off a vessel. Whenever possible, you should use a shroud as a handhold while moving between the dock and the sailboat. Be careful of tripping while stepping over lifelines. Remember a sailboat may heel significantly when you embark or disembark.

▶ **Bow and stern lines** keep the boat close to the dock but do not prevent it from surging forward or backward in the wind or waves.

▶ **Spring lines** keep the boat from moving forward and backward. *Spring lines* are referenced according to where they go from the cleat on the sailboat. For example, a spring line attached to the bow cleat that goes aft to the dock cleat is an aft spring line.

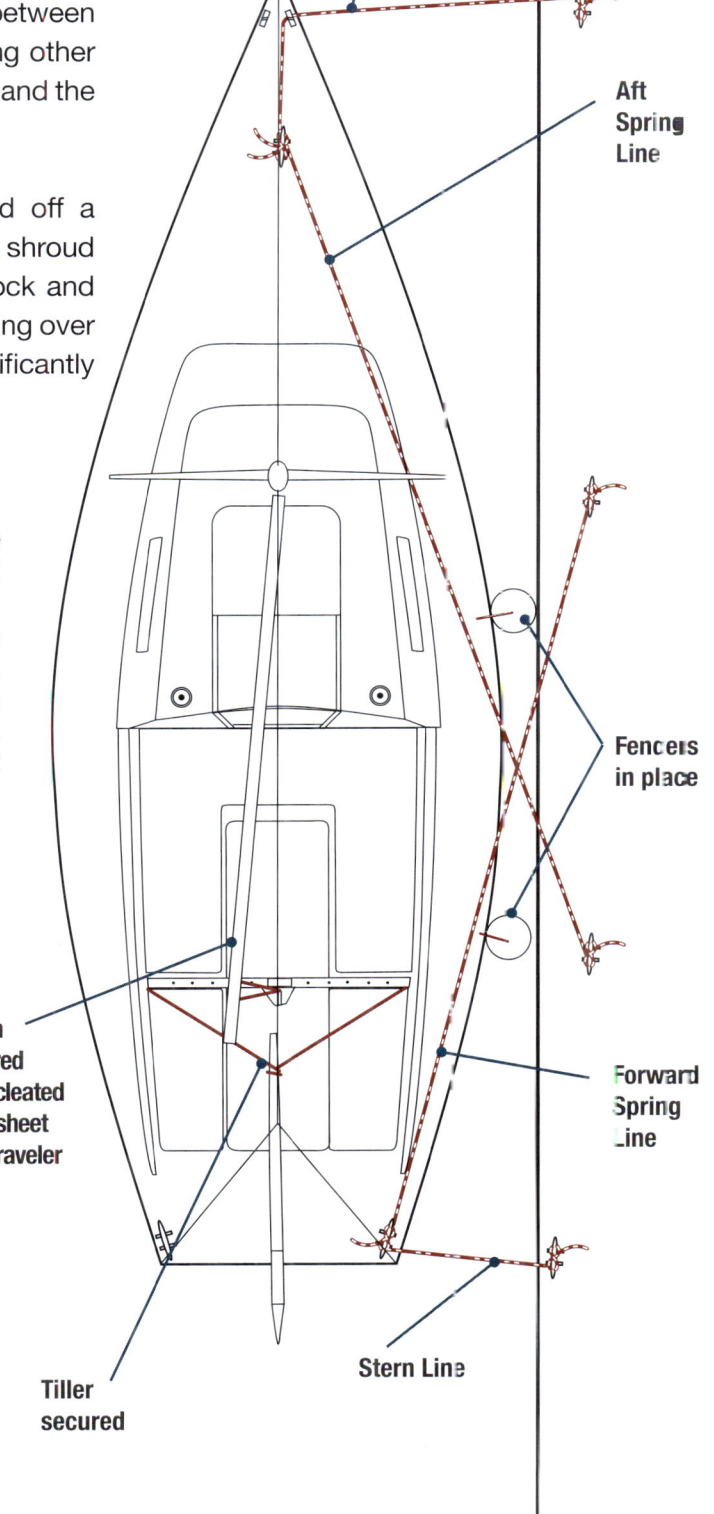

Bow Line

Aft Spring Line

Fenders in place

Forward Spring Line

Boom secured with cleated mainsheet and traveler

Tiller secured

Stern Line

Before you leave the boat, double check that the docklines are cleated securely with the right amount of tension. All cleated docklines should be secured with a cleat hitch (see photo).

LEAVING THE DOCK

Like learning how to park a car, learning how to leave or return to a dock can make beginning sailors nervous. With a little forethought and basic sailing skills, you can leave and return to a dock with confidence. Boats and docks are large objects, and the safety of your crew should be foremost.

While some marinas allow boats to depart and return only under motor, in this section, we describe leaving the dock by sail.

First decide how you will leave the dock, then explain your departure plan to the crew members. Make sure everyone knows what they should do and when.

In both examples the open sailing area is to the left. In the bottom example the boat will have to be backed out of the *slip* before it can be turned out of the No-Sail (No-Go) Zone. In preparation for leaving the dock, make sure the fenders are positioned to protect the boat while leaving the dock.

SKILL EVALUATION

☐ **Prepare to Depart** - Check the wind speed, wind direction, current, and traffic on the water for a clear departure.

☐ **Ready the Boat** - Fenders out, sail(s) raised and a crew member standing on the dock.

☐ **Position the Boat** - Crew on dock readies docklines and positions boat for clear departure.

☐ **Sail Away** - The stern line is released and the driver steers away from the dock as crew trim sails and retrieves the fenders.

LEAVING A DOCK BY SAIL

1 Now that your sails are up and luffing and you are tied to the dock with the bow pointed into the wind. A crew member is on the dock to handle the docklines. Double the stern line by uncleating it from the dock and loop it around the base of the cleat. Return the tail end to a crew member on board. Release the *bow line* first, and then step aboard at the shrouds while pushing the bow away from the dock.

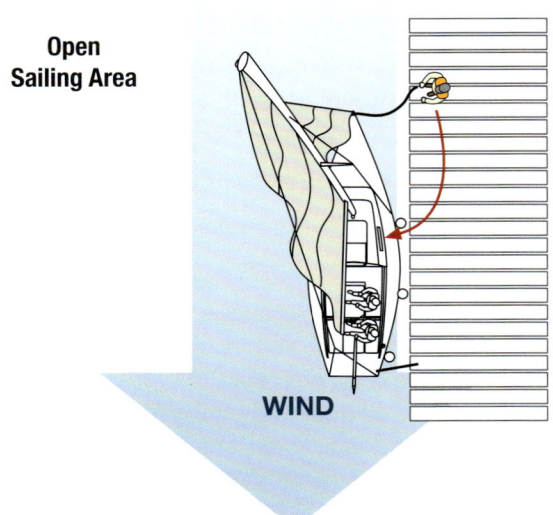

Open Sailing Area

WIND

LEAVING A SLIP BY SAIL

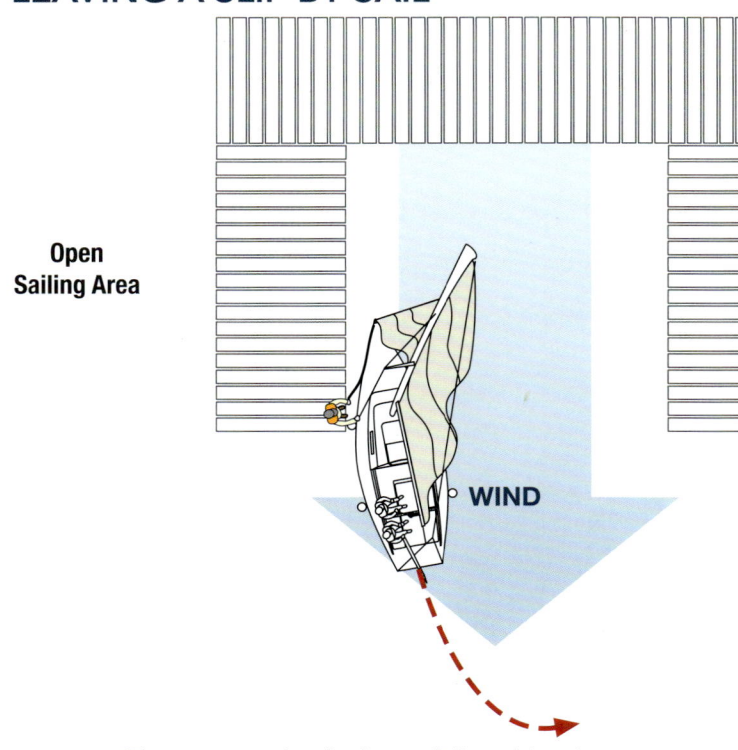

Open Sailing Area

WIND

1 The crew on the dock carefully guides the boat by hand around the end of the dock.

2 Sheet in the jib on the dock side until the sail becomes backwinded and the boat slowly rotates out of the No-Sail (No-Go) Zone. Then release the stern line.

3 Finally, sheet in the jib on the other side and trim the mainsail to propel you forward. Stow fenders and docklines. Enjoy your sail!

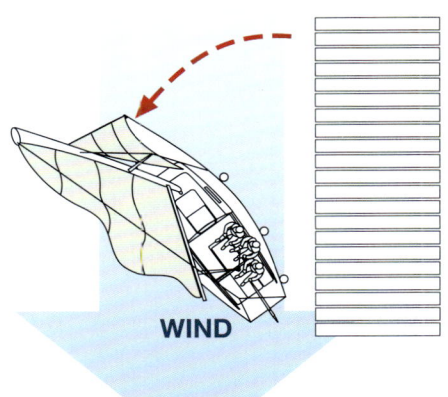

WIND

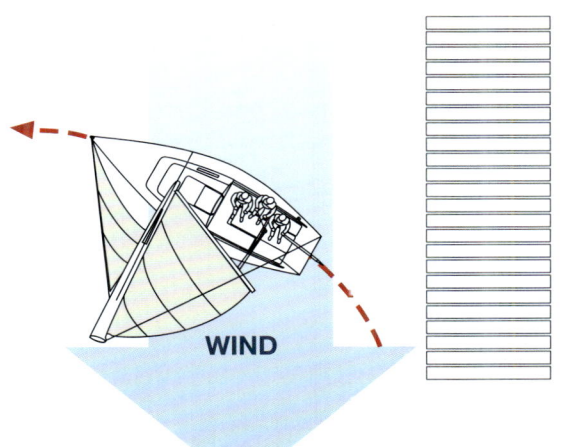

WIND

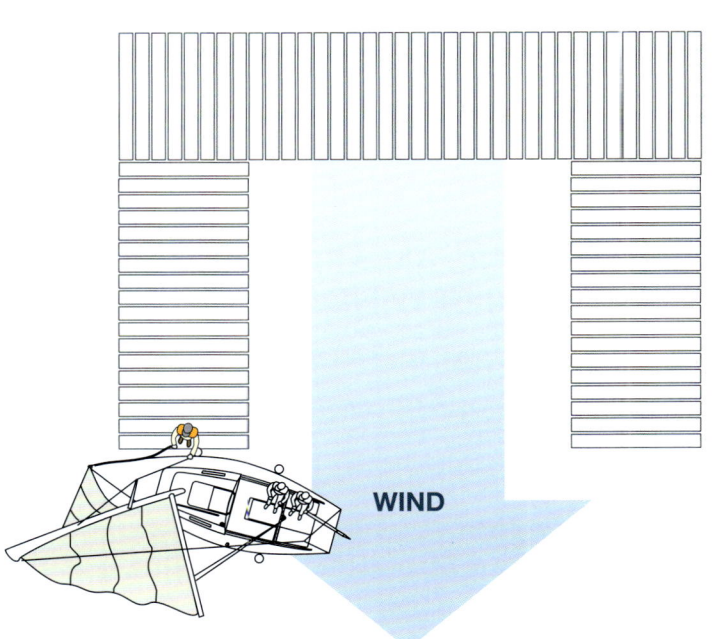

WIND

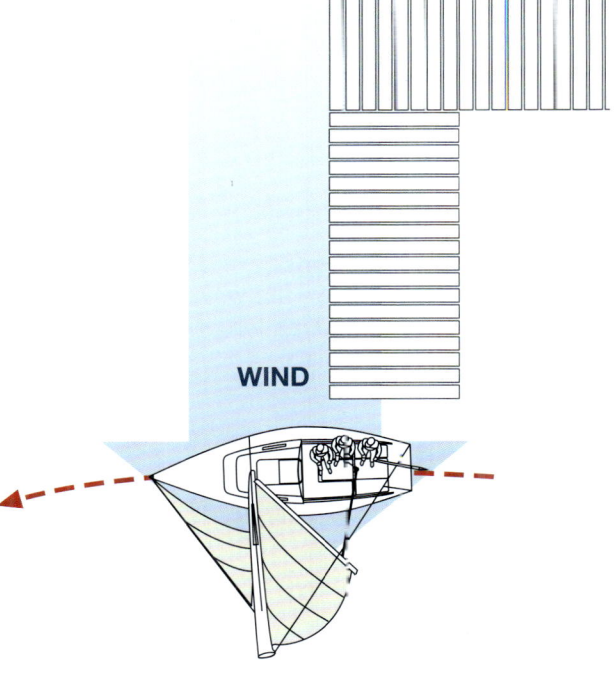

WIND

2 The bow is maneuvered past the end of the dock. The boat is guided alongside the dock towards the sailing area. The crew pushes off from the dock and steps on the boat holding onto the shrouds.

3 The sails are sheeted in. Then fenders and docklines are stowed.

RETURNING TO THE DOCK

Prepare the boat before returning to the dock. Have the fenders hung at the right height to safeguard the hull. Have the docklines attached properly to the boat and strung under the lifelines so they are ready to be used. Decide upon a plan for a controlled landing and inform the crew of their responsibilities. Be sure to have an escape plan if the landing isn't going well. Once you are ready to approach the dock, do it carefully.

WHEN NEARING A SIDE DOCK

Ease out your sails on your approach to slow the boat ❶. As you come closer, steer up into the wind, letting the sails luff. Coast to a stop along the dock ❷. If the dock is short or has limited space, you will want to make your approach more slowly.

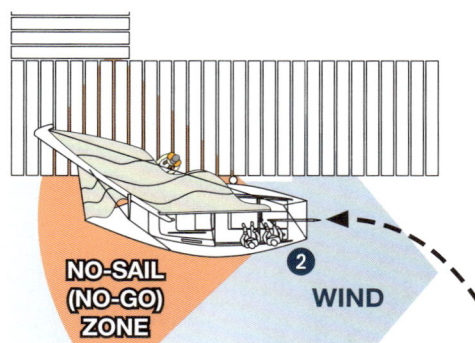

NO-SAIL (NO-GO) ZONE

WIND

☐ **Prepare to Land** - Skipper checks the wind speed, wind direction, current, and traffic on the water.

☐ **Ready the Boat** - Crew hangs fenders and readies the docklines.

☐ **Land** - Approach with sails luffing or lowered and stop within one boat length of the landing area.

MAKING AN APPROACH TO AN UPWIND SLIP

❶ Ease the sails to slow your speed. If your speed is slightly high, you can do a series of shallow S-Turns to slow your sailboat. ❷ Once you are sure your speed is correct (fast enough to get you into the slip, but not fast enough to bang your bow), head into the slip.

KEY POINTS TO REMEMBER

When docking up wind:

▶ Ease sails out to slow your sailboat.

▶ Sheet sails in to increase the speed of your sailboat. If you go too slow, you can't steer.

PUTTING IT ALL TOGETHER

SUMMARY

- Steer by pushing or pulling the tiller in the opposite direction you want the bow to go.
- On a beam reach, the wind will be coming over sailboat at 90 degrees to your course, and sails will be trimmed about halfway out.
- If stuck in irons, back wind the jib by sheeting one jib sheet in tightly. Move the tiller to the opposite side of the sailboat. The sailboat will back up and turn. When out of irons, resume sailing by releasing and trimming the jib on the other side and centering the tiller.
- Before tacking, the driver looks around for hazards, and tells the crew, "Ready to Tack".

- When tacking, the sailboat's bow is turning through the wind. Initiate the tack by pushing the tiller towards the boom.
- Control your speed by trimming the sails in or easing them out. Control the heel of the sailboat by using crew weight and sail trim.
- Prepare the sailboat for docking by rigging the fenders and docklines. Brief the crew on their responsibilities, including how and where to step of the sailboat and secure docklines.
- When docking, always have an escape plan

KEY TERMS AND CONCEPTS

1. Whenever a sailboat changes direction, it is also turning relative to the wind, either **heading up** (toward) or **bearing away** (away) from the source of the wind.
2. When using a tiller to avoid collisions, remember to move the "**Tiller Towards Trouble**".
3. **Safety Position:** stopping on a close reach with the sails fully luffing.
4. "**When in doubt, let it out**" and "**Out until it luffs, in until it stops luffing**"
5. When docking, never place your hands or feet between the boat and the dock. Use a fender!

CHECK YOUR UNDERSTANDING

1. What will moving crew's body weight and adjusting sail trim affect?

   ○ a. Flatten the sails

   ○ b. Change the angle of heel

   ○ c. Dock the sailboat

   ○ d. Amount of sail area

2. What should be done when heading up?

   ○ a. Pull the tiller away from the boom and ease out the sails.

   ○ b. Push the tiller toward the boom and ease out the sails.

   ○ c. Pull the tiller away from the boom and sheet in the sails.

   ○ d. Push the tiller toward the boom and sheet in the sails.

Chapter 5

Upwind to Downwind: Intermediate Sailing Techniques

There are four fundamental sailing maneuvers: heading up, bearing away, tacking, and jibing. The details of heading up and bearing away were outlined in the previous chapter. In this chapter, we will explore the fine points of tacking close hauled, jibing and learn how to perform these maneuvers more precisely. The roles of both driver and crew will also be explained in detail. Finally, we will review what you have learned through a visual sailing course that travels upwind, across the wind, and downwind while also practicing successful tacking and jibing maneuvers along the way.

SAILING UPWIND

Although a sailboat cannot sail directly into the wind, it can sail upwind, or close to where the wind is coming from. Sailing about 45 degrees from the direction of the wind is about the closest a sailboat can sail upwind (although some high-performance sailboats can sail as close as 30 to 35 degrees).

Sailing upwind is fun and exhilarating. You can feel waves passing under the hull, wind and spray in your face.

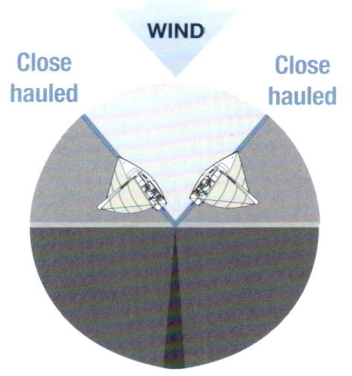

WIND

Close hauled | Close hauled

If you try to sail too close to the wind, your sails will luff and lose power, and the sailboat will slow down or come to a stop. This 90-degree area is called the No-Sail (No-Go) Zone for obvious reasons.

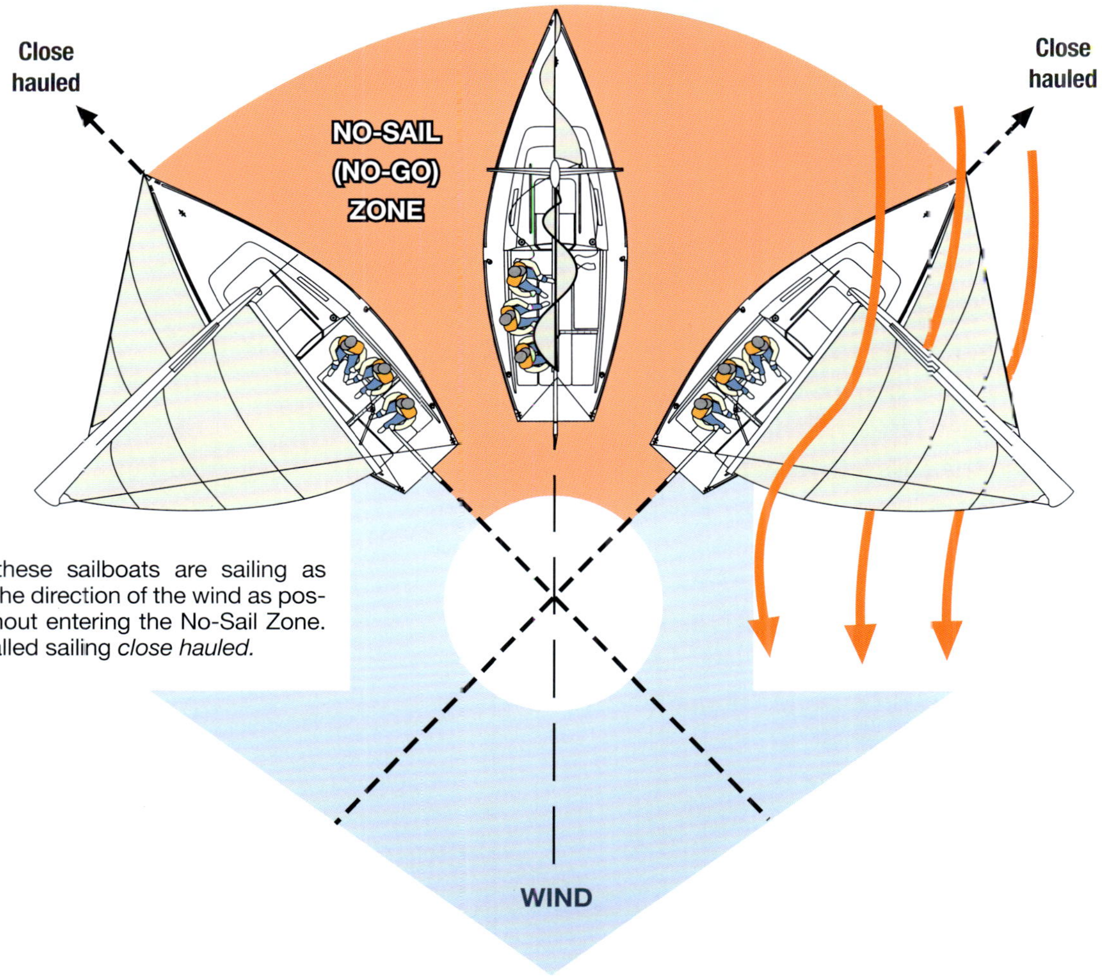

Close hauled

NO-SAIL (NO-GO) ZONE

Close hauled

Two of these sailboats are sailing as close to the direction of the wind as possible without entering the No-Sail Zone. This is called sailing *close hauled*.

WIND

☐ **Heading** - Steer a steady, upwind course with good sail trim.

☐ **Driver Position** - Sit on the windward side with good posture. Sit forward and clear of the tiller.

☐ **Steering** - Adjusting steering with tiller and sail trim with sheets at the same time communicating between driver & crew.

Sailing Upwind (Close Hauled) Tips

▶ Feel the wind in your face (when looking forward).
▶ Sheet in the sails all the way.
▶ Steer to the jib using the *telltales* (Chapter six). and the luff of the sail to achieve smooth air flow.
▶ Driver sits on the windward (high) side opposite the boom.
▶ Crew trim sails and move from one side to the other to help keep the sailboat from heeling too much or too little.

TACKING UPWIND (CLOSE HAULED)

A sailboat cannot sail directly into the wind. To make progress toward the wind it must sail a zig-zag course, similar to switch-backs on a steep hill. When a sailboat switches from a "zig" to a "zag," it is called a tack. You have already learned how to tack from reach to reach, you are now going to learn how to tack upwind by switching from one close hauled course (ex: *port tack*) to the other (ex: *starboard tack*). During an upwind tack the driver slows down the turn by centering the tiller earlier than on a reach to reach tack. By centering the tiller earlier you will complete the tack on a close hauled course.

Steps to Tacking Close Hauled

❶ At the beginning of the tack, the sailboat is sailing close hauled with the wind coming over the port side of the boat.

❷ In the middle of the tack, the boat crosses the No-Sail (No-Go) Zone, and the sails luff, losing their power.

❸ The driver slows down the turn by straightening the tiller slowly when the luffing jib passes in front of the mast and is on the new side. Then the crew trims the jib in fully.

❹ In the final part of the tack, the boat is picking up speed with the wind coming over the starboard side of the sailboat. The sailboat's direction changed about 90 degrees and is on a close hauled course.

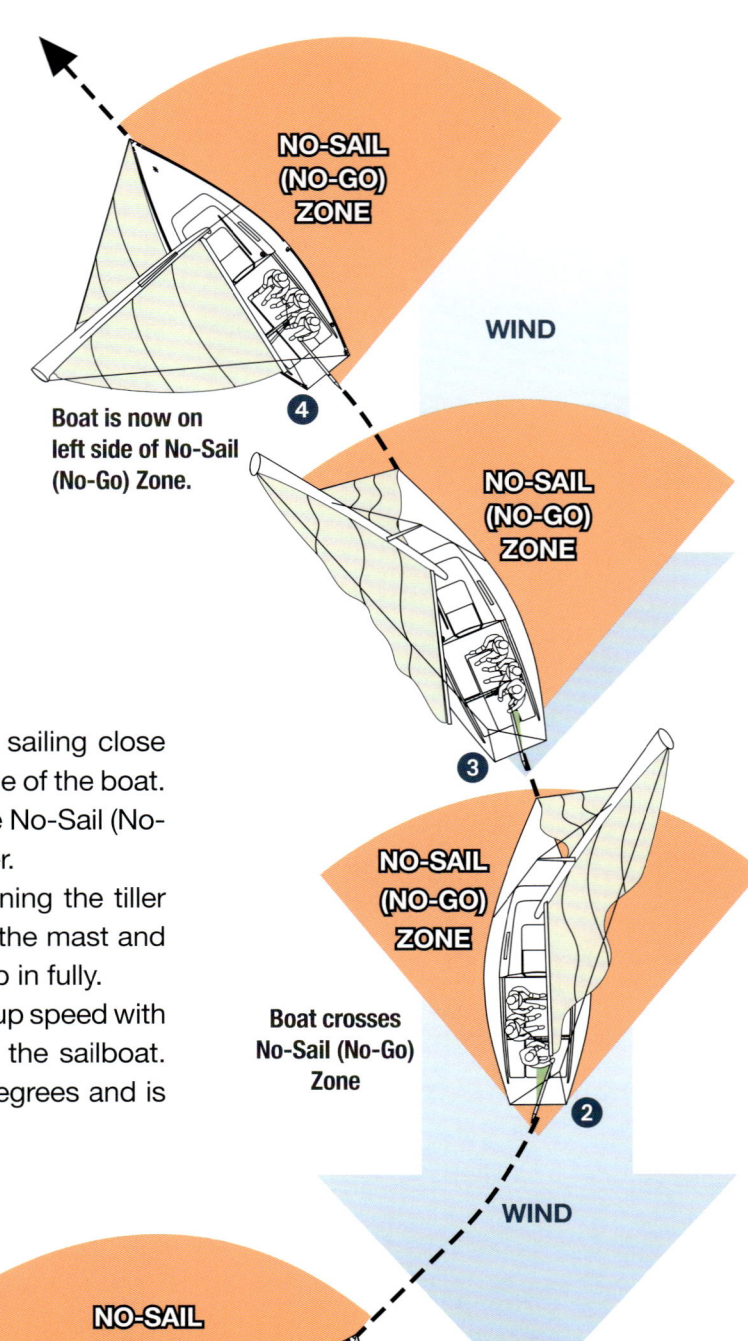

NO-SAIL (NO-GO) ZONE

WIND

Boat is now on left side of No-Sail (No-Go) Zone.

NO-SAIL (NO-GO) ZONE

NO-SAIL (NO-GO) ZONE

Boat crosses No-Sail (No-Go) Zone

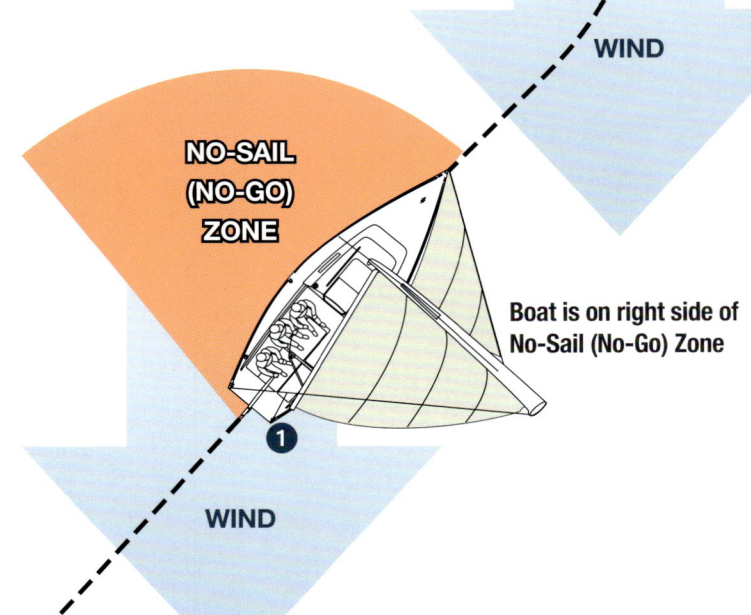

WIND

NO-SAIL (NO-GO) ZONE

Boat is on right side of No-Sail (No-Go) Zone

WIND

SAILING DOWNWIND

Sailing downwind is the most comfortable and relaxing point of sail. You are sailing in approximately the same direction as the wind and waves, the ride is smooth, and the boat stays upright.

Sailing a *deep broad reach* is defined as sailing as far down wind as possible with both sails on the same side and still full of wind. It is faster, safer, and more comfortable than sailing directly downwind (with the wind coming over the stern of the boat and the sail on opposite sides).

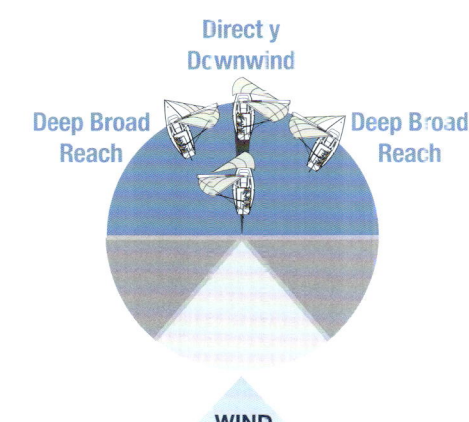

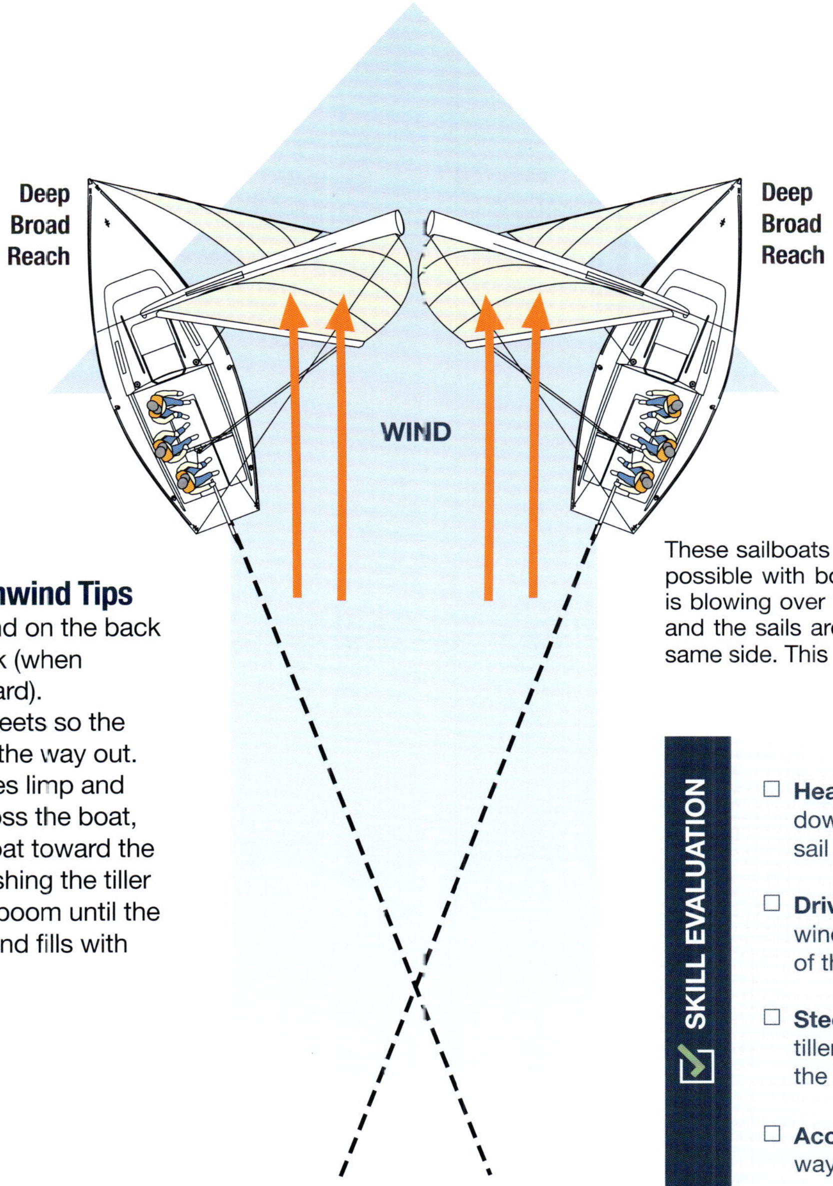

Directly Downwind

Deep Broad Reach   **Deep Broad Reach**

WIND

Deep Broad Reach

WIND

Deep Broad Reach

Sailing Downwind Tips

► Feel the wind on the back of your neck (when facing forward).

► Ease the sheets so the sails are all the way out.

► If the jib goes limp and starts to cross the boat, head the boat toward the wind by pushing the tiller toward the boom until the jib returns and fills with wind again.

These sailboats are sailing as far downwind as possible with both sails full of wind. The wind is blowing over the back corner of the sailboat and the sails are eased all the way out on the same side. This is called a *deep broad reach*.

SKILL EVALUATION

☐ **Heading** - Steer a steady, downwind course with good sail trim.

☐ **Driver Position** - Sit on the windward side, forward and clear of the tiller.

☐ **Steering** - Adjusting steering with tiller and sail trim with sheets at the same time

☐ **Accidental Jibes** - Identify three ways to prevent an accidental jibe.

☐ **Sailing by the Lee** - Identify when your mainsail leech is going soft.

JIBING

A *jibe* (sometimes spelled gybe) is a fundamental sailing maneuver. Like a tack, the jibe turns the sailboat so that both the wind and the sails cross from one side of the sailboat to the other. The difference is that during a tack you steer the bow through the No-Sail (No-Go) Zone and during a jibe you steer the stern through the No-Sail (No-Go) Zone.

REMEMBER:
STAY SEATED AND BE READY TO DUCK UNDER THE BOOM AS IT CROSSES THE SAILBOAT.

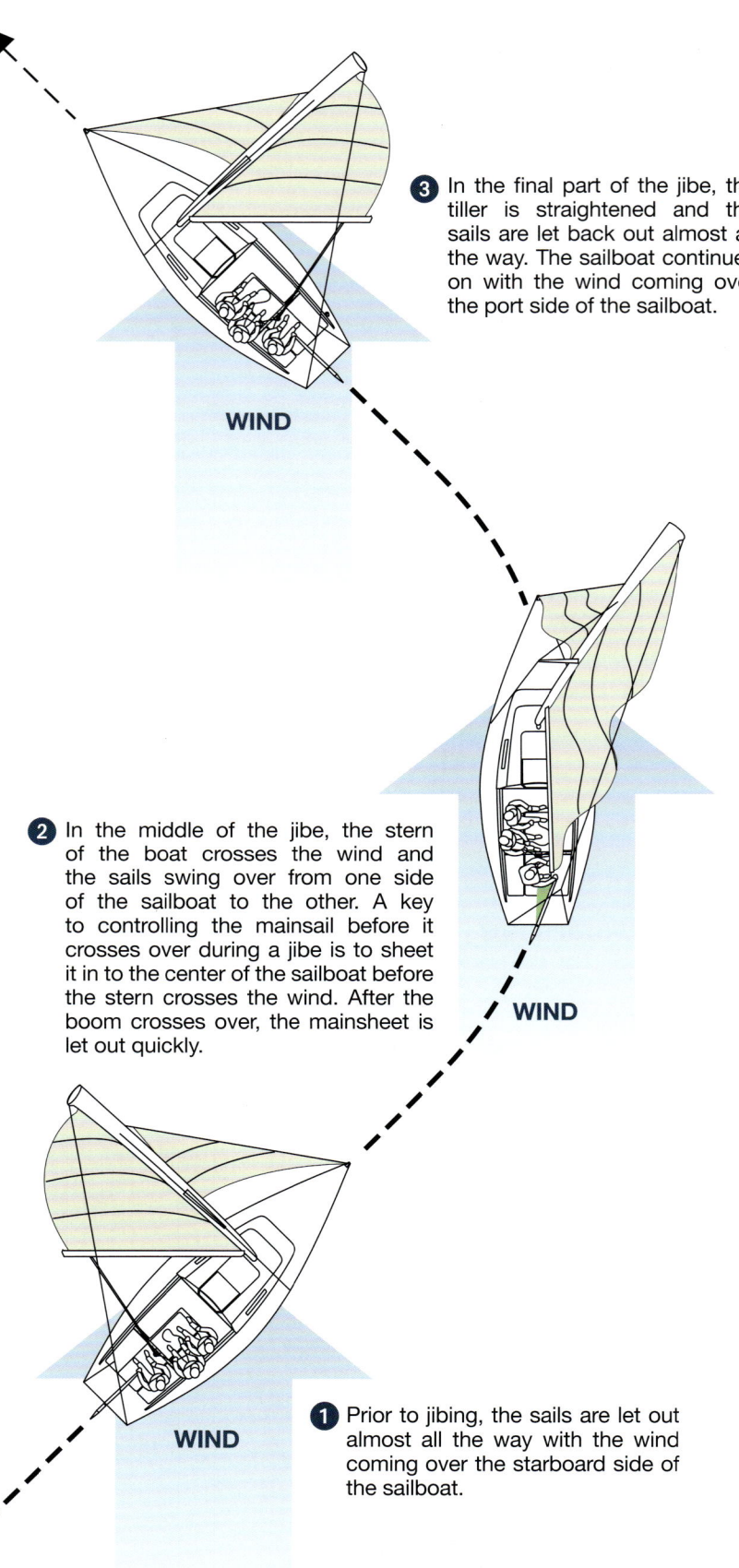

3 In the final part of the jibe, the tiller is straightened and the sails are let back out almost all the way. The sailboat continues on with the wind coming over the port side of the sailboat.

WIND

2 In the middle of the jibe, the stern of the boat crosses the wind and the sails swing over from one side of the sailboat to the other. A key to controlling the mainsail before it crosses over during a jibe is to sheet it in to the center of the sailboat before the stern crosses the wind. After the boom crosses over, the mainsheet is let out quickly.

WIND

1 Prior to jibing, the sails are let out almost all the way with the wind coming over the starboard side of the sailboat.

WIND

DANGEROUS UNCONTROLLED JIBES!

The sailors in these illustrations have forgotten to sheet in the mainsail, resulting in an uncontrolled jibe. The force of the boom rapidly swinging across the cockpit can break rigging or hit a crew member. In illustrations positions **②** and **③**, it is still possible to avoid the uncontrolled jibe if the driver heads up to the original course. The key thing to do if the uncontrolled jibe occurs **④** is to quickly duck under the boom's path. **The alert sailor should shout out a warning, "Duck!"**

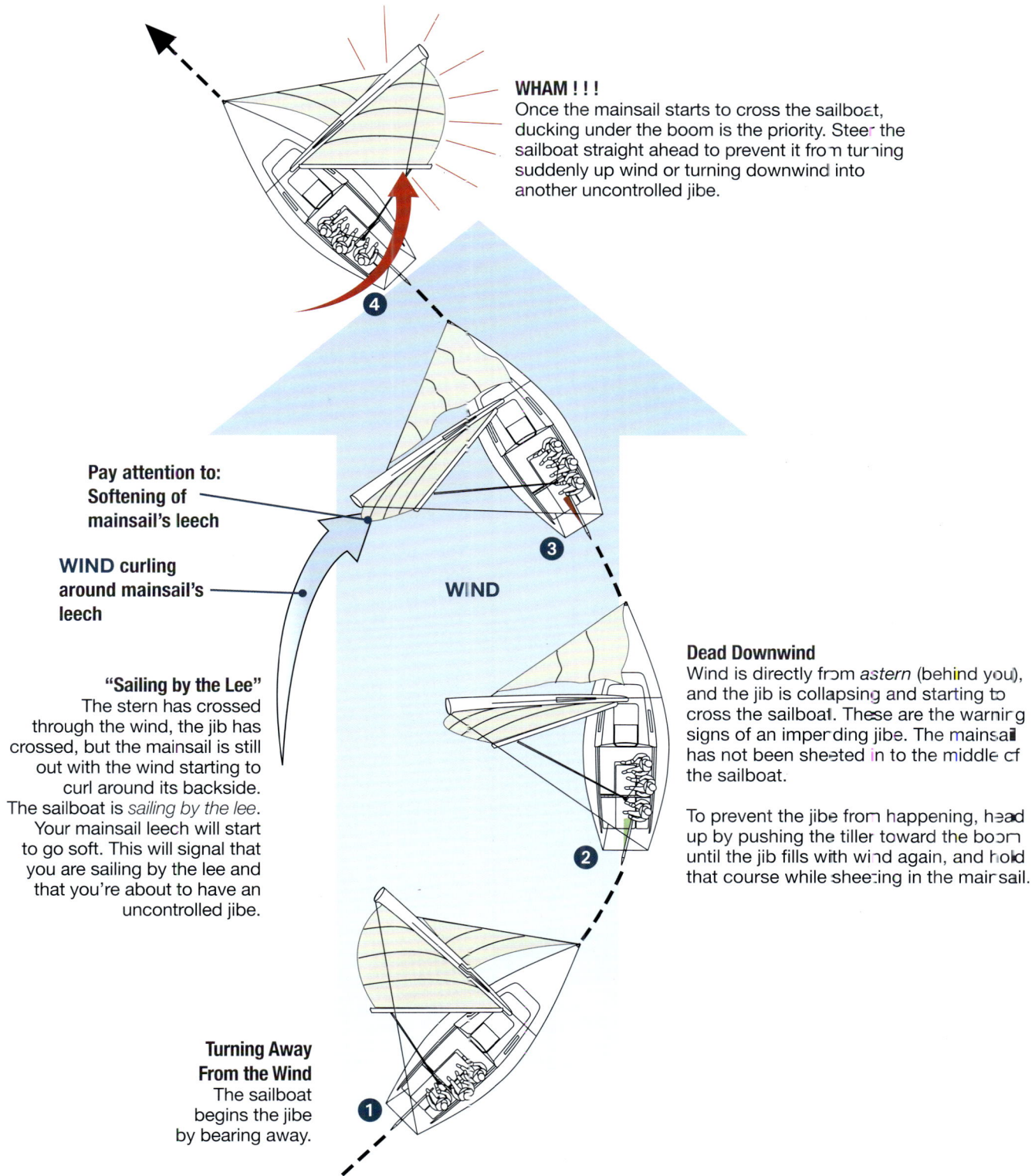

WHAM ! ! !
Once the mainsail starts to cross the sailboat, ducking under the boom is the priority. Steer the sailboat straight ahead to prevent it from turning suddenly up wind or turning downwind into another uncontrolled jibe.

Pay attention to:
Softening of mainsail's leech

WIND curling around mainsail's leech

WIND

"Sailing by the Lee"
The stern has crossed through the wind, the jib has crossed, but the mainsail is still out with the wind starting to curl around its backside. The sailboat is *sailing by the lee*. Your mainsail leech will start to go soft. This will signal that you are sailing by the lee and that you're about to have an uncontrolled jibe.

Dead Downwind
Wind is directly from *astern* (behind you), and the jib is collapsing and starting to cross the sailboat. These are the warning signs of an impending jibe. The mainsail has not been sheeted in to the middle of the sailboat.

To prevent the jibe from happening, head up by pushing the tiller toward the boom until the jib fills with wind again, and hold that course while sheeting in the mainsail.

Turning Away From the Wind
The sailboat begins the jibe by bearing away.

JIBING STEP-BY-STEP

There are four (4) key elements to a safe and controlled jibe.

❶ Steer a steady *deep broad reach* (close to, but not a run), as you prepare the sailboat for the jibe.
❷ Control the mainsail.
❸ Turn the sailboat SLOWLY through the jibe.
❹ Stop the turn as soon as the mainsail has crossed the sailboat.

Note that three of these four key elements have to do with steering. It is very easy to become preoccupied with the boom and lose track of where you are steering the sailboat. The following sequence of events from ❶ at the bottom of this page to ❹ at the top of the next page will help you understand what needs to be done and stay focused when jibing.

STAY ALERT!

When sailing on a run, remember to be alert to wind shifts so you can control the mainsail and avoid an uncontrolled jibe.

❶ **Prepare to Jibe**
The driver checks the wind direction, holds course on a deep broad reach, selects a reference to steer for when the jibe is completed, and then calls out, "*Prepare to jibe!*" The driver holds course as the mainsail is sheeted in until it is close to the sailboat's centerline. The crew takes the slack out of the lazy jib sheet, uncleats and holds the working jib sheet, and responds with, "*Ready!*"

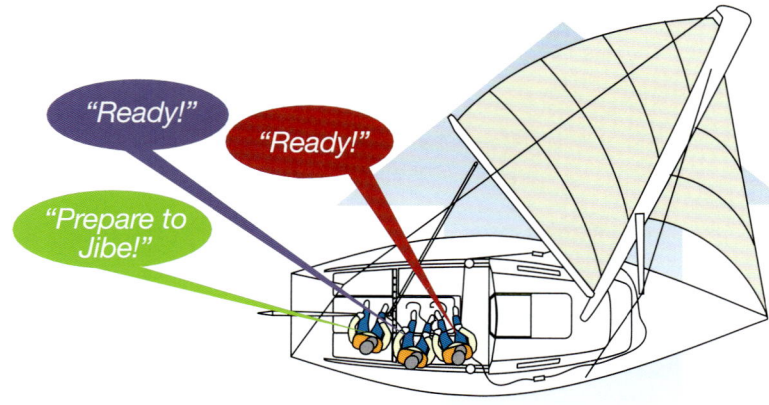

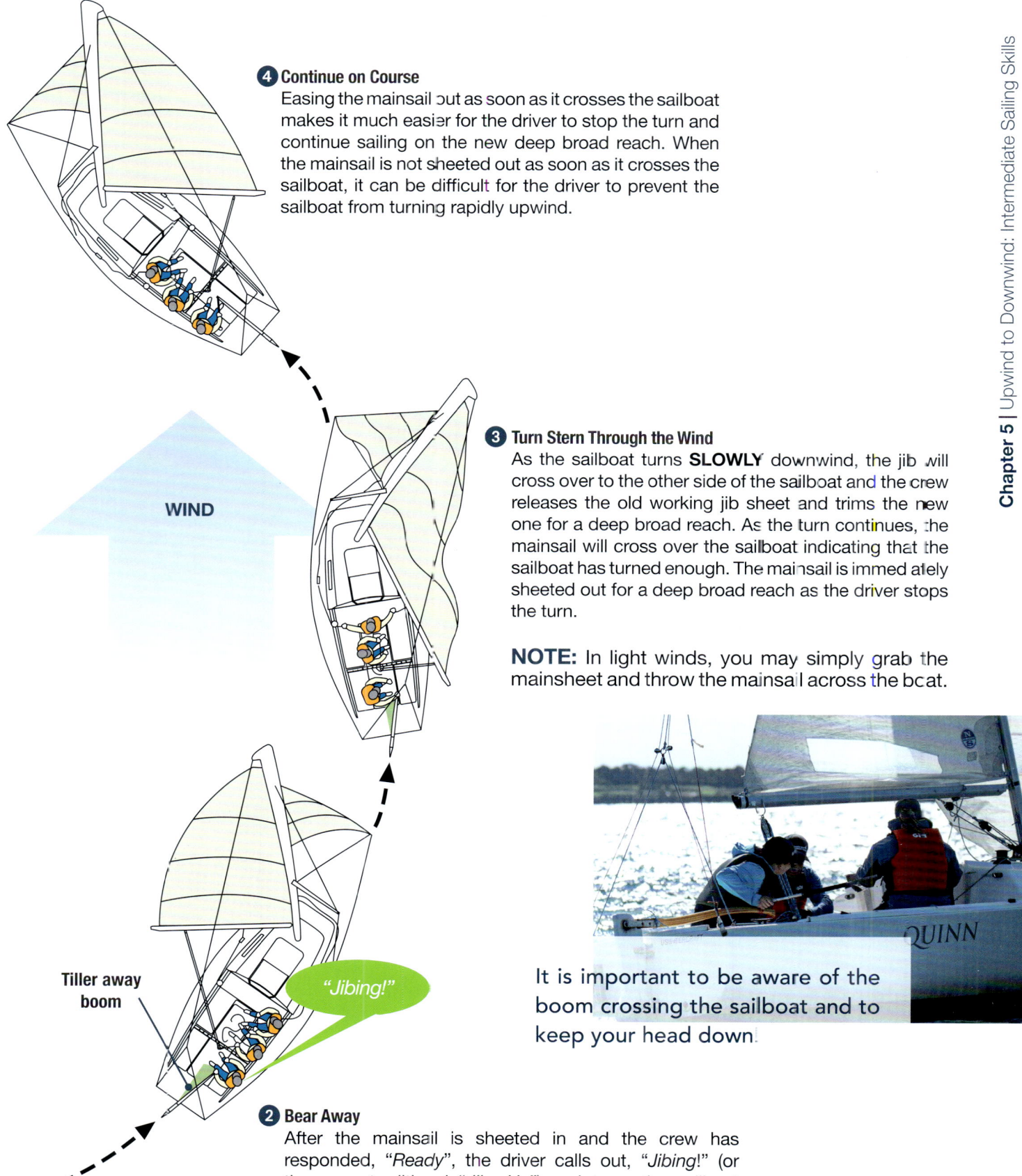

4 Continue on Course

Easing the mainsail out as soon as it crosses the sailboat makes it much easier for the driver to stop the turn and continue sailing on the new deep broad reach. When the mainsail is not sheeted out as soon as it crosses the sailboat, it can be difficult for the driver to prevent the sailboat from turning rapidly upwind.

WIND

3 Turn Stern Through the Wind

As the sailboat turns **SLOWLY** downwind, the jib will cross over to the other side of the sailboat and the crew releases the old working jib sheet and trims the new one for a deep broad reach. As the turn continues, the mainsail will cross over the sailboat indicating that the sailboat has turned enough. The mainsail is immediately sheeted out for a deep broad reach as the driver stops the turn.

NOTE: In light winds, you may simply grab the mainsheet and throw the mainsail across the boat.

It is important to be aware of the boom crossing the sailboat and to keep your head down.

Tiller away boom

"Jibing!"

2 Bear Away

After the mainsail is sheeted in and the crew has responded, "*Ready*", the driver calls out, "*Jibing!*" (or the more traditional "*Jibe-Ho*") and turns the sailboat **SLOWLY** away from the wind (tiller away from the boom).

GETTING THERE AND RETURNING

Now let's put everything you have just learned together by sailing upwind, across the wind, and downwind. We will start by sailing upwind to a *buoy* with a series of tacks. Then we'll sail across the wind on a reach to another buoy. After rounding the second buoy, we'll sail downwind using a series of jibes. After jibing around the third buoy, we will sail a reach, this time on starboard tack back to our starting point.

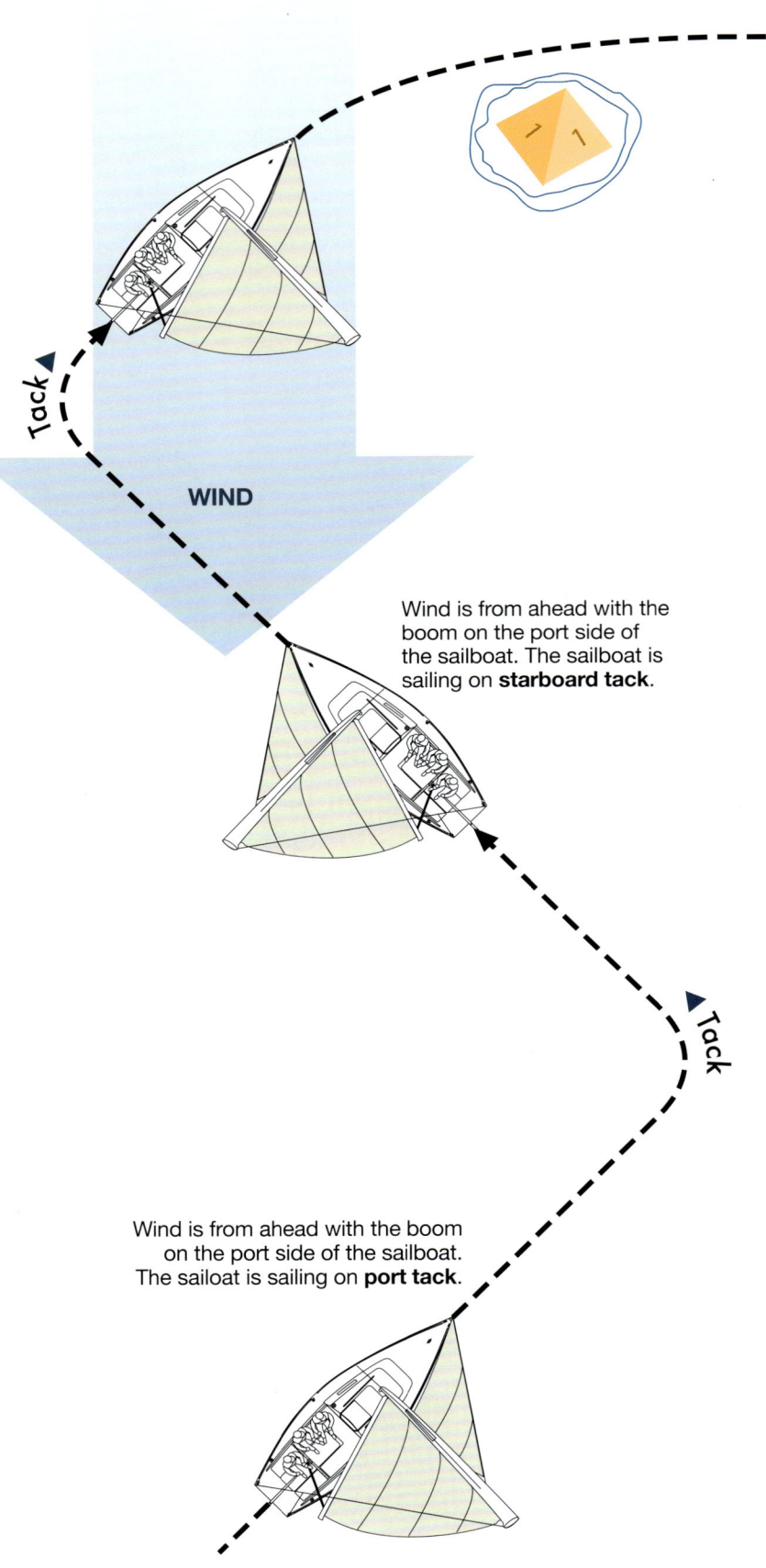

Wind is from ahead with the boom on the port side of the sailboat. The sailboat is sailing on **starboard tack**.

WIND

Wind is from ahead with the boom on the port side of the sailboat. The sailoat is sailing on **port tack**.

SKILL EVALUATION

☐ **Sail Trim** - Adjust sail trim as needed for each of the points of sail on a circuit.

☐ **Maintain Course** - Sail a predetermined course within +/- 10 degrees with proper sail trim.

Sailing Upwind

▶ Wind coming over the bow of boat.

▶ Sails are sheeted in all the way.

▶ Driver steers boat toward the wind as much as possible.

▶ A sailboat may sail a series of tacks to reach a destination.

TIP

Sailing upwind is also called beating to windward, or *beating*.

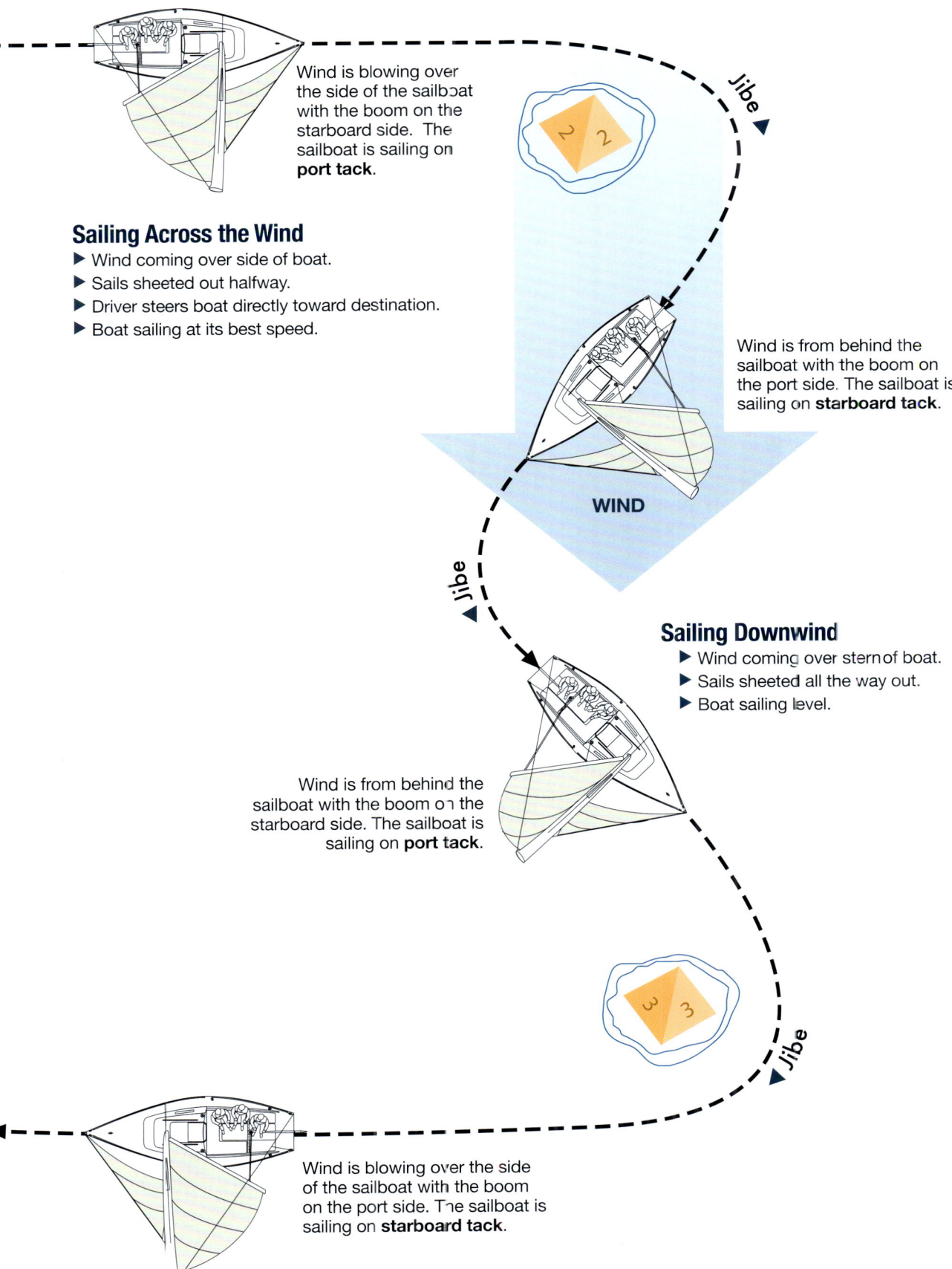

Wind is blowing over the side of the sailboat with the boom on the starboard side. The sailboat is sailing on **port tack**.

Sailing Across the Wind

▶ Wind coming over side of boat.
▶ Sails sheeted out halfway.
▶ Driver steers boat directly toward destination.
▶ Boat sailing at its best speed.

Jibe ▼

Wind is from behind the sailboat with the boom on the port side. The sailboat is sailing on **starboard tack**.

WIND

◀ Jibe

Sailing Downwind

▶ Wind coming over stern of boat.
▶ Sails sheeted all the way out.
▶ Boat sailing level.

Wind is from behind the sailboat with the boom on the starboard side. The sailboat is sailing on **port tack**.

▼ Jibe

Wind is blowing over the side of the sailboat with the boom on the port side. The sailboat is sailing on **starboard tack**.

SAILING ANGLES

TACKING ANGLES

Since tacking upwind requires course changes of approximately 90 degrees, there are several ways to arrive at an upwind destination. In open water you can sail on one tack until you are in a position to tack just once and then sail directly to your destination. In a *channel,* you may need to use a series of short tacks to reach your destination.

A handy way to estimate what your new course will be after you tack is to sight directly off the windward side of the boat and pick out a landmark. This landmark will help you reference where your bow should point after your tack.

When tacking, your course options are unlimited, but the angle of your tacks should always be the same: about 90 degrees.

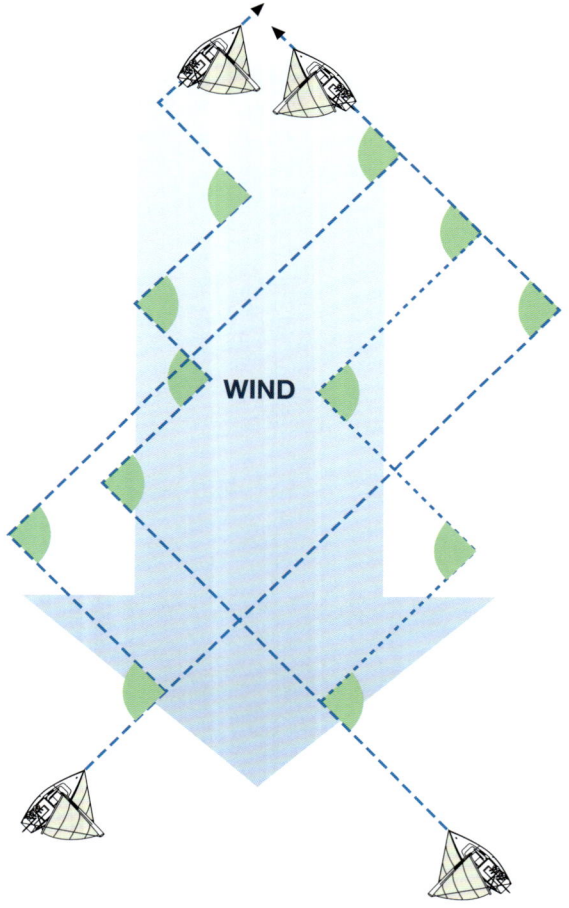

Tacking to an upwind destination is accomplished by sailing close hauled through a series of tacks.

JIBING ANGLES

Sailing downwind allows you to sail directly toward your destination. However, it is safer, more comfortable, and faster to sail on a deep broad reach and jibe, rather than sail directly downwind.

Jibing angles are a lot more flexible and less structured than tacking angles. With the wind coming from behind, you do not have to contend with the No-Sail (No-Go) Zone.

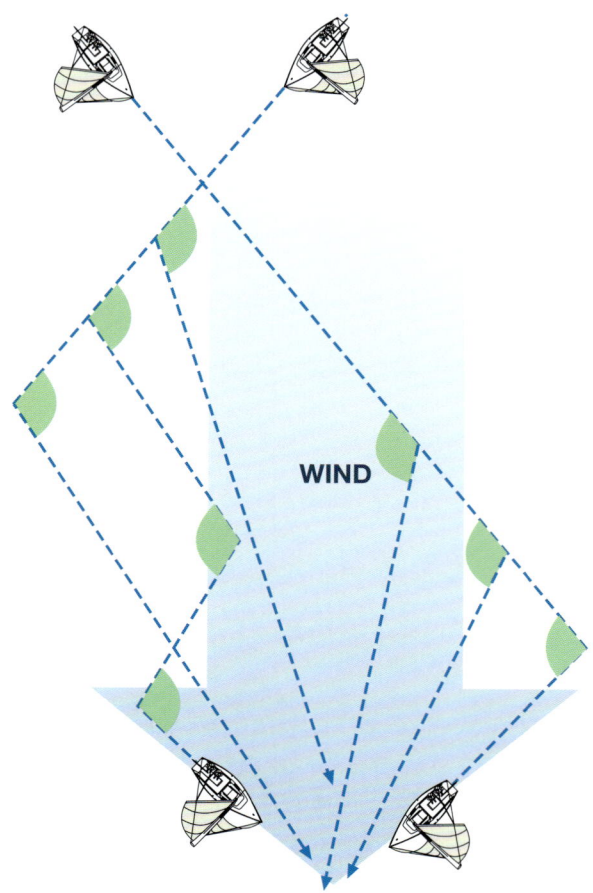

Similar to tacking upwind, you can either use just one or a series of jibes to head downwind.

KEEP IN MIND

When tacking, we turn through an angle of approximately 90 degrees. When jibing, however, the angle is much smaller, about 45 degrees.

PUTTING IT ALL TOGETHER

SUMMARY

- When sailing upwind with your course about 45 degrees from the wind's direction is called sailing close-hauled. This angle allows you to sail as close to the wind as possible while avoiding the No-Sail (No- Go) Zone.
- You cannot sail directly into the wind; instead navigate a zig-zag course, tacking upwind.
- When tacking close-hauled to close-hauled the driver slows down the turn earlier than when tacking from reach to reach.
- When sailing downwind, sailing on a deep broad reach is faster, safer, and more comfortable than a run.

- Sailing directly downwind increases the risk of dangerous jibes. Preventing it requires awareness and accurate steering by driver.
- A jibe can happen faster and be more dangerous than a tack.
- A jibe is similar to a tack, but instead of the bow going through the wind, the stern will go through the wind.
- To jibe, pull the tiller away from the mainsail.
- When the wind changes direction, you many need to tack, jibe, and/or adjust your sails to remain on course to your destination.

KEY TERMS AND CONCEPTS

1. There are four fundamental sailing maneuvers: heading up, bearing away, tacking, and jibing.
2. **Close-hauled:** sailing as close to the source of the wind as possible without entering the No-Sail Zone.
3. **Deep broad reach**: sailing as far downwind as possible, both sails full on the same side.
4. When jibing, duck under the boom.
5. If an uncontrolled jibe occurs, quickly shout and duck under the boom as it crosses.
6. To prevent an **uncontrolled jibe**, push the tiller toward the boom and head up.
7. Stay alert to wind shifts to avoid accidental jibes, particularly when **sailing by the lee**.

CHECK YOUR UNDERSTANDING

1. What should the crew do during a close-hauled tack after the jib passes in front of the mast?

   ◯ a. Release the mainsheet out all the way

   ◯ b. Trim the jib sheet in all the way

   ◯ c. Furl or lower the jib on the deck

   ◯ d. Let the skipper know you are ready

2. During a close-hauled tack, what does the driver do to slow down the turn?

   ◯ a. Let go of the tiller

   ◯ b. Center the tiller earlier

   ◯ c. Release the jib sheet

   ◯ d. Trim the mainsail

Chapter 6

Mastering the Wind: Advanced Sailing Skills

Having seen and performed fundamental maneuvers, now we begin the process of refining and perfecting the sailor's art. We will be exploring how to shape our sails, how to use telltales to trim them efficiently, how to recognize and utilize changes in wind direction, strategies for sailing both up and down wind, and how to adjust the balance of the boat. With practice and understanding comes increasing competency, confidence, and pleasure.

BALANCE

A sailboat is a collection of forces in motion, not all of which move the sailboat in the same direction. The forces generated by the sails move the sailboat to leeward as well as forward. The sideways motion (called *leeway*) is resisted by the keel and rudder, causing the sailboat to heel as it moves forward. When all these forces are in balance, the sailboat will sail forward in a straight line. When they are not, the boat will tend to turn.

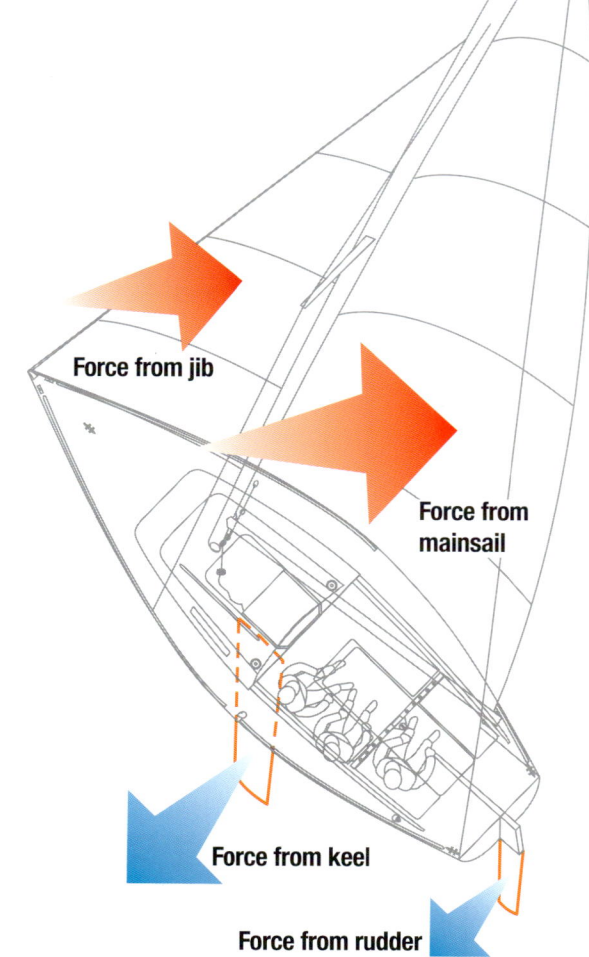

Force from jib

Force from mainsail

Force from keel

Force from rudder

The mainsail (pulling the stern to leeward) causes the sailboat to head up and the jib (pulling the bow to leeward) causes the sailboat to *bear away*. Because these forces are constantly changing and never exactly equal, small adjustments with the tiller are needed to keep the boat on course. Understanding principle of balance allows you to adjust your sails to minimize tiller corrections. As your sailing skills improve, you will use balance to get the best performance out of your sailboat and execute more advanced maneuvers.

USING TELLTALES

Sail trim is an important sailing skill, but because the wind is invisible, it can sometimes be difficult to judge if your sails are trimmed properly. Telltales are a very helpful tool in detecting wind flow across sails. Telltales provide direction on how to adjust your sails and when to change course.

SKILL EVALUATION

☐ **Close-Hauled** - Demonstrate adjusting sails and course using telltales to hold a close-hauled course.

☐ **Beam Reach** - Demonstrate adjusting sails and course using telltales to hold a reach.

☐ **Broad Reach** - Demonstrate adjusting sails and course using telltales to hold a run.

HOW TELLTALES WORK

Telltales are pieces of yarn or sail cloth attached near the luff of the jib and on the leech of the mainsail. When sailing close-hauled with sails sheeted in, the driver steers to the telltales. On a reach, the driver holds course and sails are trimmed to the telltales.

▶ If both telltales stream straight back, it means the wind is flowing smoothly over both sides of the sail.

▶ If the leeward telltale is fluttering, sheet out the sail toward the telltale or turn the boat away from the telltale (head up) until it flows smoothly.

▶ If the windward telltale is fluttering, either sheet in the jib toward the telltale or turn the boat away from the telltale (bear away) until it stops fluttering and flows smoothly.

▶ To adjust your course to the telltales, remember: "Tiller Toward the Tattling Telltale"

▶ To adjust your sail trim to the telltales, remember: "Trim Toward the Tattling Telltale"

JIB SAIL TRIM

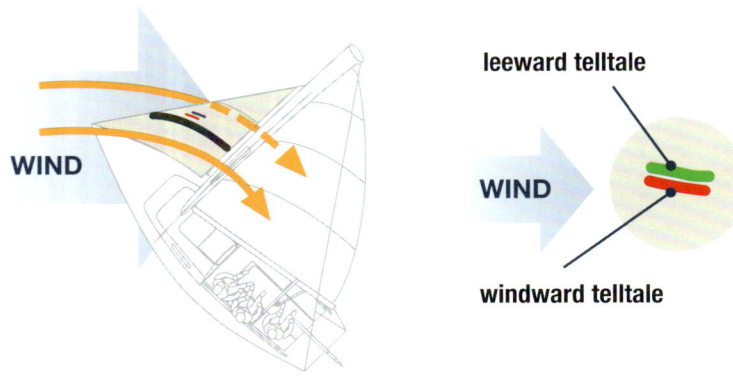

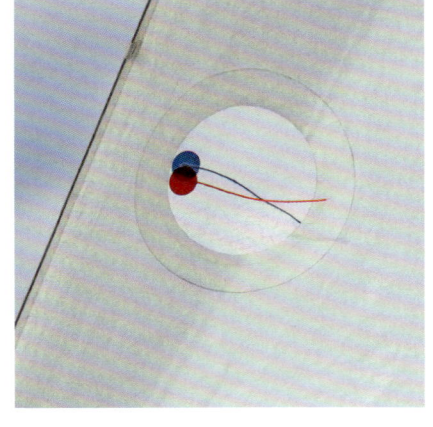

Air flow is smooth on both sides of the jib, and the telltales are both streaming back.

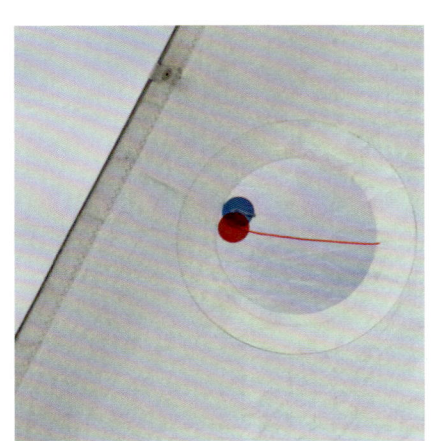

This jib is sheeted in too tight. Air flow is turbulent on the outside (leeward) side of the sail as indicated by the fluttering telltale. Ease the jib sheet out or head up to get smooth air flow.

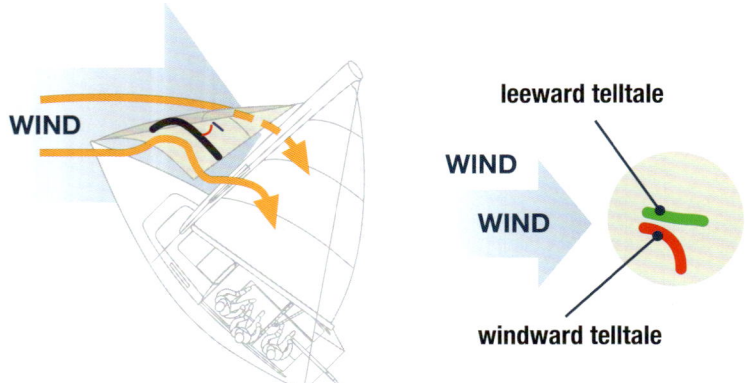

This telltale on the windward side is fluttering, indicating turbulence on that side of the sail. Sheet in the jib or bear away until the telltale stops fluttering.

MAINSAIL TRIM

JUST RIGHT

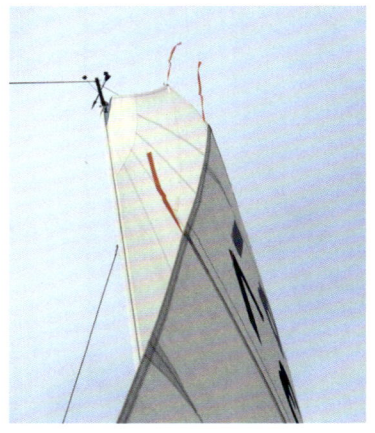

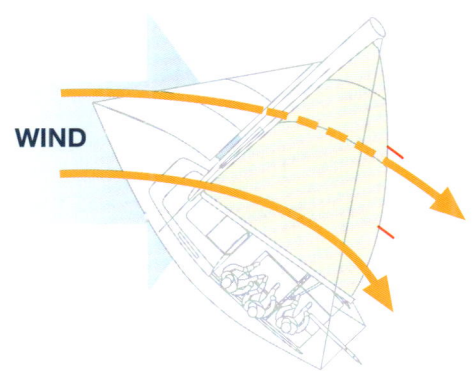

WIND

The mainsail is trimmed properly when you ease it until it luffs, then trim it in just until it stops luffing. The telltales will be streaming off the leech indicating that airflow is smooth on both sides of the mainsail.

TOO TIGHT

Telltale curled forward on the leeward side.

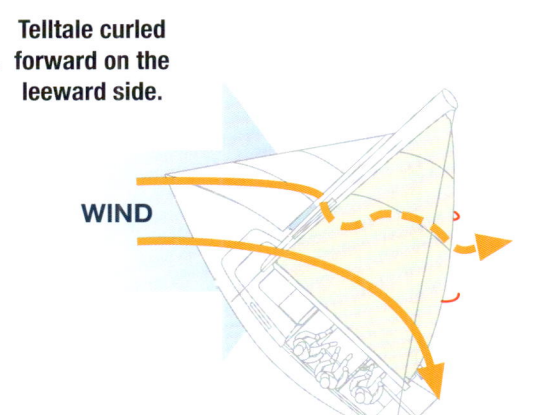

WIND

When the main is trimmed too tight, it is stalled and not being used efficiently. Leech telltales indicate over-trimming when they curl forward on the *leeward side* of the mainsail (where you may not be able to see them).

TOO LOOSE

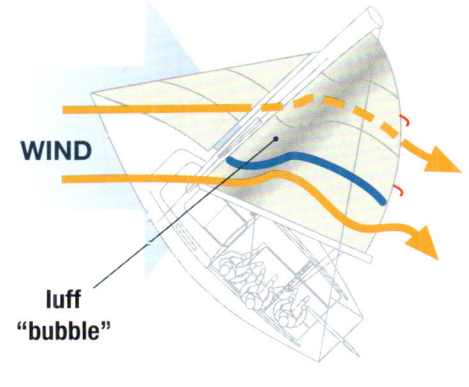

WIND

luff "bubble"

The luff bubble and the fluttering leech telltales are good indicators that the mainsail needs to be sheeted in more.

STEERING WITH TELLTALES

Telltales are a helpful aid to assist you with steering an optimum course when sailing upwind. Usually several pairs of telltales can be found on the luff of the *headsail*. Use the lowest set of telltales to fine tune your course and to efficiently sail your boat to windward.

TOO HIGH

When sailing closer to the wind, the boat heels less because there is less power in the sails. *The windward telltale will flutter (fly up or down from parallel).* At this point, smoothly steer back down away from the wind until the jib stops luffing and you feel your boat speed pick up again.

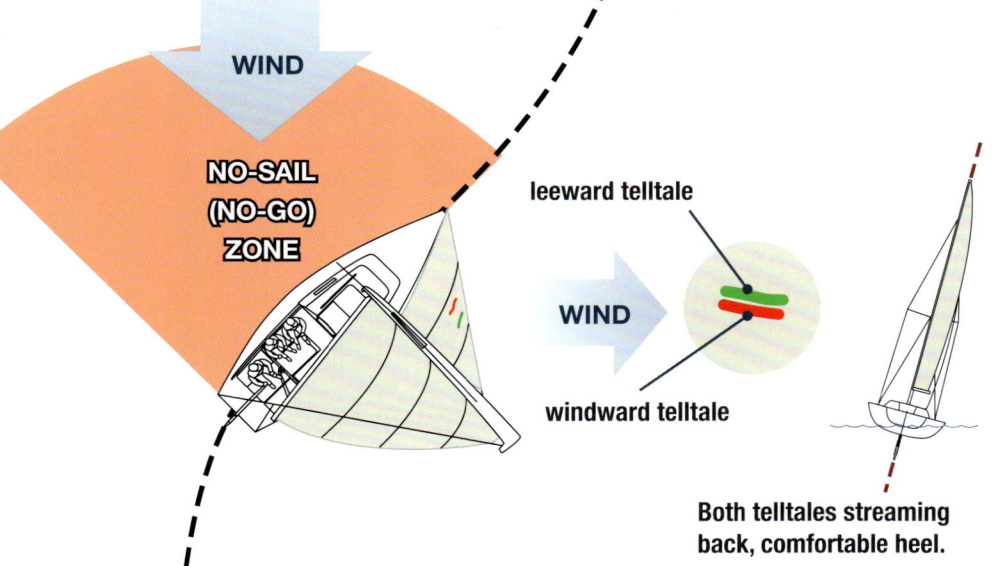

leeward telltale

WIND

windward telltale

WIND

NO-SAIL (NO-GO) ZONE

Windward telltales fluttering, less heel.

WIND

NO-SAIL (NO-GO) ZONE

JUST RIGHT

With perfect sail trim on the edge of the No-Sail (No-Go) Zone, the sails are working most efficiently. Both the windward and leeward telltales will stream straight aft (back).

leeward telltale

WIND

windward telltale

Both telltales streaming back, comfortable heel.

WIND

NO-SAIL (NO-GO) ZONE

TOO LOW

When sailing too low, efficiency is reduced. The boat will not feel very different, other than increased heel. You have to watch the telltales to make course corrections. Head up until both telltales are streaming straight back.

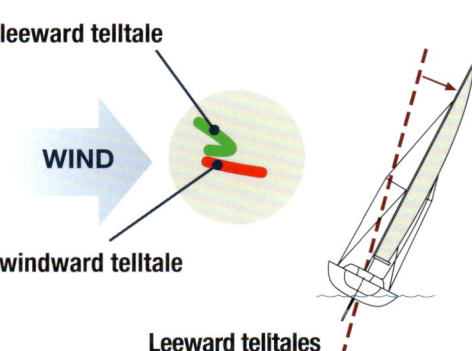

leeward telltale

WIND

windward telltale

Leeward telltales fluttering, too much heel.

SAILING IN THE GROOVE

As you learn to sail up wind, you will develop an advanced technique called "sailing in the groove." The *groove* is an invisible sailing angle where your sailboat is making the best progress toward the wind (*to windward*). Sails will be trimmed in for close hauled and the sailboat is steered to the perfect angle to the wind. Finding the groove and staying there can be a bit of a challenge at first, but sailors soon learn how to "feel it" when their sailboat is in the groove. The best references for staying in the groove are your sailboat's speed, how much it tips (*angle of heel*), and the use of the jib telltales.

The No-Sail (No-Go) Zone extends about 45 degrees off both sides of the eye of the wind.

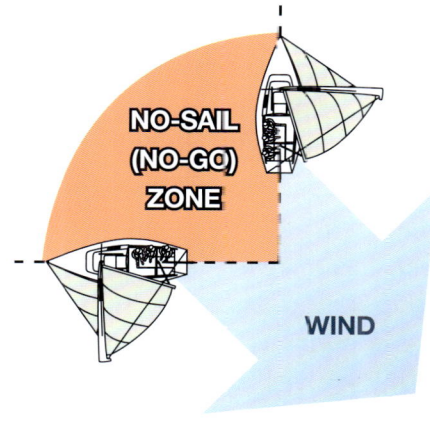

NO-SAIL (NO-GO) ZONE

WIND

Telltales stream back when wind flow is smooth and flutter upward when flow is turbulent.

WIND

NO-SAIL (NO-GO) ZONE

What is "The Groove"?
Experienced helmsmen don't sail a perfectly straight course upwind. They subtly "snake" a course along the edge of the No-Sail (No-Go) Zone—first sailing closer to the wind to see if the sails are on the verge of luffing, then heading back away from the wind to fill the sails with wind. This technique is called *sailing in the groove.*

WIND SHIFTS UPWIND

Even the steadiest breezes will shift (change direction). These shifts, ranging from subtle to quite substantial, play a significant role in how you sail upwind. When the wind shifts, your No-Sail (No-Go) Zone shifts with it. This affects the course you can sail. When the wind shifts aft, you are able to head up and sail more directly toward your destination. When the wind shifts forward, you must bear away and sail a less direct course to your destination. If the wind shift is large enough, you should tack because the new tack will allow you to sail closer to your destination than your current one.

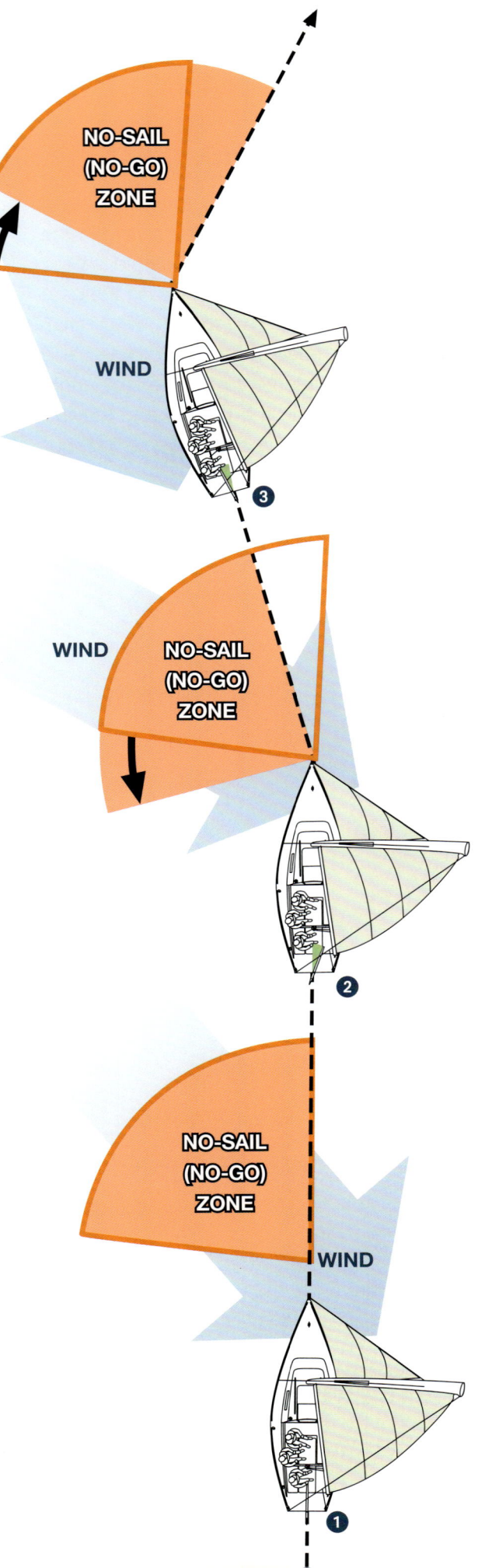

WIND SHIFT TIPS

▶ A wind that shifts aft and allows you to head up is called a *lift*.

▶ A wind shift that shifts forward and forces you to bear away is called a *header*.

(Follow sequence from bottom ❶ to top ❸)

❶ **Sailing a Close hauled Course**
This sailboat is sailing upwind on a close hauled course.

❷ **Lift (wind shifts aft)**
The wind has shifted aft, which also moves the No-Sail (No-Go) Zone aft. This allows the driver to head up.

❸ **Header (wind shifts forward)**
The wind has shifted forward from the original direction, shifting the No-Sail (No-Go) Zone forward. The boat's course is now in the No-Sail (No-Go) Zone and the driver must bear away until the boat is on a close-hauled course again.

WIND SHIFTS AND DISTANCE

Wind shifts *(headers* and *lifts)* do more than force you to change your course. They also shorten or lengthen the distance you will need to sail to reach a destination upwind. The example here shows how tacking when headed shortens the distance sailed to an upwind destination.

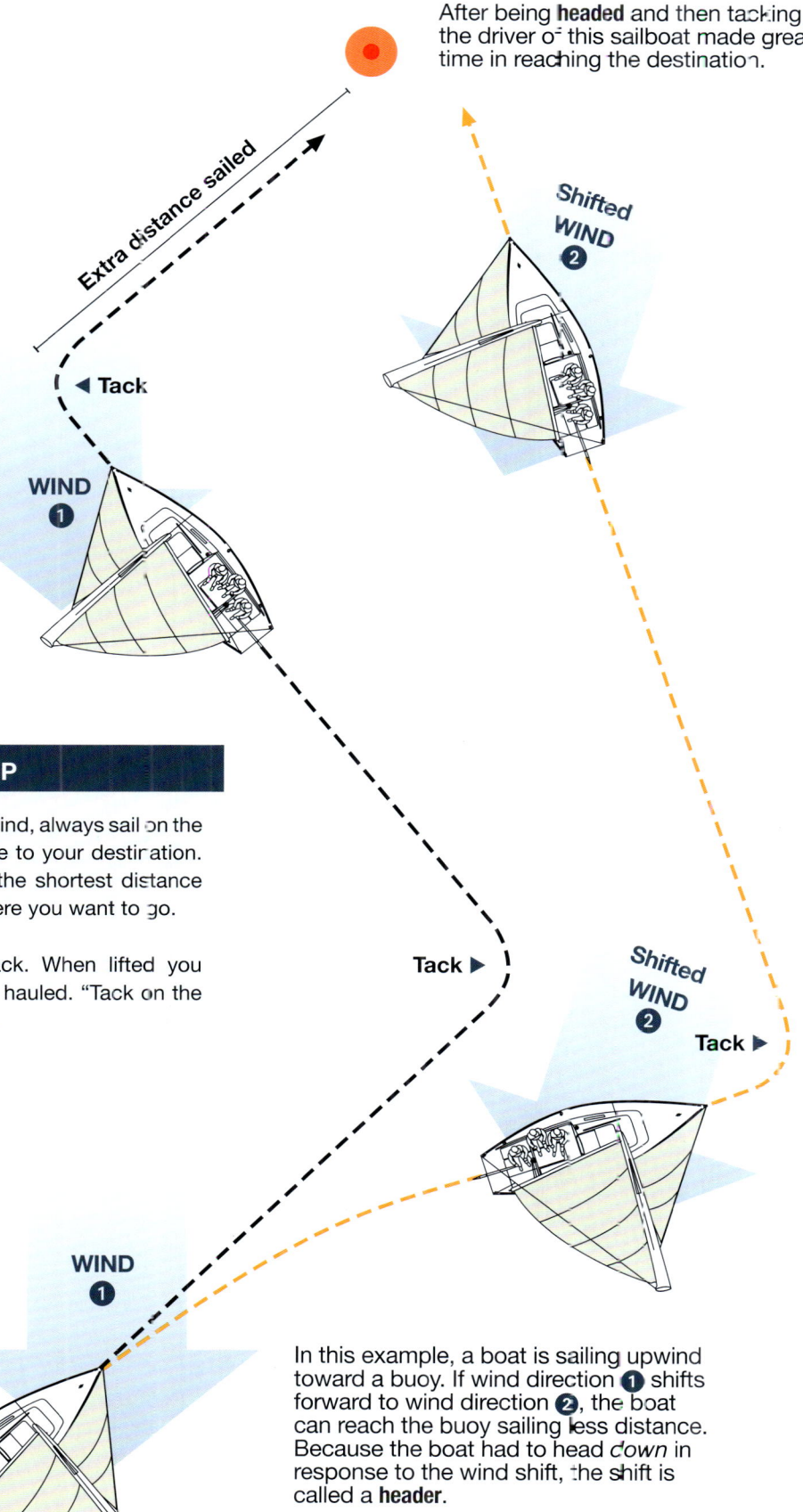

After being **headed** and then tacking, the driver of this sailboat made great time in reaching the destination.

Extra distance sailed

◄ Tack

Shifted **WIND** ❷

WIND ❶

Tack ►

Shifted **WIND** ❷

Tack ►

WIND ❶

EXPERT TIP

▶ When sailing upwind in shifty wind, always sail on the tack that has the closest angle to your destination. That way, you will be sailing the shortest distance (and the fastest course) to where you want to go.

▶ When headed you should tack. When lifted you should head up back to close hauled. "Tack on the headers, head up on the lifts".

In this example, a boat is sailing upwind toward a buoy. If wind direction ❶ shifts forward to wind direction ❷, the boat can reach the buoy sailing less distance. Because the boat had to head *down* in response to the wind shift, the shift is called a **header**.

ADJUSTING SAIL SHAPE

Sails are not flat. They have curvature (called *draft*) built into them. The amount and position of this draft can be adjusted to match the wind speed. In light winds, you want a full sail shape and in stronger winds a flatter shape. This will keep the boat under control and sailing well. Any surplus energy does not contribute to boat speed but only increases heel and makes steering more difficult.

The Cunningham adjusts mailsail luff tension. As wind speed increases and the sailcloth stretches, the position of the draft moves aft in the mainsail. Tightening the Cunningham moves the draft forward, back to its proper position.

Tightening the outhaul depowers the mainsail by flattening the lower (and largest) portion of the mainsail.

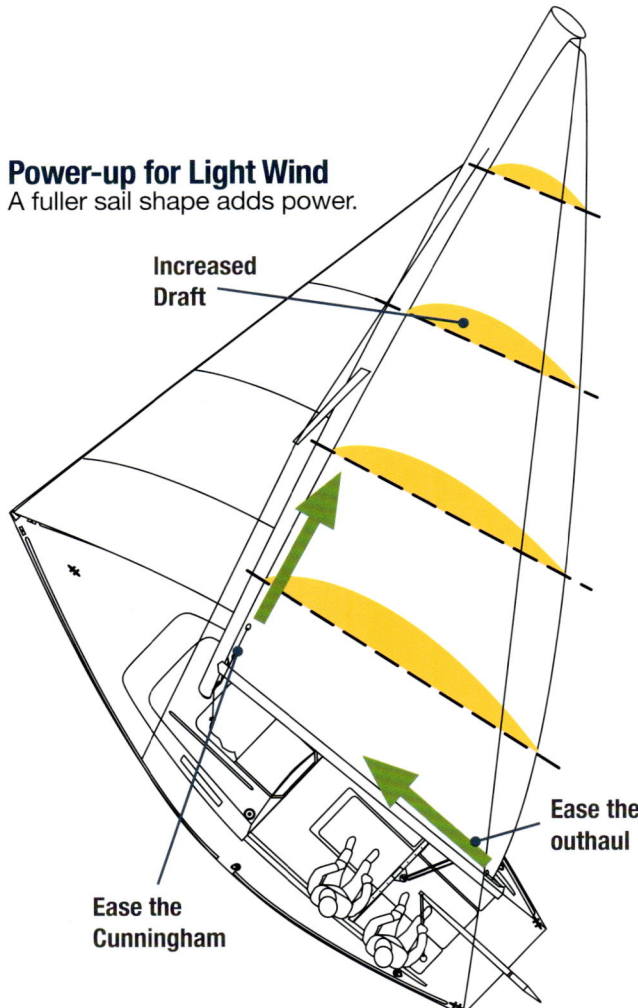

Power-up for Light Wind
A fuller sail shape adds power.

Increased Draft

Ease the Cunningham

Ease the outhaul

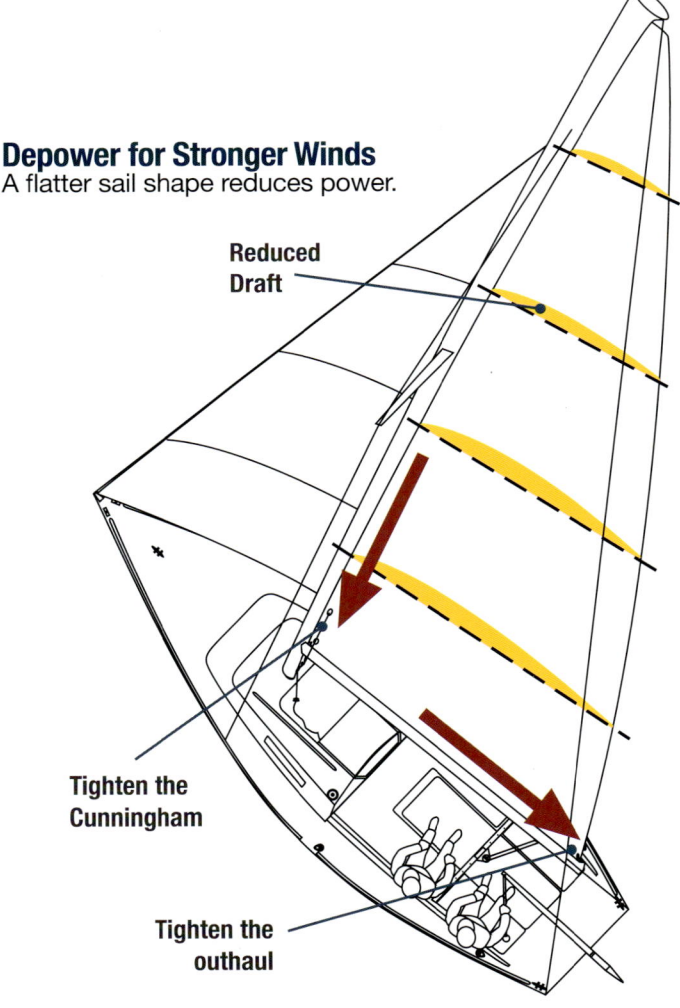

Depower for Stronger Winds
A flatter sail shape reduces power.

Reduced Draft

Tighten the Cunningham

Tighten the outhaul

DEPOWERING SAILS

To keep stronger winds from overpowering your sailboat, you can *ease* out the sails slightly to spill the excess wind. Adjusting sail trim, either permanently as winds increase or just momentarily during gusts will keep the sailboat balanced, easy to steer, and sailing at its best.

Depowering with the Traveler

Easing the traveler allows the boom and the sail to move to leeward without changing the shape of the sail. This decreases pressure on the sail, reduces heel, and makes steering easier.

Depowering with the Mainsheet

Easing the mainsheet a bit causes the boom to rise and move to leeward. The top of the mainsail then twists away from the wind, reducing power.

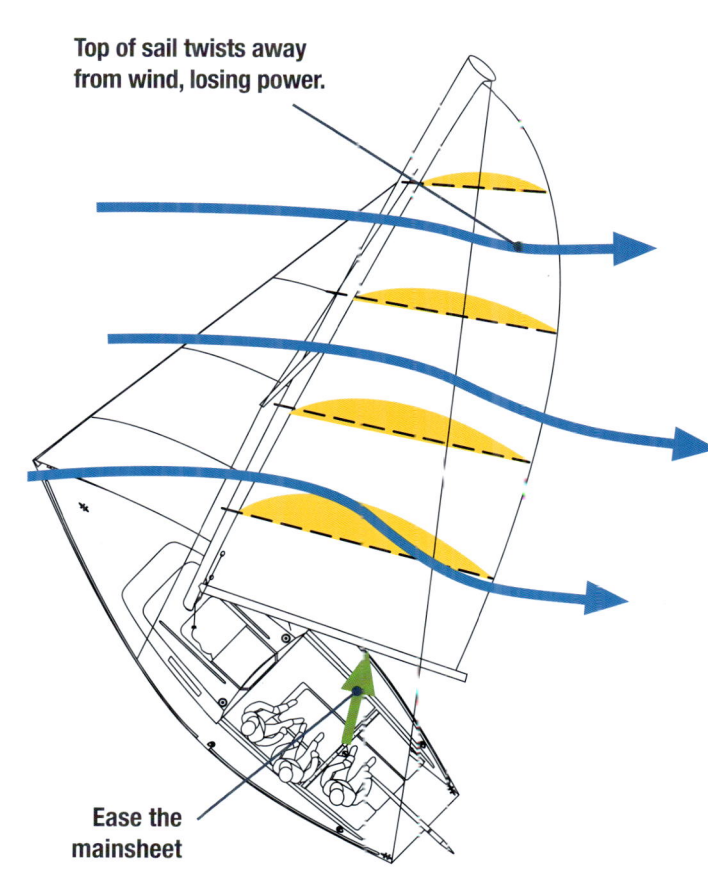

Entire sail rotates away from the wind, losing power.

Ease the traveler

Top of sail twists away from wind, losing power.

Ease the mainsheet

REDUCING SAIL AREA

As the wind speed increases, a point is reached where the sail shaping tools have been utilized completely. It is now time to reduce your sail area or "shorten sail". Your boat will sail just as fast and with less heel.

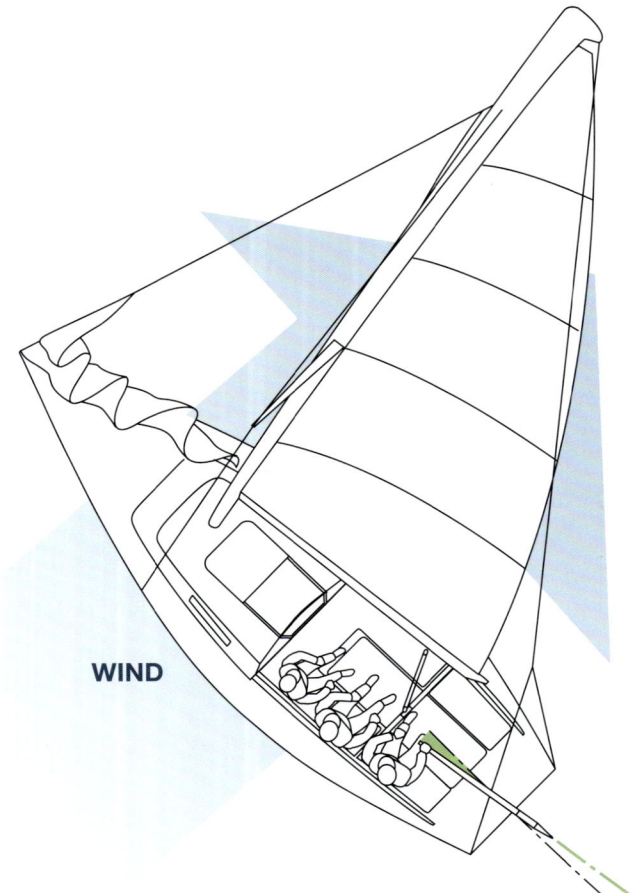

WIND

◄ Lowering the Jib

The easiest way to reduce sail is to simply lower or roll up the jib. With just the mainsail up, however, the boat is no longer in balance. The wind pressure on the mainsail will tend to rotate the bow of the boat toward the wind. To compensate, you will need to steer with the tiller pulled slightly to windward to keep the boat sailing straight. Not all boats will sail as well to windward with the jib down.

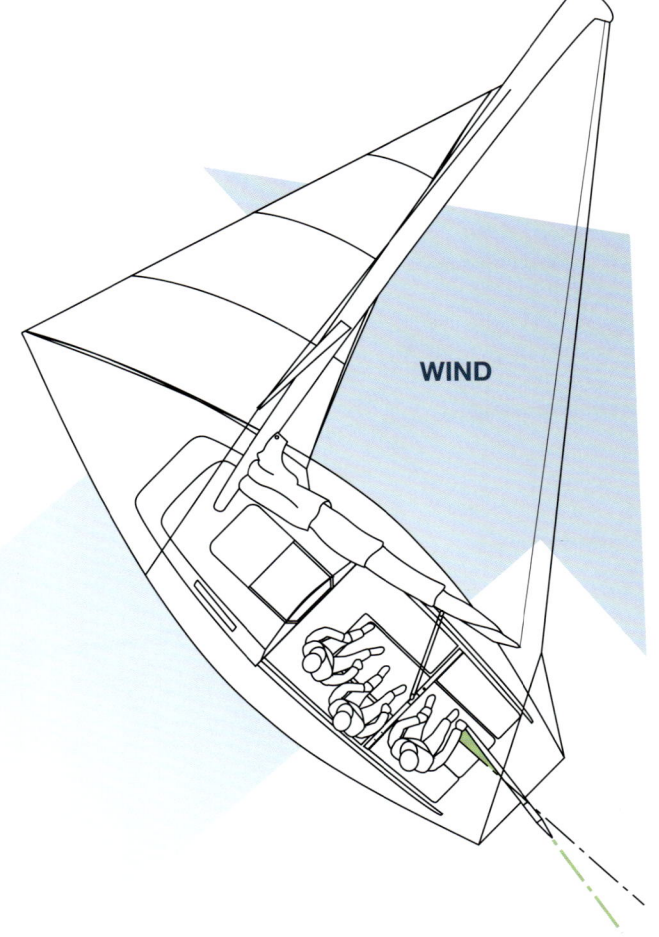

WIND

Lowering the Mainsail ►

The most significant way you can reduce sail is to lower the mainsail. With just the jib up, however, the boat is no longer in balance. The wind pressure on the jib will tend to rotate the bow of the boat away from the wind. To compensate, you will need to steer with the tiller pushed slightly to leeward to keep the boat sailing straight. Most sailboats will not sail to windward well, if at all with just a jib.

REFING

The size of the mainsail may be reduced by lowering it partially and securing it in that position using the lines and fittings supplied for that purpose. This process is most easily accomplished while sailing on a close reach under jib only with the mainsail luffing or when heaving-to.

SKILL EVALUATION

☐ **Time** - If you think about reefing, do it.

☐ **Sequence** - Tack, head, clew.

☐ **Proper Tension** - Luff first then foot.

☐ **Sail Ties** - Attach sail ties under the foot of the sail, not around the boom if possible.

☐ **Reverse** - Perform the steps in the opposite order to *shake out a reef.*

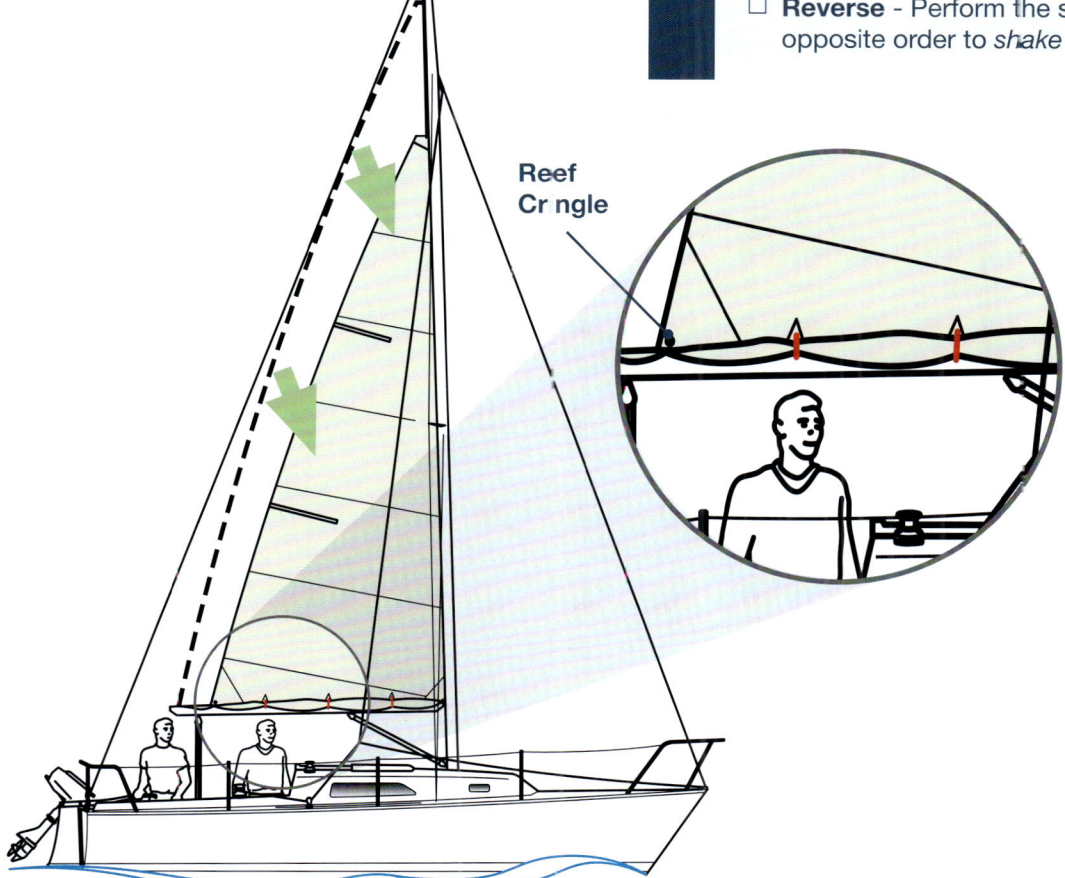

Reef
Cringle

1. Loosen the mainsheet and boom vang to unload the forces off the sail.

2. Lower the main halyard until your desired *reefing cringle* (grommet) is near the point where the mast and boom meet. Secure the new tack, usually by placing it in the hook at the gooseneck.

3. Raise the main halyard and winch it up until it is taut.

4. Tighten the reef line until the new foot of the mainsail is tight along the boom.

5. Pull the excess sail out on the windward side of the boom. Roll it up. **Secure it with sail ties that go around just the sail and not the boom,** if possible. If you must pass the sail ties around the boom, they should be tied loosely. However, the sail tie used to secure the sail at the clew should go around the boom. It will then act as a safety line should your reef line break. Make sure not to capture any of the mainsheet in the sail ties.

6. Tighten the boom vang and sheet in the mainsail.

7. Reverse the order to shake out (remove) the reef

BACKING THE JIB

There are times when a sailor intentionally backwinds or "backs" the jib. This means that the jib is intentionally sheeted on the "wrong" side of the sailboat, the windward side. This causes the bow to be pushed to leeward.

There are multiple situations in which you may want to backwind the jib:

▶ As you have seen, it can be useful when sailing off a dock.

▶ You can also backwind the jib to help push the bow through a tack on a light-wind day, by not immediately releasing the jib sheets as the boat passes through the no-sail zone.

▶ When a boat is caught in irons, backwinding the jib can force the bow to turn in the direction you want it to, getting you out of irons and sailing in a safe direction.

▶ It is also used when heaving-to, as described on this page.

HEAVING-TO

If you want or need to stop sailing, for instance to check a chart, or relax for lunch the best way is to *heave-to.* Heaving-to holds your position with the sails and rudder countering each other as the boat drifts forward and to leeward. Always check that you have plenty of room to drift downwind before heaving-to.

❶ To heave-to, sail closehauled and sheet the jib in so that it is as flat as possible.

❷ Head up into the No Sail (No-Go) zone as if you were going to tack, until the jib becomes backwinded. Do not release the jib sheet.

❸ Hold this straight into the wind course with the jib backwinded and the mainsail luffing. As the boat slows, it will take more and more tiller angle to maintain this *head-to-wind* course. Eventually, the sailboat will stop, the backwinded jib will complete the tack for you, and the tiller will be hard over on the new lee side.

❹ Secure the tiller and trim the mainsail so the boat lies on a close reach.

This sailboat is hove-to with the wind coming over the port side. The jib is sheeted to the port (windward) side, while the mainsail remains on the starboard (leeward) side, and the tiller is held hard to leeward.

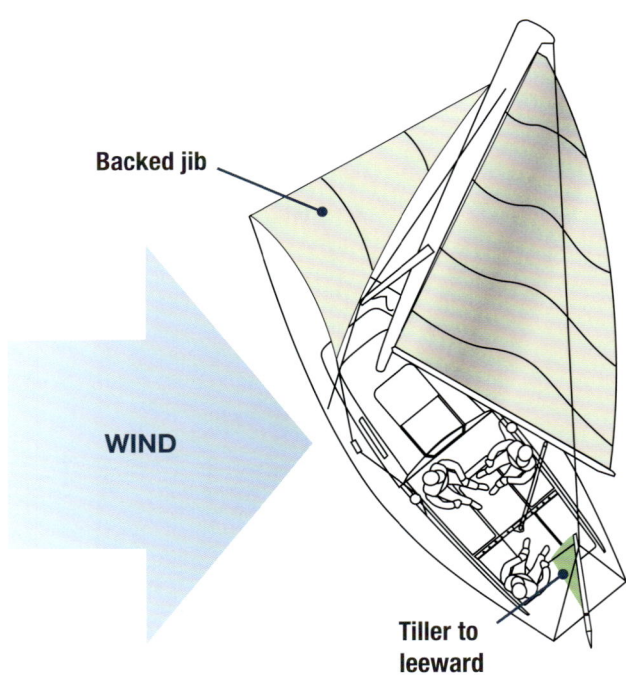

Backed jib

WIND

Tiller to leeward

HEAVING-TO TIP

▶ Be patient! Allow the sailboat to come to a complete stop while you are head to wind.

▶ Adjust mainsail trim so the sailboat maintains a close reach. Experiment to find out what works for your sailboat.

PUTTING IT ALL TOGETHER

SUMMARY

- Small tiller adjustments are normal when steering a steady course.
- If your sailboat constantly wants to turn upwind or downwind, the trim of your mainsail and/or jib needs to be adjusted.
- Telltales will alert you when your sails are too tight or loose.
- As the wind shifts direction, the No-Sail Zone shifts with it. Shifting aft allows heading up. Shifting forward requires bearing away. Substantial shifts may require tacking or jibing to stay on course.

- Proper sail shape is necessary to keep your sailboat under control and must be adjusted as wind speed changes. A fuller sail adds power, and a flatter sail reduces power.
- The Cunningham and outhaul adjust mainsail shape.
- To depower further, reduce sail area by furling or lowering the jib or reefing the mainsail.
- Backing the jib by intentionally sheeting it on the same side the wind is coming from is useful when caught in irons, sailing off a dock, or heaving-to.

KEY TERMS AND CONCEPTS

1. Adjust your course or sail trim with the telltales using the saying: "**Tiller Toward the Tattling Telltale.**"
2. When the telltales on both sides of the jib are streaming straight back, it's trimmed correctly.
3. A wind that shifts aft and allows you to head up is called a **lift**.
4. A wind shift that shifts forward and requires you to bear away is called a **header**.
5. Tightening the **Cunningham** adjusts mainsail luff tension, moving the draft forward.
6. Tightening the **outhaul** depowers the mainsail by flattening the lower portion of the mainsail.

CHECK YOUR UNDERSTANDING

1. What action should be taken if the leeward telltale is fluttering while sailing upwind?

   ○ a. Head up until the telltale flows smoothly back.
   ○ b. Keep changing course until the telltales stop fluttering.
   ○ c. Bear away until the telltale flows smoothly back.
   ○ d. Move the tiller away from the tattling telltale.

2. How does a significant forward wind shift (header) affect your sailing close-hauled?

   ○ a. You can head up and sail more directly toward your destination.
   ○ b. You must bear away and sail a less direct course to your destination.
   ○ c. You can hold current course until the wind shifts back.
   ○ d. The No-Sail (No-Go) Zone remains unchanged.

Chapter 7

Ancillary Skills & Situational Awareness

John Muir once said, "When one tugs at a single thing in nature, he finds it attached to the rest of the world." And so... there are many things that, while they are not strictly sailing skills, they are related to the operation of a sailboat. In this chapter we will be looking at these ancillary skills; such things as anchoring/mooring, weather and wind awareness, the outboard motor, the Rules of the Road, and navigation.

DOCKING IN CHALLENGING CONDITIONS

You don't always leave and return to the dock under the ideal conditions described earlier. Awareness of the wind conditions, forethought, and knowledge of sail handling are necessary for approaching and departing docks, particularly when weather conditions offer a challenge.

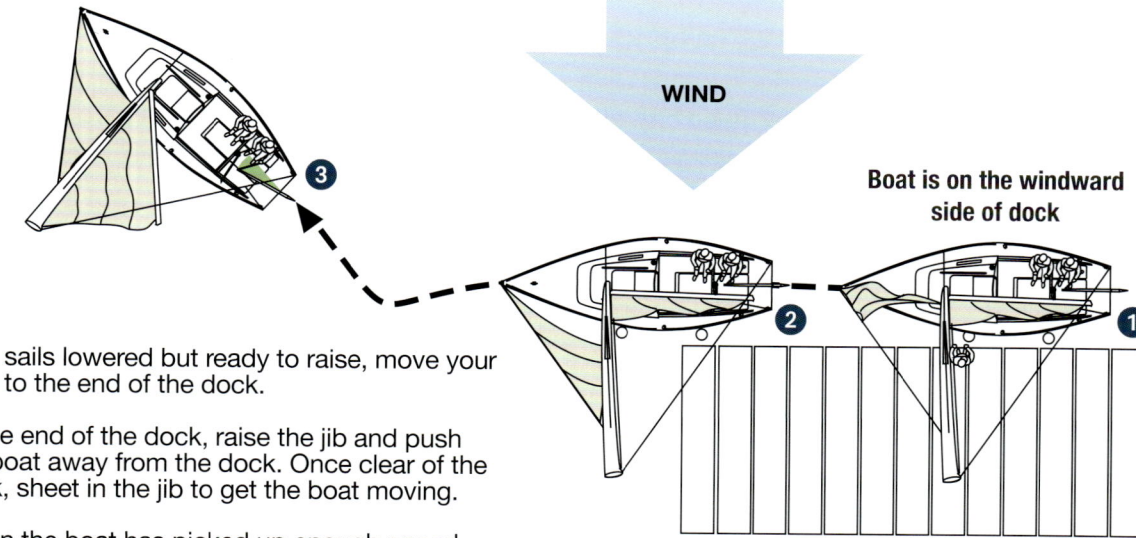

WIND

Boat is on the windward side of dock

❶ With sails lowered but ready to raise, move your boat to the end of the dock.

❷ At the end of the dock, raise the jib and push the boat away from the dock. Once clear of the dock, sheet in the jib to get the boat moving.

❸ When the boat has picked up enough speed, come to a close reach and hoist the mainsail. Once the mainsail is up, turn to your course.

Backward Departure

There may be times when you will have to sail the boat backward to leave the dock.

1 Back away from the dock
Push the boom out all the way in the direction you want the bow to turn (in this case to the port), and back the jib on the opposite side. Center the tiller. Cast off the bow line. The boat will sail backwards, away from the dock.

2 Turn away from the dock
As soon as the boat has cleared the dock, turn the tiller toward the mainsail (the same direction you want the bow to turn).

3 Sail away from the dock
When the sailboat has turned out of the No-Sail (No-Go) Zone, release the jib sheet and trim it on the correct (leeward) side, trim in the mainsheet, and center the tiller.

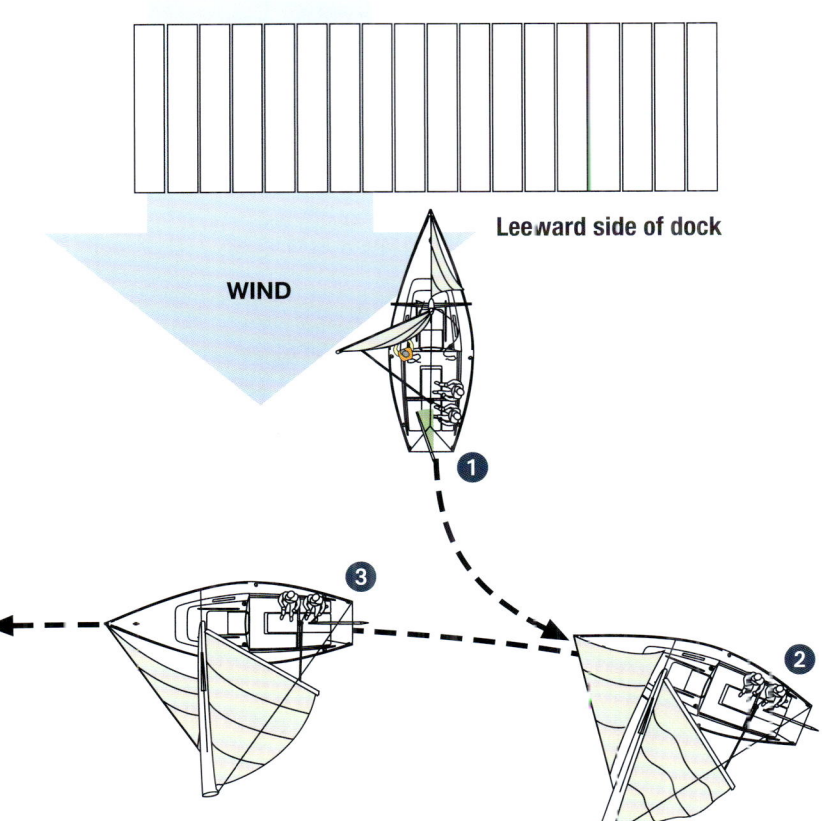

WIND

Leeward side of dock

Approaching the Windward Side of the Dock

To return to the windward side of the dock, lower the mainsail when the sailboat is up wind of the dock. Then steer down to the dock. Whether to leave the jib up depends on the conditions and the sailboat. In light air, keep the jib up, luffing it as necessary to maintain the ability to steer. If it's windy, either *furl* or lower the jib so you don't approach the dock too quickly.

❶ Brief your crew and deploy fenders.

❷ When about 4-5 boat lengths upwind of your landing spot, turn into the wind, lower and safely secure the mainsail.

❸ Turn downwind toward the dock, trimming or luffing the jib as necessary to adjust your speed.

❹ As you get near the dock, let the jib luff completely, furl or lower it. A crew member should be positioned at the shrouds to step off onto the dock and help slow the sailboat. **Remember: Do not postion any part of your body between the boat and the dock!**

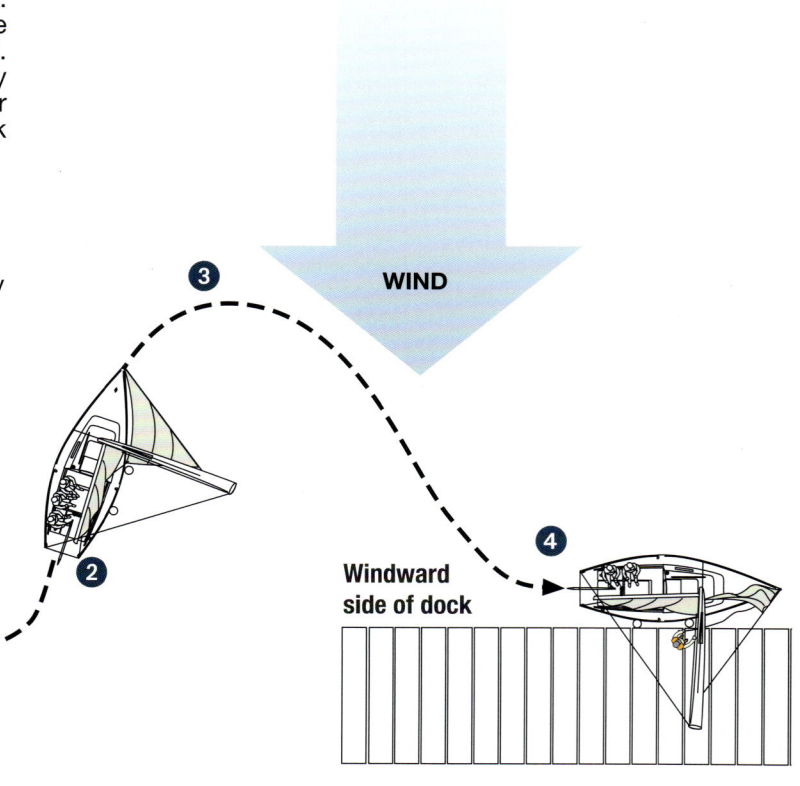

WIND

Windward side of dock

Approaching the Dock from a Downwind Course

The disadvantage of a downwind approach is that you have less control of your boat speed because you cannot luff your sails effectively, particularly the mainsail.

❶ Brief your crew and deploy fenders.

❷ Sail downwind until leeward of the dock. Allow enough distance from the dock to be able to coast to a stop.

❸ Turn upwind towards the dock with sails luffing and coast to the leeward side of the dock. If you need more speed, you can briefly sheet in the mainsail.

❹ As you near the dock, a crew member should be positioned at the shrouds to step off onto the dock and help slow the sailboat. **Remember: Do not postion any part of your body between the boat and the dock!**

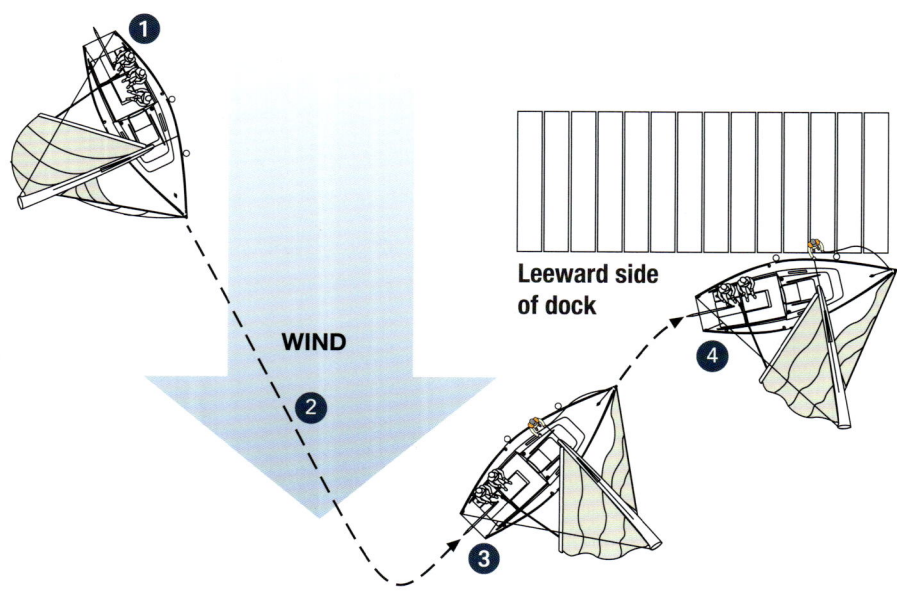

WIND

Leeward side of dock

GAS OUTBOARD MANAGEMENT

Starting Procedure

1. Lower the propeller in the water using the engine tilt and/or lifting mechanism.
2. Check for adequate fuel in the tank.
3. Open the fuel tank vent.
4. If you have an external fuel tank, check that both ends of the *fuel line* are securely attached to tank and the outboard. Some outboards will only have an integral fuel tank.
5. Pump the bulb firm.
6. Put gear lever in neutral.
7. Attach engine cut-off switch clip to engine.
8. Pull the choke out.
9. Put the *throttle* in start position.
10. Pull the starter cord slowly until you feel resistance, then give it a rapid jerk.
11. Push the choke in slowly after engine starts. If the engine doesn't start after a few starter cord pulls, push in the choke and try again.
12. When the outboard starts, check for cooling water discharge. If there is none, stop the engine.
13. If engine won't start, it may be flooded. Push the choke in, open the throttle all the way and pull the cord several times. Or, wait several minutes and try again.
14. Attach engine cut-off switch clip to driver.

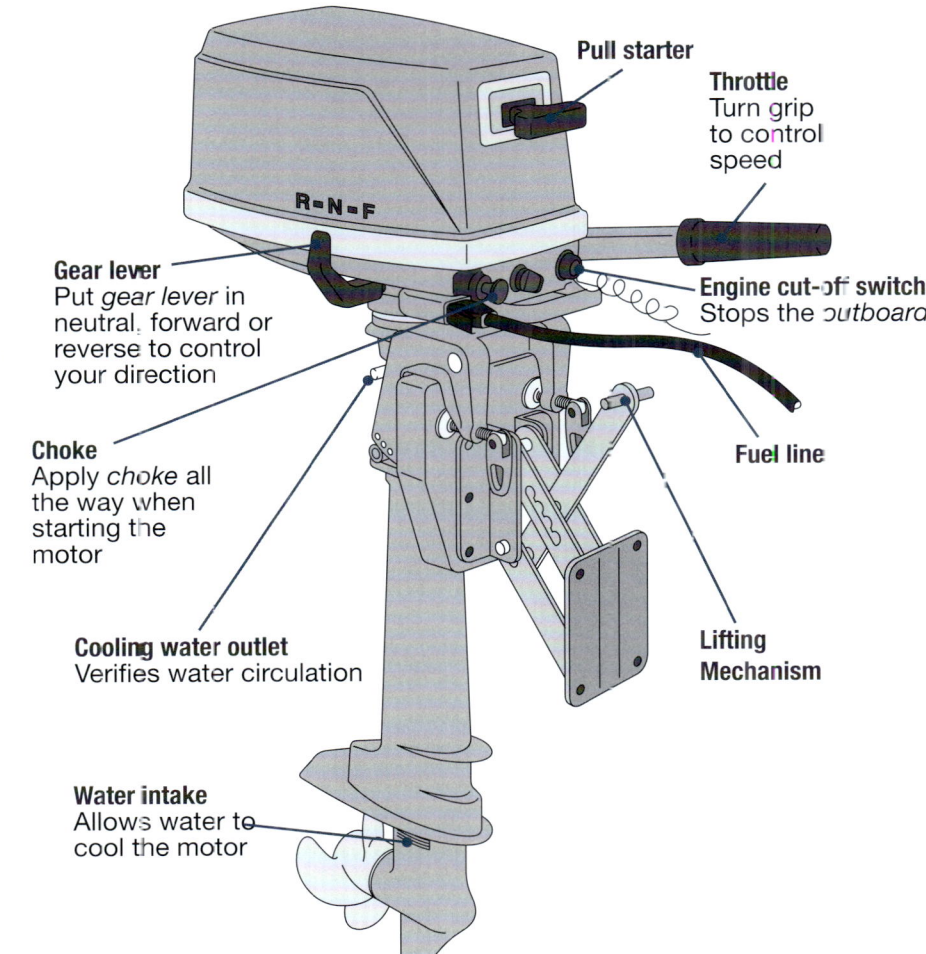

Pull starter

Throttle
Turn grip to control speed

Engine cut-off switch
Stops the outboard

R - N - F

Gear lever
Put *gear lever* in neutral, forward or reverse to control your direction

Choke
Apply *choke* all the way when starting the motor

Fuel line

Cooling water outlet
Verifies water circulation

Lifting Mechanism

Water intake
Allows water to cool the motor

SKILL EVALUATION

☐ **Power** - Check gas.

☐ **Safety Lanyard** - Attach engine cut-off switch clip.

☐ **Check Engine** - Make sure engine is down and in neutral.

☐ **Start Engine** - Pull cord (Check choke)

☐ **Cooling Water** - Ensure there is cooling water discharge.

ANCHORING UNDER SAIL AND POWER

As in docking, preparation is the key to successful anchoring. Before anchoring furl or take down the jib. Make sure the foredeck is clear, except for the anchor and *rode* (chain and/or line). Secure the *inboard* end of the rode to the boat. Lay out the rode so that it will run freely. If there is a bow *pulpit,* make sure the anchor and rode will run under it.

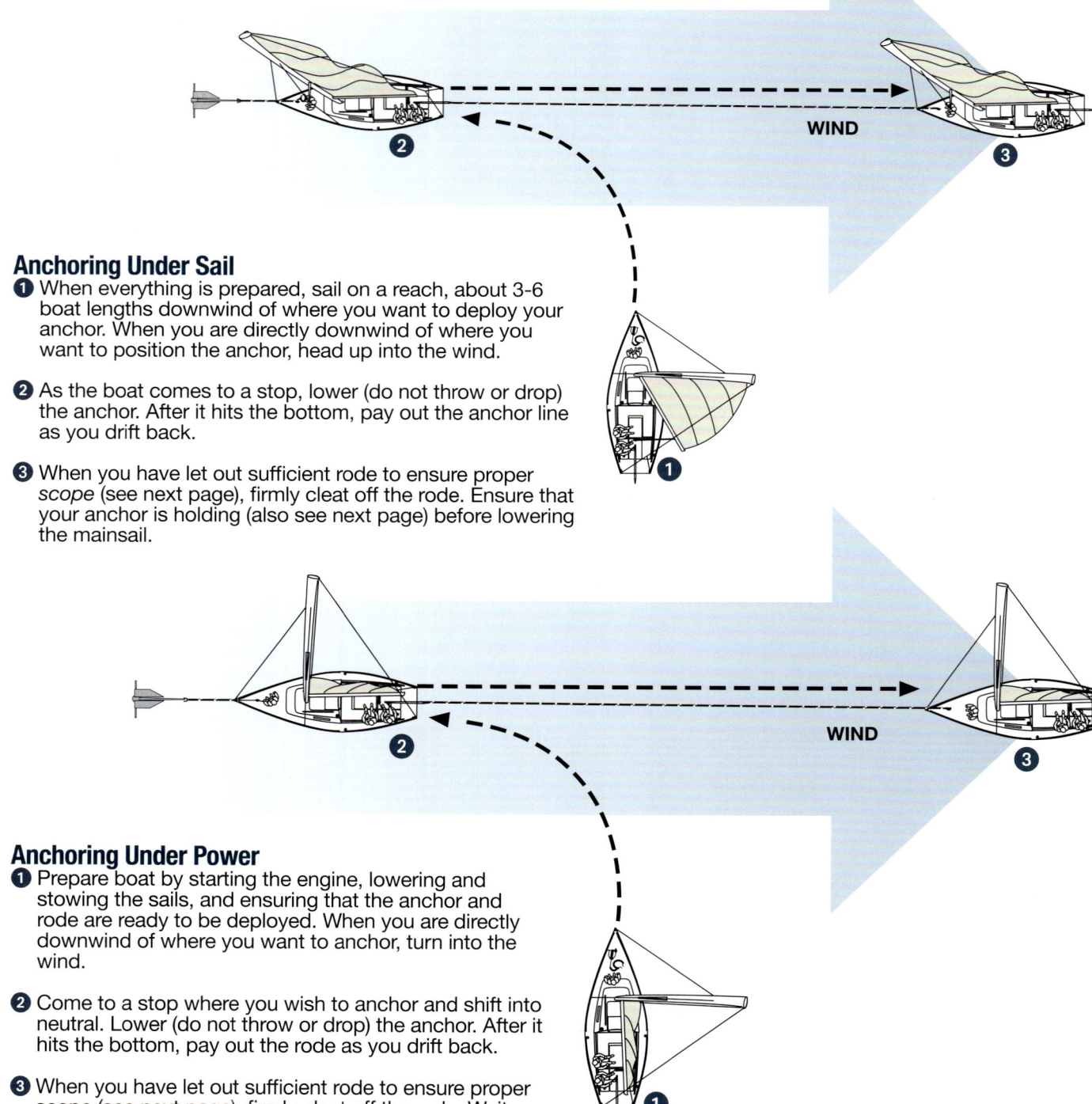

Anchoring Under Sail

❶ When everything is prepared, sail on a reach, about 3-6 boat lengths downwind of where you want to deploy your anchor. When you are directly downwind of where you want to position the anchor, head up into the wind.

❷ As the boat comes to a stop, lower (do not throw or drop) the anchor. After it hits the bottom, pay out the anchor line as you drift back.

❸ When you have let out sufficient rode to ensure proper *scope* (see next page), firmly cleat off the rode. Ensure that your anchor is holding (also see next page) before lowering the mainsail.

Anchoring Under Power

❶ Prepare boat by starting the engine, lowering and stowing the sails, and ensuring that the anchor and rode are ready to be deployed. When you are directly downwind of where you want to anchor, turn into the wind.

❷ Come to a stop where you wish to anchor and shift into neutral. Lower (do not throw or drop) the anchor. After it hits the bottom, pay out the rode as you drift back.

❸ When you have let out sufficient rode to ensure proper scope (see next page), firmly cleat off the rode. Wait a minute or so, then shift into reverse and GRADUALLY apply moderate power to bury the anchor into the seabed (aka setting the hook) and ensure that it is holding (also see next page). Then GRADUALLY throttle back to idle and turn off the engine.

Scope

Scope is the ratio of anchor rode to the depth of the water, plus *freeboard* (the the height of the deck above the water) and any rise of tide. A scope of 5:1 or 7:1 is considered normal. This means that if you are going to anchor where the water is 10 feet deep, your freeboard is 2 feet, and the tide will rise 3 feet, you should pay out 105 feet of rode (10 + 2 + 3) x 7 or 15 x 7 = 105. Charts provide the water depth at a low level called Mean Lower Low Water (MLLW), and the tide tables will tell you what the change will be during the period you are anchored.

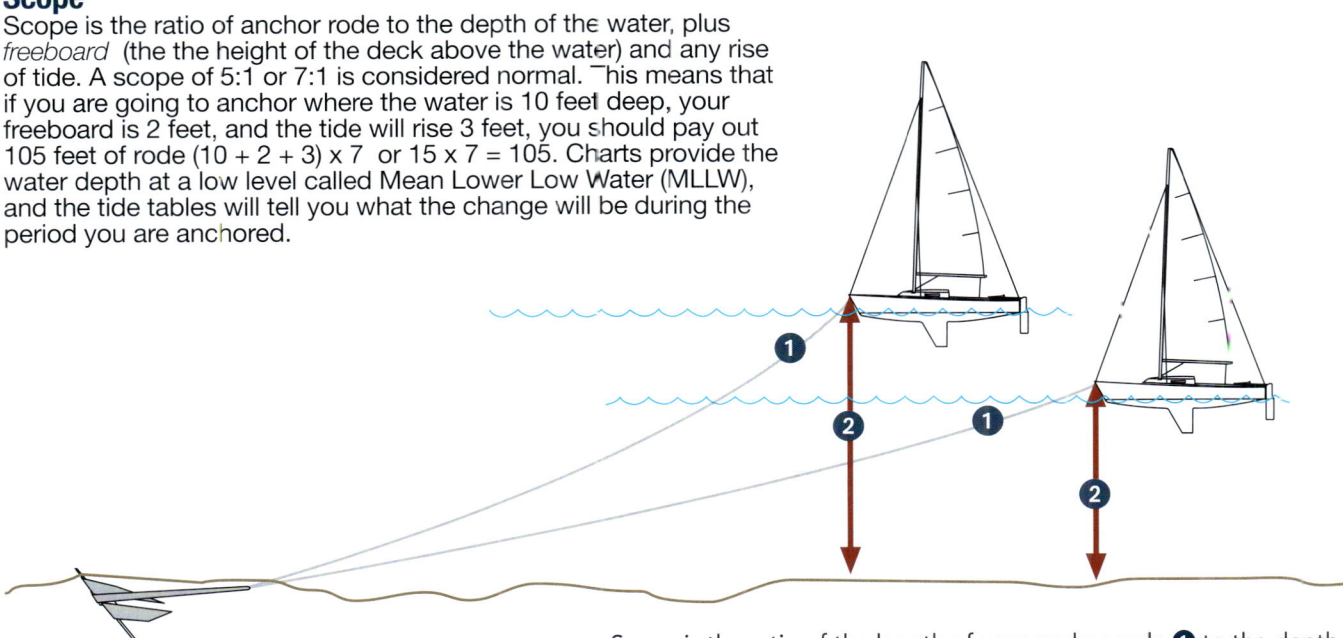

Scope is the ratio of the length of your anchor rode ❶ to the depth of the water plus freeboard and allowing for any tidal rise ❷.

Is your anchor holding?

It's good seamanship to make sure your anchor has a secure hold on the bottom. Navigation apps have an anchor alarm feature that will signal if your sailboat moves more than the distance you select.

Another, non-electronic method is to locate two objects *abeam* (perpendicular to the middle of the sailboat) that are aligned. The objects can be on shore, such as a fence post or telephone pole or floating, for instance, a bucy. Do NOT use moveable objects, such as another boat! If the objects abeam remain in alignment, your anchor is holding If the wind shifts, select new objects.

SKILL EVALUATION

- ☐ **Approach** - Properly plan your approach.

- ☐ **Mooring** - Properly tie to a mooring.

- ☐ **Anchors** - Properly deploy, set and retrieve the achor.

- ☐ **Scope** - Calculate proper scope based on depth.

- ☐ **Check Holding** - Determine if the anchor is holding with a GPS or sighting if the two objects are aligned.

The Danforth (or fluke type) anchor is very common. It is strong, lightweight, holds well in mud and sand, and is easy to store.

PICKING UP A MOORING UNDER SAIL AND POWER

A *mooring* is a buoy that is permanently anchored to the bottom with a chain. There may be a pendant (a floating or buoyed line) attached to the chain just below the buoy, which can be used to secure your sailboat. Because the anchor or weight is much heavier than could be handled on board, moorings are more secure than anchoring and require less scope and swing room. This also allows more boats to be stored in a smaller area. In locations with limited dock space, many boats are kept on moorings.

To pick up a mooring under sail, furl or lower the jib so the foredeck is clear. In a crowded mooring field, it may be necessary to sail to a point directly downwind of the mooring, turn straight into the wind, and coast to a stop within reach of the mooring. This is known as *"shooting the mooring"*. If you have too much boat speed and overshoot the mooring, it can become entangled in your keel and/or rudder. To avoid this, if possible, approach the mooring on a close reach, luffing the mainsail as necessary to control boat speed, and come to a stop with the pendant within reach on the upwind side of the bow.

Under power, approach from downwind and bring the boat to a stop with the mooring ball within reach of the crew on the bow.

ATTACHING TO THE MOORING

The design of mooring balls varies widely in how a boat is attached to them. There may simply be a ring on the top of the mooring ball through which you thread your dock line and cleat both ends on board. Some mooring balls have a floating pendant (line) attached that you pick up with your boat hook. Once you have the pendant in your hands, be VERY careful about what you do with the boat hook. Carelessly laying it on the deck may result in it rolling into the water and sinking.

WIND

Pendant or dock line

Mooring Ball

Mooring Chain

Anchor/weight

Close Reach Approach

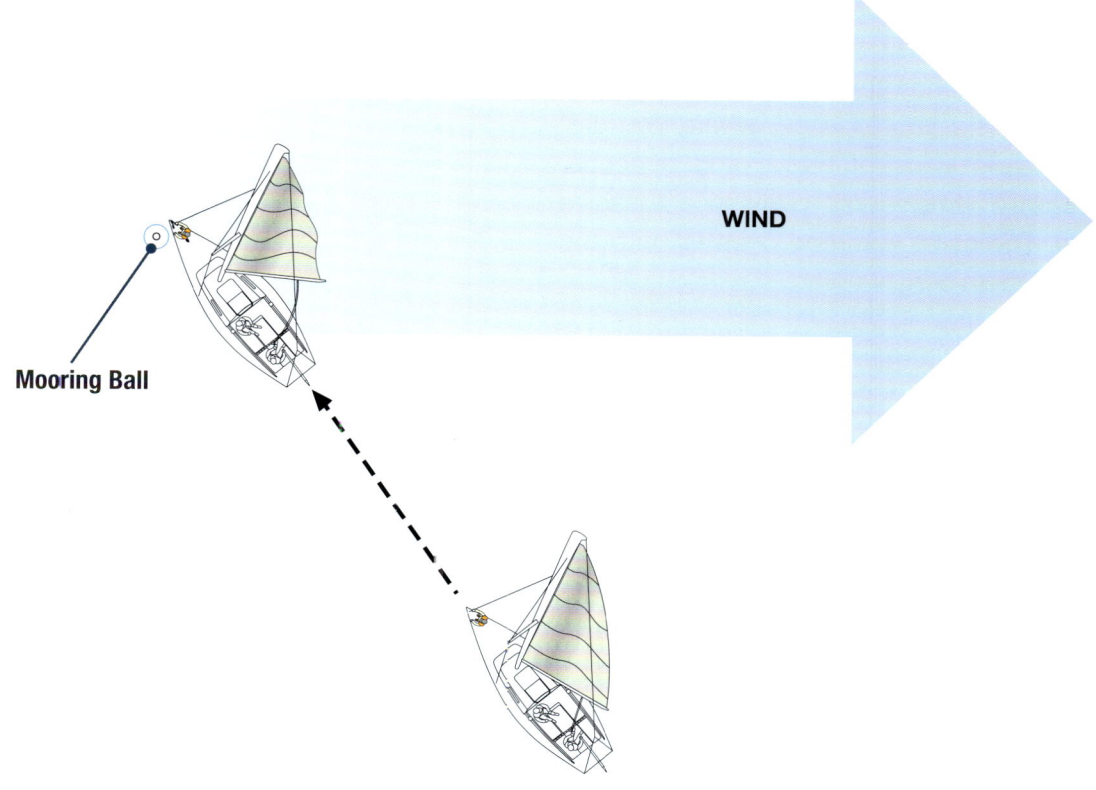

WIND

Mooring Ball

Shooting the Mooring Approach

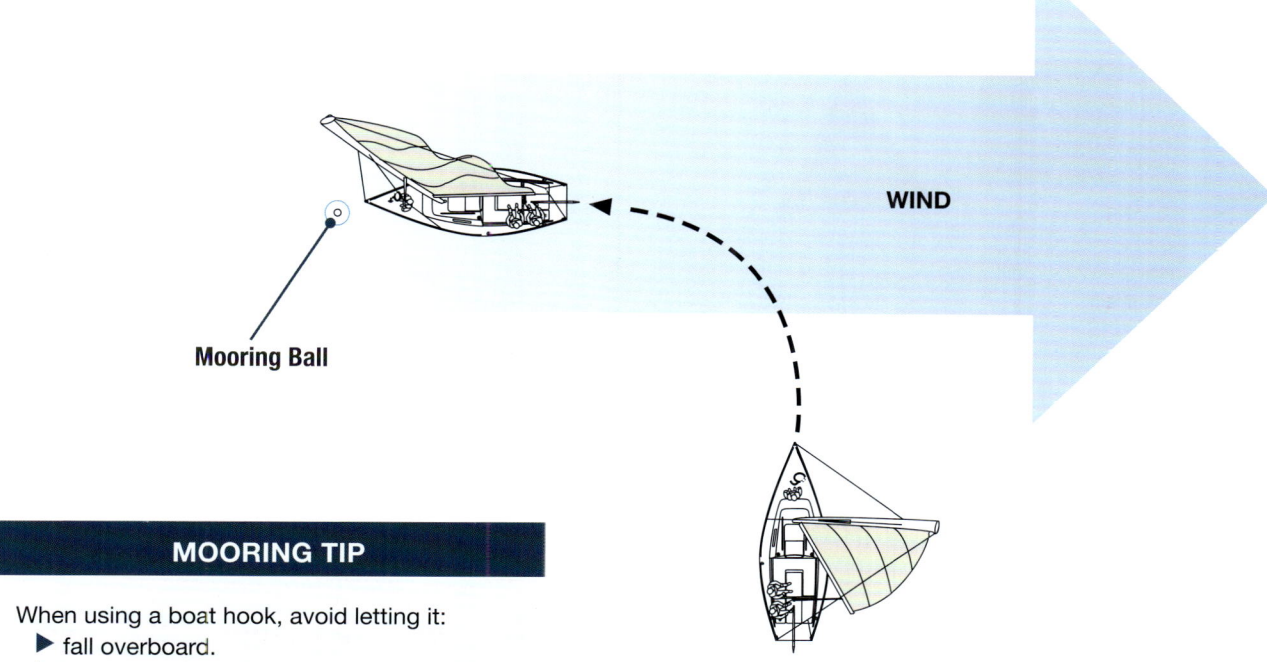

WIND

Mooring Ball

MOORING TIP

When using a boat hook, avoid letting it:
▶ fall overboard.
▶ become entangled on the mooring ball.

BASIC NAVIGATION AIDS

Aids to Navigation (ATONs) are *buoys* (floating aids) and beacons (fixed or non-floating aids) that indicate channels, show the location of submerged hazards, and help you to know where you are. There are many kinds of buoys and beacons, ranging from a simple unlit buoy to a massive lighthouse. The most common ones fall into the categories shown here.

The basic rule to remember in U.S. waters is "*Red, Right, Returning.*" This means keep the <u>Red</u> aids to your <u>Right</u> (starboard) side when you are <u>Returning</u> from open water or entering a harbor or marina. Keep the green aids on your right when leaving.

ATONs have distinct shapes, colors, numbers, and (sometimes) lighting characteristics to help you to identify them. Their position is shown on nautical charts. Study a chart of your local sailing area to become familiar with the navigation aids you will be encountering.

Green or red **lighted buoys** are spaced relatively far apart and located near the entrances of harbors. Each has a distinct flashing pattern that is indicated on a chart so it can be readily identified. Lighted buoys are especially helpful for navigating at night.

A **can** is an odd-numbered, green buoy that is used to mark the left side of a channel when entering (returning to) a harbor. It has a flat top. When you leave a harbor, cans mark the right side of the channel.

A **nun** is an even-numbered, red buoy used to mark the right side of a channel when entering (returning to) the harbor. It has a pointed top. When you leave the harbor, nuns mark the left side of the channel.

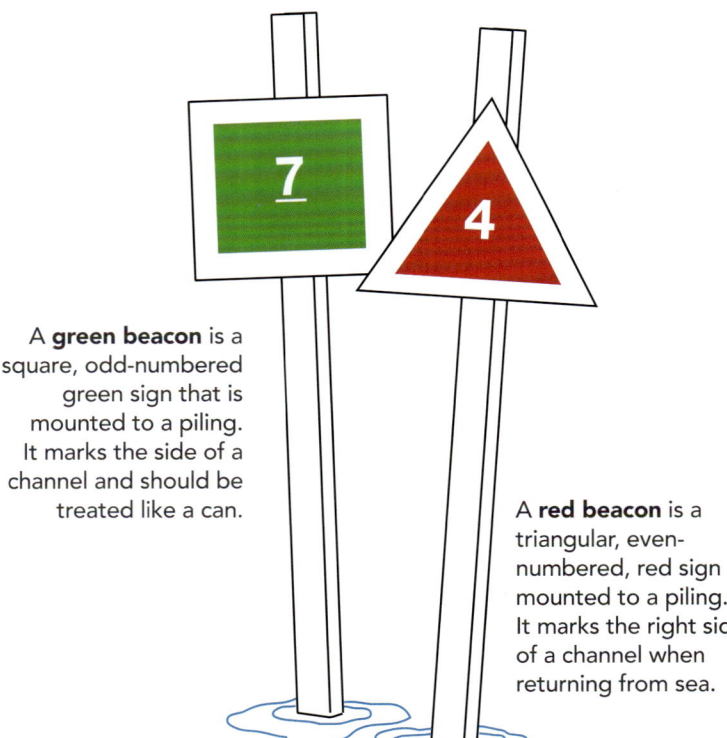

A **green beacon** is a square, odd-numbered green sign that is mounted to a piling. It marks the side of a channel and should be treated like a can.

A **red beacon** is a triangular, even-numbered, red sign mounted to a piling. It marks the right side of a channel when returning from sea.

SKILL EVALUATION

☐ **Chart** - Demonstrate using a chart to identify ATONs, depth, and hazards.

☐ **ATONs** - Identify common aids to navigation on the water.

☐ **Avoiding Collisions** - Demonstrate avoiding hazards or obstructions while on the water.

☐ **Red, Right, Returning** - Demonstrate keeping red buoys and beacons on your starboard side when returning to harbor.

READING A CHART

A chart shows not only the ATONs, but also the shorelines, *soundings* (water depths), obstructions, shoals, the positions of wrecks, and the nature of the seabed. In addition, it indicates the positions of landmarks, lighthouses, and much more. Paper charts indicate the unit used for soundings. When using an electronic chart, search the app to determine how soundings are displayed.

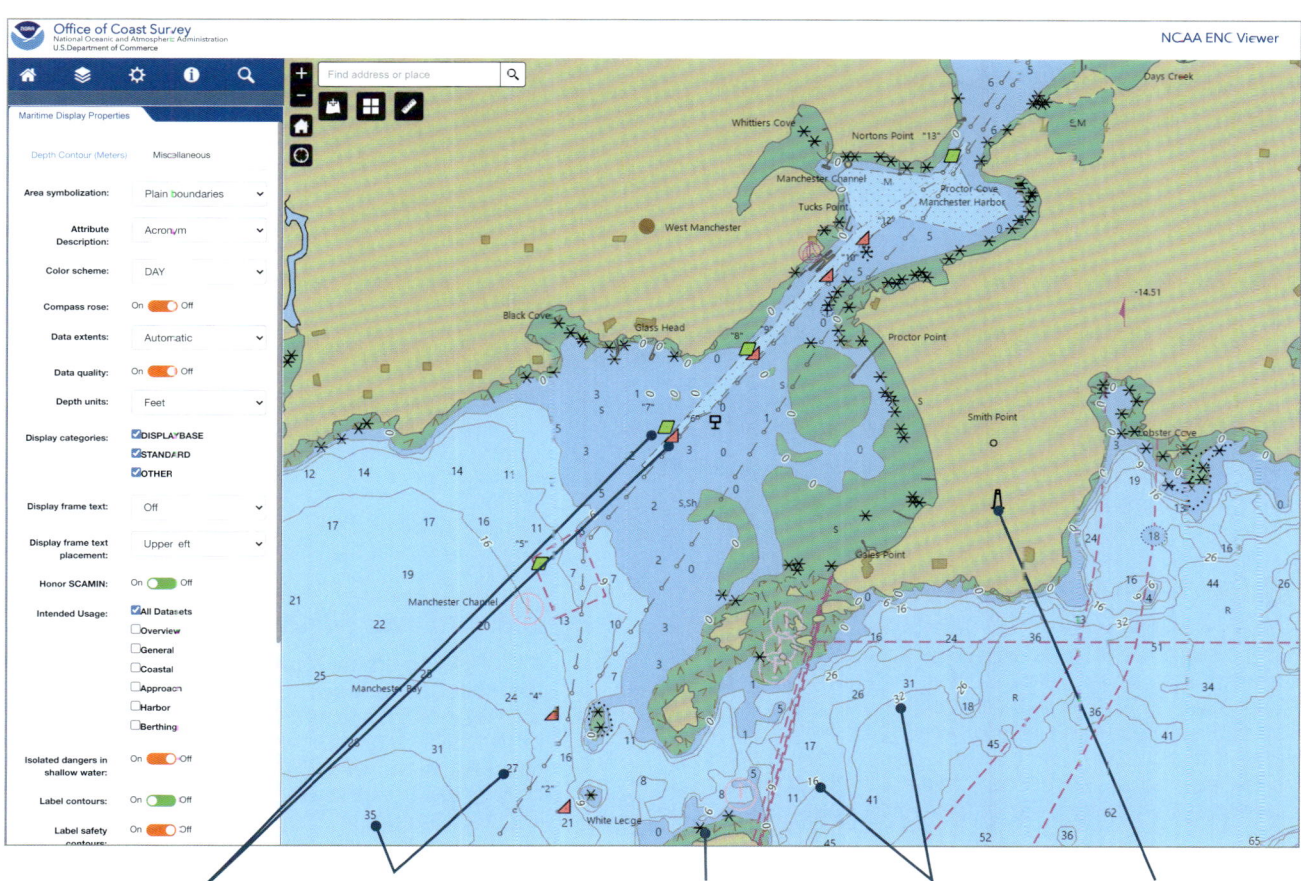

These shapes represent **buoys**. They are colored red and green and mark the edges of a narrow channel through shallow water. In keeping with the saying **"Red, Right, Returning"**, you see red nuns on the right and green cans on the left when returning to Manchester harbor.

The small numbers scattered throughout the water are **soundings** at low tide at those particular points.

Charts also indicate **noteworthy bottom topography**, such as hazardous rocks (shown as an *), wrecks, and other hidden dangers.

A **contour line** follows a constant water depth.

Charts also indicate **onshore landmarks** that can be used as navigation references. Here a tower is indicated.

ELECTRONIC CHART TIPS

Because electronic charts are customizable by the user, insure you understand your settings. For example:

▶ Units used for soundings (e.g., feet, meters)
▶ What the various colors represent
▶ How the chart is oriented (e.g., North up or boat heading up)

INTRODUCTION TO THE NAVIGATION RULES

The purpose of the Navigation Rules is to avoid collisions. When two vessels meet, the Rules designate one vessel as *stand-on* and the other vessel as *give-way*. The stand-on vessel is required to maintain course and speed. The give-way vessel is required keep out of the way of the stand-on vessel and should make all changes to its course and/or speed early and obvious. It is safest to pass astern of a stand-on vessel.

NOTE: It is every vessel's obligation to avoid collisions. If it becomes necessary, even the stand-on vessel may have to maneuver to avoid a collision.

The following three Rules govern how sailboats interact with each other and are listed in order in which they are to be applied.

❶ Overtaken over Overtaking

When *overtaking* another vessel, you are the give-way vessel, and must change course to maneuver around the slower vessel ahead. The vessel being overtaken is the stand-on vessel and should hold its course. It doesn't matter who is on which tack or who is to windward or leeward. Even when a sailboat is overtaking a powerboat, this rule still applies; the sailboat must keep clear of the powerboat.

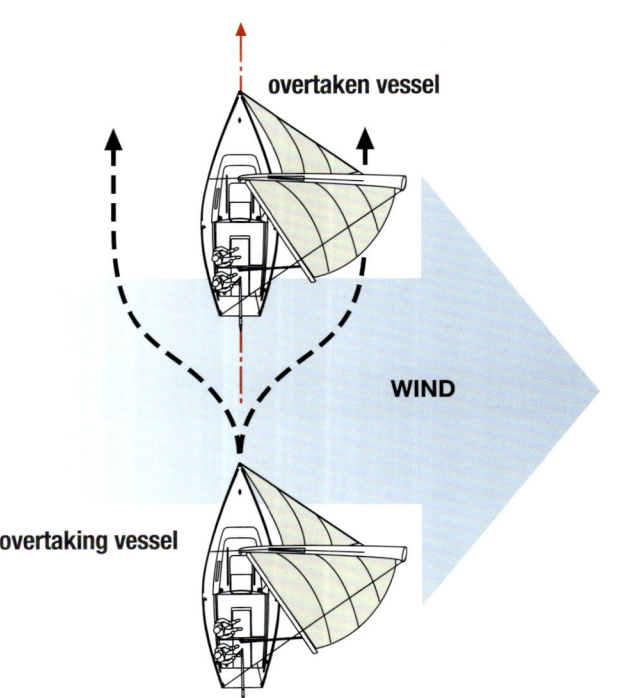

❷ Opposite Tacks (Starboard over Port)

As sailboats on opposite tacks approach each other, the sailboat on starboard tack is the stand-on vessel and should hold its course. The sailboat on port tack is the give-way vessel and it should alter course to keep clear of the sailboat on starboard tack. It doesn't matter who is windward or leeward.

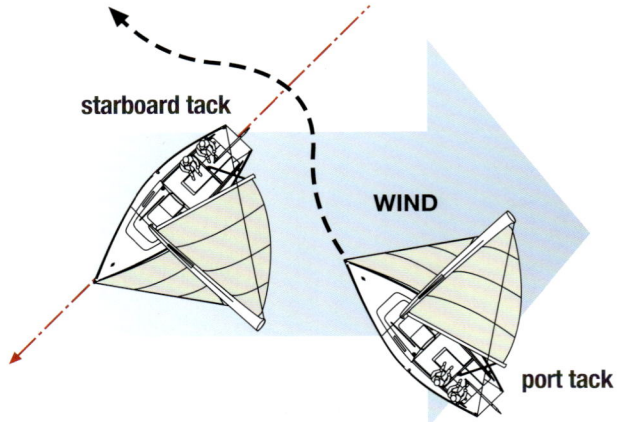

❸ Leeward over Windward

As sailboats on the same tack approach each other, the sailboat to leeward is the stand-on vessel and should hold its course. The sailboat to windward is the give-way vessel, and it should alter course to keep clear of the leeward sailboat. This Rule only applies if it is not an *Overtaking* or Opposite Tacks situation.

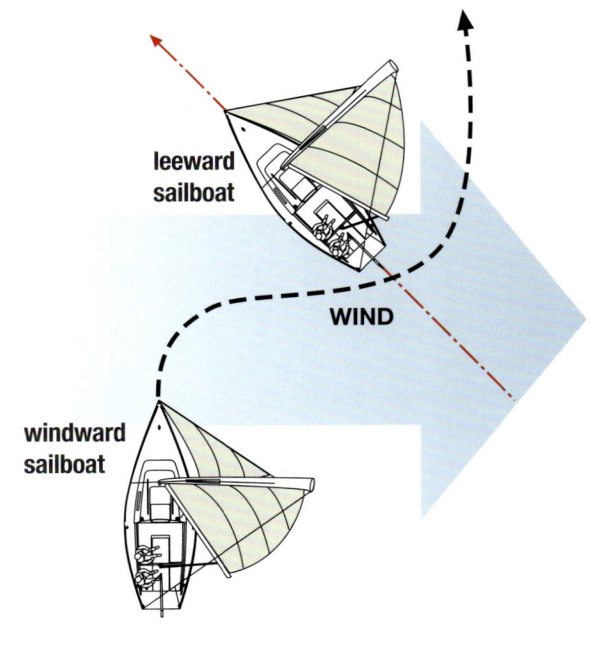

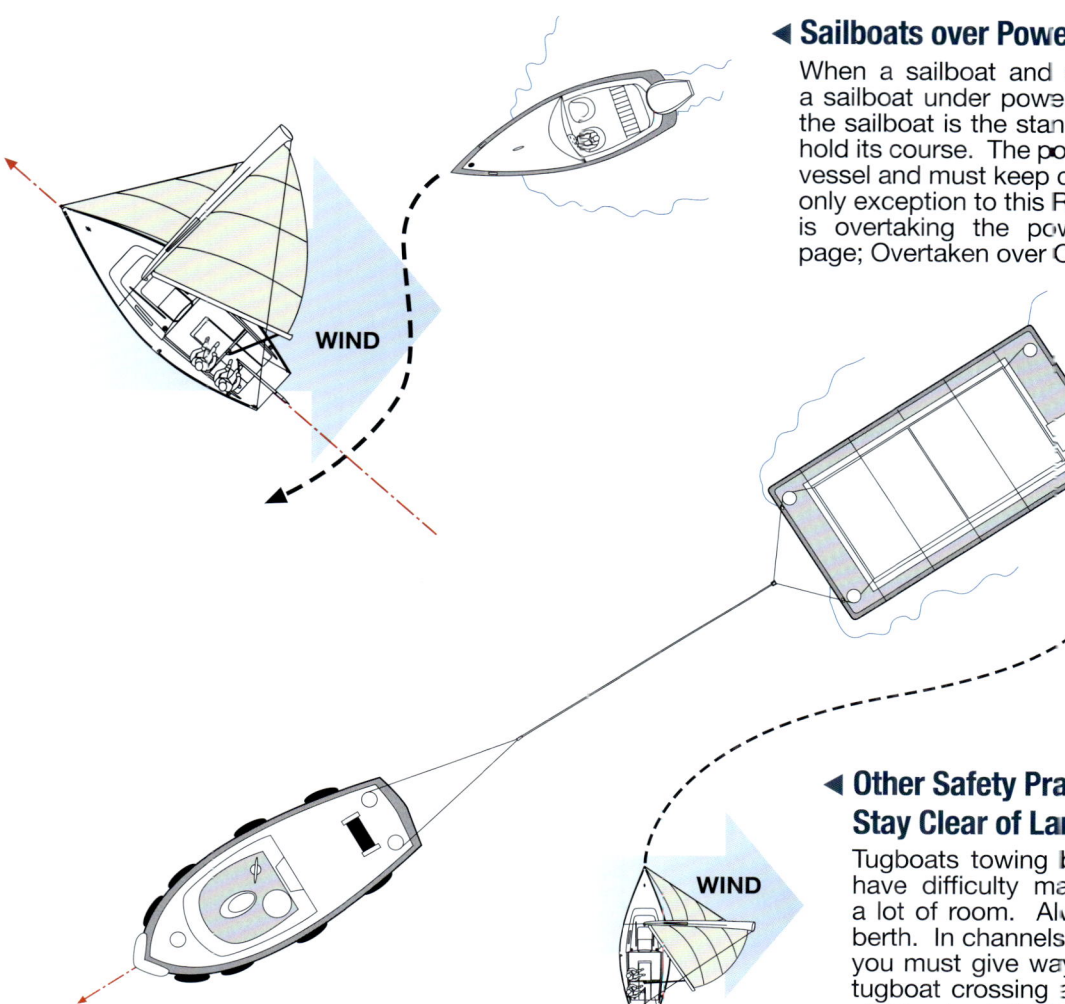

◄ Sailboats over Powerboats

When a sailboat and a powerboat (including a sailboat under power) approach each other, the sailboat is the stand-on vessel and should hold its course. The powerboat is the give-way vessel and must keep clear of the sailboat. The only exception to this Rule is when the sailboat is overtaking the powerboat. (see previous page; Overtaken over Overtaking)

◄ Other Safety Practices:
Stay Clear of Large Vessels

Tugboats towing barges and large ships have difficulty maneuvering and require a lot of room. Always give them a wide berth. In channels they are stand-on, and you must give way to them. If you see a tugboat crossing ahead, look well astern of it to check if a barge is being towed.

NEVER try to cross between a tug and what it is towing, even if the cable seems submerged!

In general, the priority for stand-on vessels, from top to bottom is:

1 A disabled vessel

2 A vessel restricted in its ability to maneuver, such as a tanker in a channel, a dredge, or a tug and tow.

3 A vessel engaged in commercial fishing

4 A sailboat

5 A powerboat

AVOID COLLISIONS AND BE SAFE!

All course changes should be made early and obvious. If you aren't SURE you can safely cross ahead of another vessel, aim astern to cross its wake. When you are the give-way vessel, make your actions (changing course and/or speed) obvious to the other vessel.

Remember: You are always responsible for avoiding a collision, even if you are the stand-on vessel. The Rules require you to maneuver to avoid a collision.

SKILL EVALUATION

☐ **Starboard and Port** - Identify stand-on and give-way between starboard and port sailboats.

☐ **Leeward and Windward** - Identify stand-on and give-way between leeward and windward sailboats.

☐ **Overtaken and Overtaking** - Identify stand-on and give-way between overtaken and overtaking vessels.

WEATHER AWARENESS

The US Sailing Basic Keelboat certification prepares you to sail on familiar waters, during daylight hours, in light to moderate breezes. For sailing in such conditions, you will need the area's short-term weather forecast. There are many sources of this information; an app on your phone, local radio and television broadcasts, and the nationwide broadcasts by the National Weather Service (NWS) on the marine VHF-FM radio. Many harbormasters also post the forecast at their office and display various pennants and flags (see below) to warn of strong winds. It is also worthwhile to learn about any regional or local weather patterns, such as the shifty winds of lake sailing, the strong afternoon breezes on San Francisco Bay, or the mid-west's afternoon thunder showers.

SKILL EVALUATION

☐ **Wind Strength & Direction** - Identify wind strength and direction using a forecast.

☐ **Weather Forecast** - Identify multiple resources to obtain a forecast.

☐ **Foul Weather** - Determine from a weather forecast when it is safe to go out on the water.

National Weather Service Marine Forecast

PZZ133-090045-
Northern Inland Waters Including The San Juan Islands-
334 AM PST Fri Dec 8 2023

TODAY...W wind to 10 kt. Wind waves 1 ft or less. A chance of showers in the morning.

TONIGHT...SE wind to 10 kt becoming E 10 to 20 kt after midnight. Wind waves 1 ft or less building to 1 to 3 ft after midnight. A slight chance of rain after midnight.

SAT...SE wind 20 to 30 kt rising to 30 to 40 kt in the afternoon. Wind waves 3 to 5 ft building to 5 to 7 ft in the afternoon. A chance of rain in the morning then rain in the afternoon.

SAT NIGHT...SE wind 25 to 35 kt easing to 15 to 25 kt after midnight. Wind waves 4 to 6 ft subsiding to 2 to 4 ft after midnight.

FORECAST OF WIND STRENGTH AND DIRECTION

A complete marine weather forecast will include both the predicted wind speed and direction. (Note that wind is named for the direction from which it comes.) Both of these pieces of information, i.e., speed and direction, are needed to properly plan your sail. They influence whether you are going sailing or not, your dock departure and arrival plans, where you can raise and lower sails, as well as where there is protected water, and the location of lee shores.

FOUL WEATHER

One of the more difficult dilemmas for the new sailor is recognizing when the conditions are beyond (or are likely to soon be beyond) their limited knowledge and experience or, as it has been succinctly stated, "when to say when". Sailing is supposed to be fun, and it ceases to be when you are in conditions beyond your comfort zone. **Remember: When in doubt, don't go out!**

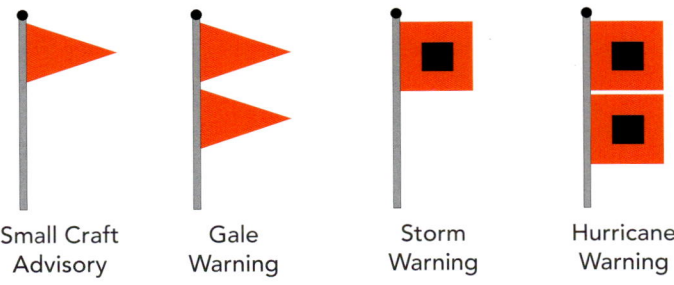

Small Craft Advisory   Gale Warning   Storm Warning   Hurricane Warning

LAND EFFECTS ON WIND

Wind speed and direction can be affected by nearby land features. Islands, tall buildings, even anchored ships cast wind shadows (areas of less or no wind) on their leeward sides. These objects can also cause the wind to change direction as it flows around or over them. Sailing into one of these wind shadows greatly depowers a sailboat and may require you to retrim your sails.

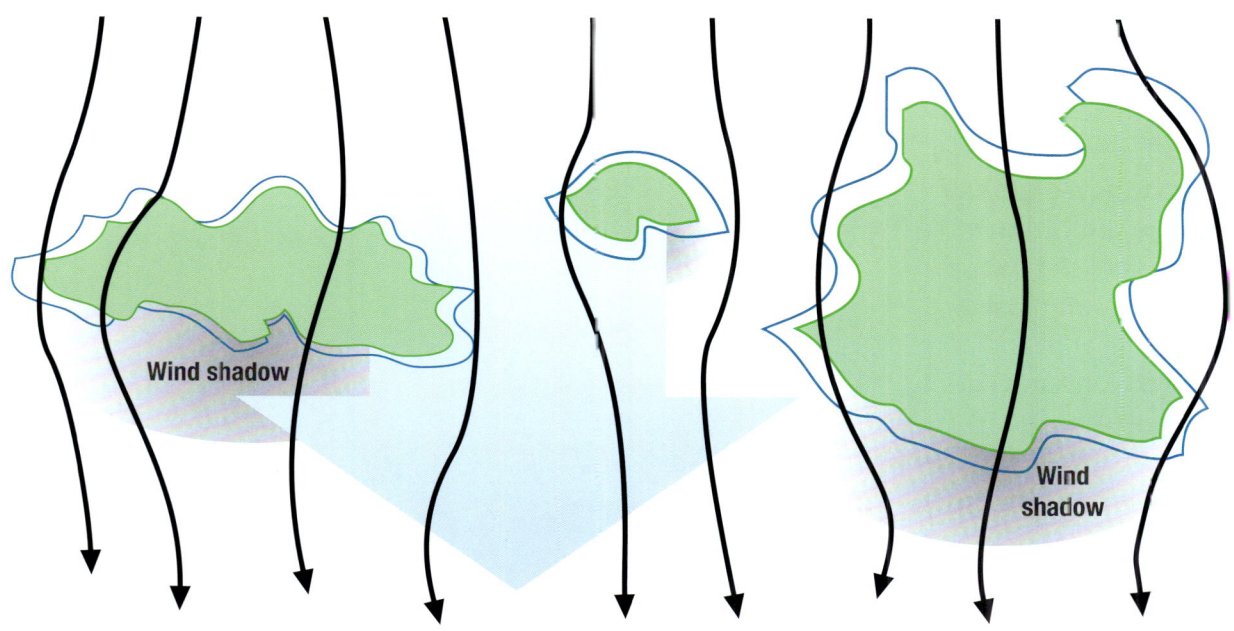

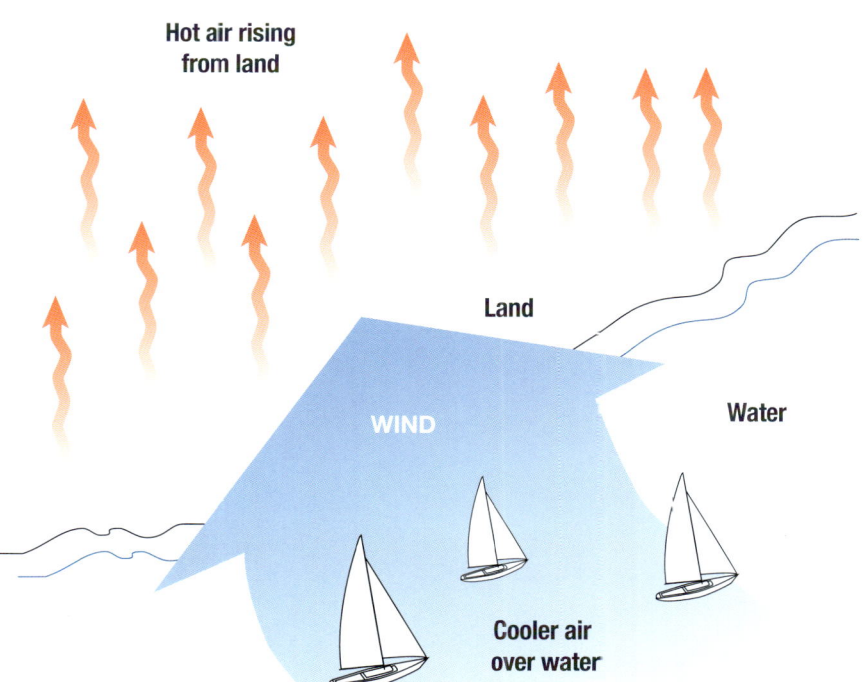

Thermal Winds

Local winds are often caused by differences in temperature between the land, which heats up quickly, and the adjacent water, the temperature of which remains constant. As the air over the land warms, it rises, and cooler, denser air is drawn in from over the water to fill the void. These winds are commonly referred to as *onshore breezes* or *sea breezes*.

The most famous example of this is on San Francisco Bay, where hot air rising out of the Sacramento Valley, about 75 miles inland from the bay, creates a vacuum that draws 25-*knot* winds in through the Golden Gate almost every summer afternoon.

WATER AWARENESS

Tide is the *vertical* change in water level caused by the gravitational attraction of the sun and moon. These heavenly bodies pull the earth's water into a bulge. As any location on earth rotates under this bulge, the sea level rises; as that location moves out from under the bulge, sea level falls. There are two high and two low tides each day on the East and West Coasts of the U.S. and only one each per day in the Gulf of Mexico.

Current is *horizontal* movement of water. In coastal areas, current is caused by the rise and fall of the tide. Current is also caused by gravity (as in river flow), wind, and ocean circulation patterns. This water movement can either assist or hinder your progress when sailing. A wise sailor will utilize favorable currents and avoid adverse ones.

Wind and current flowing in opposite directions can create uncomfortable waves that are short, steep, and closely spaced. When wind and current are flowing in the same direction, the water surface will be much smoother and calmer.

With tide and current prediction apps or tables, you can anticipate the depth and movement of the water where you will be sailing or anchoring.

COMPENSATING FOR CURRENT

When sailing across a *current* you can compensate for its effect. Instead of steering directly toward your goal, steer for a point upcurrent, and let the current carry you back to your desired course.

Adjusted Course
This boat has compensated for the current by aiming upcurrent of its destination and is carried to its destination.

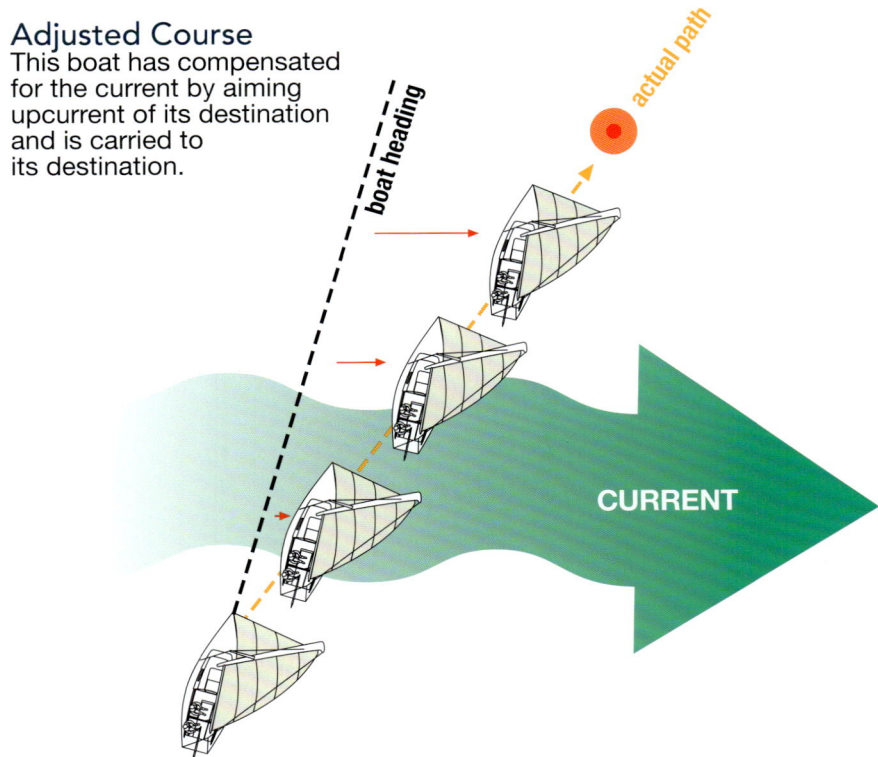

Non-Adjusted Course
This boat aimed directly for its destination but was carried downstream by the current.

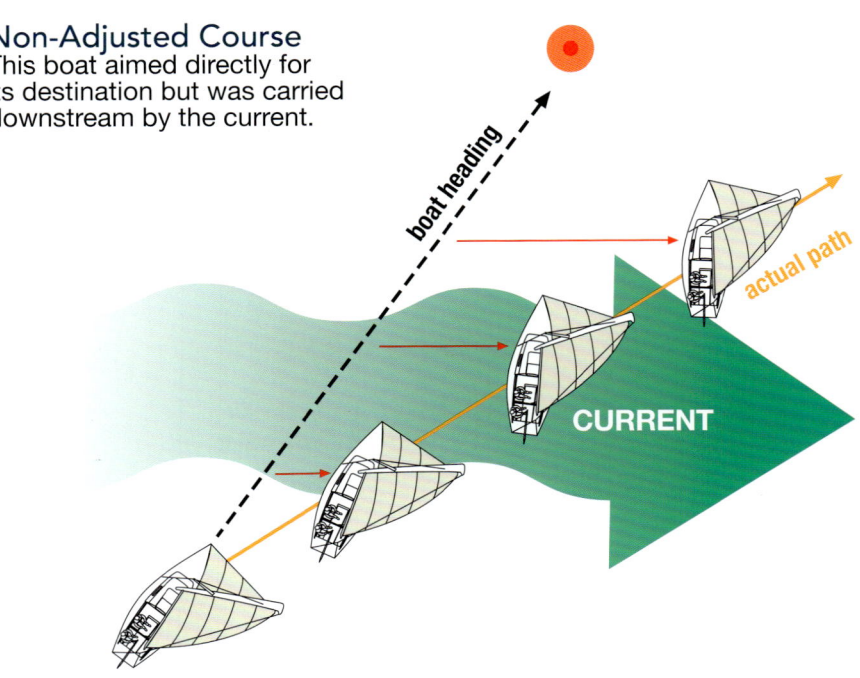

PUTTING IT ALL TOGETHER

SUMMARY

- When approaching a dock, the disadvantage of a downwind approach is that you have less control of boat speed; you cannot luff your sails effectively, particularly the mainsail.
- To start the outboard; ensure adequate fuel, pump the bulb, attach safety lanyard, choke out (if needed), pull starter cord, and check for cooling water discharge after start.
- Successful anchoring requires proper scope: anchor rode length in relation to water depth, freeboard, and tidal rise.
- When picking up mooring, stop with the mooring ball within reach of the bow. Use a boat hook carefully when necessary.
- Aids to Navigation (ATONs) are buoys and beacons that indicate channels and show the location of some submerged hazards.
- Charts enable identification of ATONs, shorelines, soundings, obstructions, and seabed characteristics.
- Stay weather-aware for safe sailing; use various sources like phone apps, local media, and weather channels on VHF radio.

KEY TERMS AND CONCEPTS

1. Remember the phrase "**Red, Right, Returning**." This means keep the Red ATONs to your right when you are returning from open water or entering a harbor.
2. When two vessels meet, the rules designate one vessel as **stand-on** and the other vessel as **give-way**.
3. All vessels must avoid collisions; stand-on vessels should be ready to maneuver.
4. **NEVER** try to cross between a tug and what it is towing, even if the cable seems submerged!
5. Compensate for the current by steering toward a point upcurrent and then let it carry you back to your desired course.

CHECK YOUR UNDERSTANDING

1. What recommendation is given regarding the position of Red and Green ATONs based on the "Red, Right, Returning" rule?

   ◯ a. Keep Red ATONs on your left when entering a harbor

   ◯ b. Keep Red ATONs on your right when returning from open water

   ◯ c. Keep Green ATONs on your right when returning from open water

   ◯ d. Keep Green ATONs on your right when approaching a lighthouse

2. How can sailors identify Aids to Navigation (ATONs)?

   ◯ a. By their size and weight

   ◯ b. By their proximity to lighthouses

   ◯ c. By their speed and movement

   ◯ d. By their shapes, colors, and numbers

Chapter 8

Health, Safety, & Emergencies

Sailing is an outdoor activity that exposes sailors to both excessive heat and cold. Sailors need to be aware of the symptoms of such exposure and the treatments for it. This chapter focuses on knowing what safety equipment is required to be aboard, how to retrieve someone who has fallen into the water, how to use a marine VHF-FM radio (you may be out of cellphone range), and how to attract attention should you need assistance.

Knowing the steps to take to minimize damage if you run *aground* and the basic procedures for accepting a tow are also covered. Being prepared and exercising seamanship ensures you will be ready for unexpected scenarios like equipment failure or adverse weather conditions.

FLOAT PLAN & CREW BRIEFING

FLOAT PLAN
'*Filing a float plan*' simply means telling someone on shore when you go sailing and leaving them basic information about your sail. The purpose is for them to have useful information to give to authorities or others in case you get into difficulties.

Float plans for daysails may include very basic information. This includes: your planned itinerary, name and description of your sailboat, who's on board, when you plan to return, and a contact cell phone on board. As your sailing adventures increase in time and distance, so does the amount of information that is appropriate to leave in a float plan.

SKILL EVALUATION

- ☐ **Float Plan** - Create a float plan including name of boat, people on board, destination and the planned time of return.

- ☐ **Communicate** - Run *crew briefing* with crew prior to departure.

  - ▶ **Safety** - Locate and check all the safety equipment.

  - ▶ **Set Expectations** - Share what everyone should expect for wind and water conditions that day and what roles they may have on the sailboat.

  - ▶ **Rescue** - Review rescue procedures and maneuvers.

An appropriate shoreside contact is a friend or family member you trust to follow up if you don't return on time. (Float plans are NOT filed with the US Coast Guard; they do not accept them.) Agree with your contact on a time that they will start making calls if you have not checked in with them. For example, if they can't reach you, they may next call your marina or boat rental company. Of course, be sure to check in with your contact promptly, and let them know of any change in your plans.

If sailing through a school or a charter company, their pre-sail paper work may include you completing a float plan prior to your day out on the water.

The QR code to the right is the U.S.C.G.'s template for a detailed float plan.
http://www.floatplancentral.org/

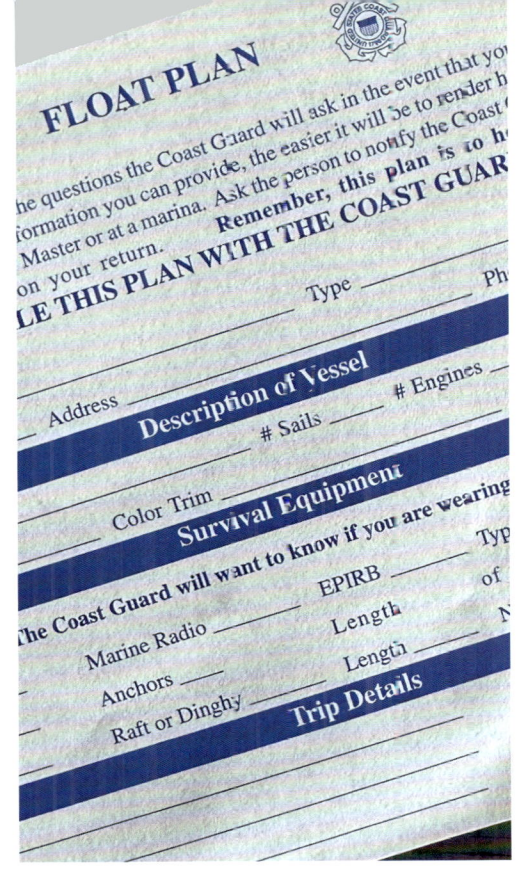

CREW BRIEFING

Part of the fun of sailing is sharing it with others! When you invite family and friends to join you on board, you'll want to give them a brief description of what to expect, which may include:

▶ Suggesting what to bring, such as extra layers of clothing, sunglasses, water, sunblock, and appropriate shoes.
▶ Wearing a life jacket, and how to adjust it comfortably.
▶ Understanding a keelboat can tip (heeling), but that doesn't mean it will tip over.
▶ How to safely board and move around the boat.
▶ The need to stay seated and avoid being hit by the boom.
▶ Using sun protection and staying hydrated.
▶ How they can help you, perhaps by helping keep a lookout or handling lines, etc.
▶ Where emergency equipment is located and how to use it. This may include VHF radio, fire extinguisher, air horn, first aid kit, throw cushion/Lifesling, head (toilet).
▶ What to do in case of emergencies, such as someone falling overboard
▶ Alcohol and seasickness avoidance.
▶ Discuss the plan for your sail, including when you plan to be back at the dock, and anything (such as wind or current) that may affect that.

Remember that as skipper, you are responsible for your crew's safety, and this is aided by a good crew briefing.

CREW HEALTH

Sailors may be exposed to a variety of weather conditions including hot sunny days with no wind, cold rainy days with too much wind, or prolonged exposure to wind, waves, and spray. Wearing appropriate clothing, staying hydrated, being well rested, and anticipating changing conditions will decrease chances of having a heat or cold emergency or becoming seasick. Here is an introduction of how to prevent, recognize, and respond appropriately to these conditions.

SKILL EVALUATION

☐ **Cold** - Know the signs of cold exposure.

☐ **Heat** - Know the signs of heat illness.

☐ **Seasickness** - Know the prevention, signs, and remedies for seasickness.

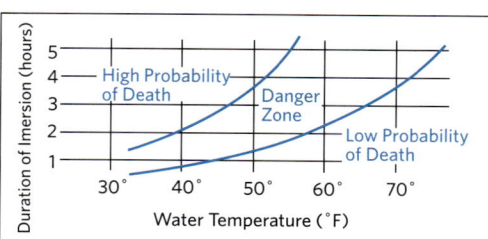

The accompanying immersion survival chart (above) shows that any water temperature can kill depending on the duration of the immersion.

HYPOTHERMIA

SIGNALS
▶ Shivering
▶ Impaired judgment
▶ Dizziness
▶ Numbness
▶ Change in level of consciousness
▶ Weakness
▶ Glassy stare; physical symptoms may vary because age, body size, and clothing will cause individual differences.

TREATMENT
Assistance should be given to anyone suffering from cold exposure:

▶ Check breathing and pulse.
▶ Move the person to a warm place.
▶ Remove all wet clothing. Gradually warm the person by wrapping in blankets or putting on dry clothes.
▶ Rapid rewarming may cause dangerous heart rhythms. Hot water bottles and chemical heat packs may be used if first wrapped in a towel or blanket before applying.
▶ Give warm, nonalcoholic and noncaffeinated liquids to a conscious person only.
▶ In severe cases, professional medical care is required. Call 911.

ASSESS COLD PATIENT

1. **From outside ring to centre: assess Consciousness, Movement, Shivering, Alertness**
2. **Assess whether normal, impaired or no function**
3. **The colder the patient is, the slower you can go, once patient is secured**
4. **Treat all traumatized cold patients with active warming to upper trunk**
5. **Avoid burns: following product guidelines for heat sources; check for excessive skin redness**

COLD STRESSED, NOT HYPOTHERMIC
1. Reduce heat loss (*e.g., add dry clothing*)
2. Provide high-calorie food or drink
3. Move around/ exercise to warm up

MILD HYPOTHERMIA
1. Handle gently
2. Have patient sit or lie down for at least 30 min.
3. Insulate/ vapour barrier
4. Give heat to upper trunk
5. Give high-calorie food/drink
6. Monitor for at least 30 min.
7. Evacuate if no improvement

CONSCIOUS
MOVEMENT NORMAL
SHIVERING
ALERT
CONSCIOUS
IMPAIRED MOVEMENT

IF COLD & UNCONSCIOUS
ASSUME SEVERE HYPOTHERMIA

NOT ALERT
NOT SHIVERING
CONSCIOUS

SEVERE HYPOTHERMIA
1. Treat as Moderate Hypothermia, and
   a) **IF** no obvious vital signs, **THEN** 60-second breathing / pulse check, or assess cardiac function with cardiac monitor
   b) **IF** no breathing / pulse, **THEN** Start CPR
2. Evacuate carefully ASAP

MODERATE HYPOTHERMIA
1. Handle gently
2. Keep horizontal
3. No standing/walking
4. No drink or food
5. Insulate/ vapour barrier
6. Give heat to upper trunk
7. Volume replacement with warm intravenous fluid (40-42°C)
8. Evacuate carefully

Funded by the Government of Canada |  Canada

BICOrescue.com

Baby it's **COLD OUTSIDE**

HEAT EXHAUSTION

SIGNALS

▶ Cool, moist, pale skin
▶ Heavy sweating
▶ Headache
▶ Dizziness
▶ Nausea
▶ Weakness, exhaustion

TREATMENT

Without prompt care, heat exhaustion can advance to a more serious condition — heat stroke. First aid includes:

▶ Move the person to a cool environment.
▶ Remove clothing soaked with perspiration and loosen any tight clothing.
▶ Apply cool, wet towels or sheets.
▶ Fan the person.
▶ Give the person a half glass (4 oz.) of cool water every 15 minutes.

HEAT STROKE

SIGNALS

▶ Red, hot, dry or moist skin
▶ Very high temperature
▶ Changes in level of consciousness
▶ Vomiting
▶ Rapid, weak pulse
▶ Rapid, shallow breathing

TREATMENT

Heat stroke is life-threatening. Anyone suffering from heat stroke needs to be cooled, and 911 should be contacted immediately. To care for heat stroke:

▶ Move the person to a cool environment.
▶ Apply cool, wet towels or sheets.
▶ If available, place ice or cold packs on the person's wrists and ankles, groin, each armpit, and neck.
▶ If unconscious, check breathing and pulse.

SEASICKNESS

Sailing can cause motion sickness.

▶ Eat before going out, but avoid greasy heavy foods and alcohol.
▶ Dress warmly.
▶ Some people use wrist bands that activate acupressure points. Others rely on over-the-counter or prescription medications such as Scopolamine.
▶ Symptoms include yawning, burping, paleness, a headache or nausea.
▶ Get on deck for fresh air and watch the horizon to calm your sensory system, or steer the sailboat.
▶ Eating salted crackers or drinking a carbonated cola might help.
▶ If you feel like you are going to vomit, move to the leeward side of the sailboat.
▶ Monitor seasick crew members.

NOTE:
US Sailing recommends you attend first aid and CPR classes, both of which are available nationwide.

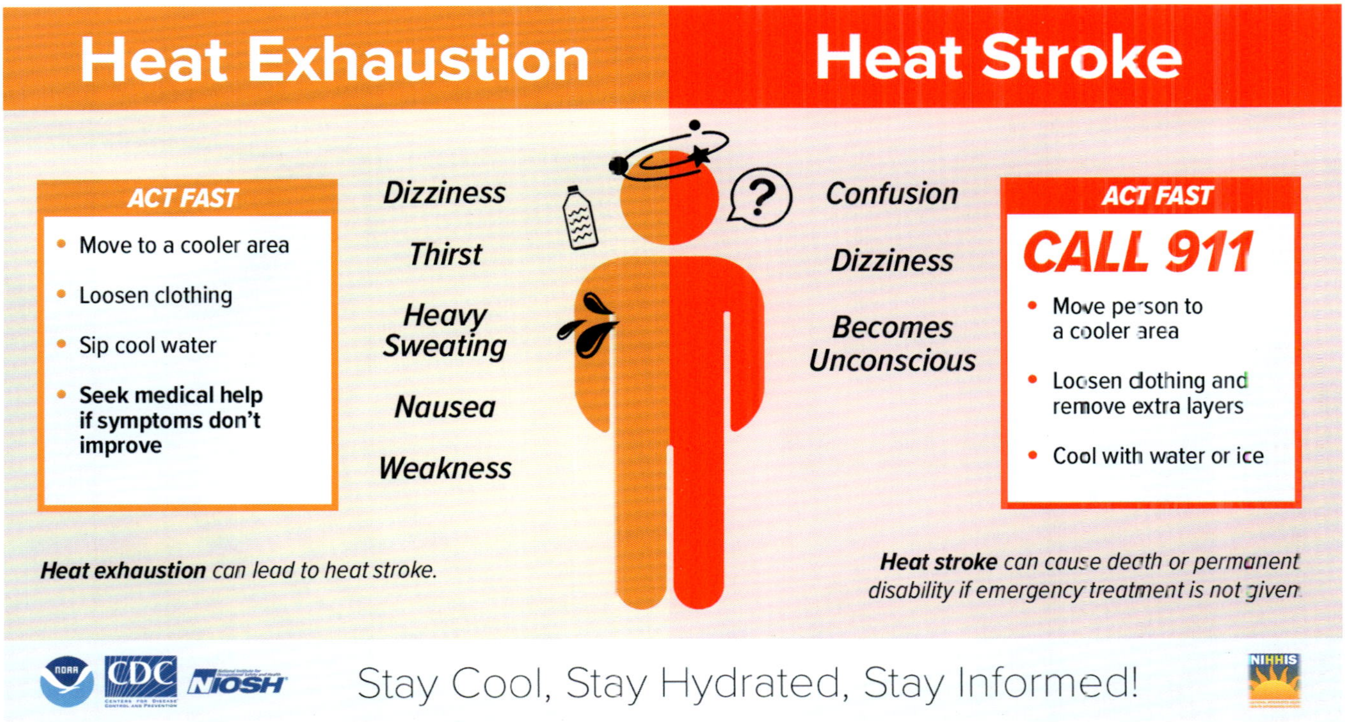

Heat Exhaustion

Heat Stroke

ACT FAST

• Move to a cooler area
• Loosen clothing
• Sip cool water
• **Seek medical help if symptoms don't improve**

Dizziness

Thirst

Heavy Sweating

Nausea

Weakness

Confusion

Dizziness

Becomes Unconscious

ACT FAST

CALL 911

• Move person to a cooler area
• Loosen clothing and remove extra layers
• Cool with water or ice

Heat exhaustion can lead to heat stroke.

Heat stroke can cause death or permanent disability if emergency treatment is not given.

Stay Cool, Stay Hydrated, Stay Informed!

OVERBOARD RESCUE

Sailors must know how to react quickly to a person in the water (PIW). While two methods of rescuing a *PIW* under sail are presented, if you have an outboard, be prepaired to use it. Make sure there are no lines in the water before starting it. Both methods involve the following eight steps:

▶ Shout **"CREW OVERBOARD!"** or **"MAN OVERBOARD"** *(MOB)*
▶ Get buoyancy to the person in water.
▶ Keep the PIW in sight.
▶ Sail back to the PIW.
▶ Stop the sailboat alongside the PIW.
▶ Make contact with the PIW.
▶ Attach the PIW to the sailboat.
▶ Bring the PIW aboard and provide aftercare.

FIGURE-8 RESCUE

The *Figure-8 rescue* method avoids jibing for better control in *heavy weather* during a recovery; however, it's crucial to maintain constant visual contact with the Person In Water (PIW). Follow these steps in a Figure-8 rescue:

1. Yell **"CREW OVERBOARD"** or **"MAN OVERBOARD"**, appoint a spotter, throw floatation.
2. Immediately get on a beam reach. Trim the mainsail and leave the jib as is.
3. Sail 3-4 boat lengths away on the beam reach.
4. Tack from the beam reach to a deep broad reach (~240°). Allow the jib to backwind.
5. Once on a deep broad reach, furl or release the jib.

☐ **Alert** - Loudly alert those around you by saying "Crew Overboard!"

☐ **Visual Contact** - Keep your eye on the person, point if possible.

☐ **Turn** - Return to the person.

☐ **Safety Position** - Stop in safety position with the person on your leeward side.

☐ **Attach** - Make contact and attach the PIW to the sailboat.

☐ **Rescue** - Retrieve PIW.

NOTES:
⊕ Most generic method; can be used from any point of sail, light or heavy winds, full crew or shorthanded, big or small boat.

⊕ Good method for new sailors, because it does not involve jibing.

6. Test your relationship to the wind and PIW by pointing the sailboat directly at the PIW. If you headed up too early and the mainsail is not luffing completely, immediately bear away to a deep broad reach again.

7. Sail downwind a short distance and test again.

8. Sail back to the PIW when the course back is a close reach, using the mainsail for power as needed. Recover the PIW on the leeward side.

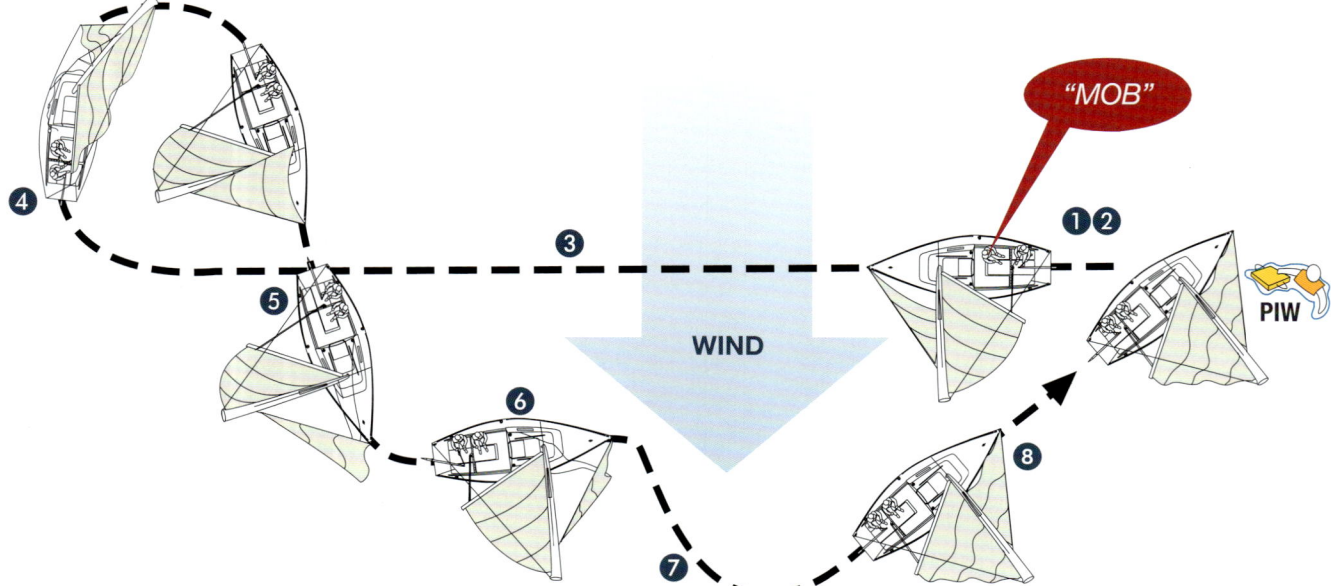

"MOB"

WIND

PIW

99

QUICK-STOP RESCUE

The hallmark of the *Quick-Stop* recovery method is the immediate reduction of boat speed by turning in a direction to windward and thereafter maneuvering at a modest speed, remaining near the PIW. This rescue requires these steps:

1 Yell **"CREW OVERBOARD"** or **"MAN OVERBOARD"**, appoint a spotter, throw floatation.

2 Immediately alter course to close-hauled and trim sails accordingly.

3 Hold your close-hauled course for approximately two (2) boat lengths.

4 Tack, but do not adjust the sails.

5 Keep the PIW directly abeam as you slowly bear away. Keep the same distance from the PIW (about 2-3 boatlengths). Do not spiral inward toward the PIW.

6 When the jib jibes, furl or release it. When the main gybes, release it.

7 Point the boat at the PIW. You should now be in a position to sail back to the PIW on a close reach, using the mainsail for power as needed. Recover the PIW on the leeward side.

NOTES:

⊕ The boat remains close to the PIW.

⊕ In most cases, the only thing that you have to do to the sails is release them.

⊖ In heavy air, it may be difficult for light boats to bear away without easing the main.

⊖ Most applicable when already closed-hauled.

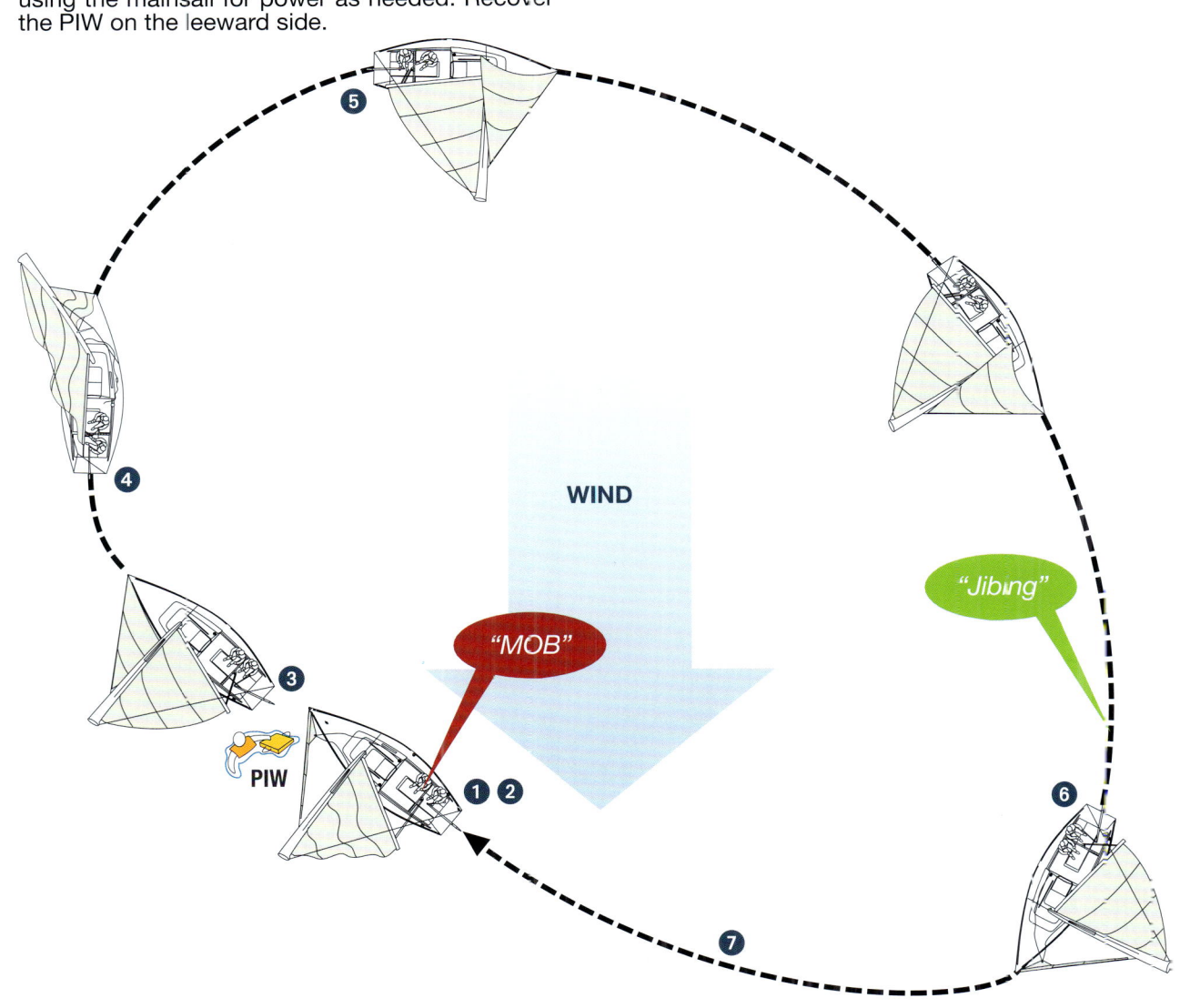

ATTACHMENT

After maneuvering the boat back along-side the PIW, it is imperative that the PIW be attached to the sailboat. This should be done so that the sailboat and PIW do not drift apart, necessitating another return. Do not rely on the PIW holding onto a line. In descending order of preference, here are some methods:

▶ Use a Lifesling, if you have one.
▶ Use the "D" rings of an inflatable harness (if being worn) to secure the PIW to the sailboat.
▶ Tie a bowline around the PIW.
▶ Once the PIW is attached, you may need to drop the sails. Do not leave the PIW tied to the sailboat unattended.

RETRIEVAL

This is considerably easier if there are more than two crew members left aboard to assist. On a sailboat with low freeboard, the crew can often drag the PIW aboard. In flat water, and if the sailboat has a scoop/swim platform, the PIW can be lifted up over the stern. If shorthanded, you may need to improvise some method to aid in the retrieval:

▶ A line over the side with a bowline tied in the end to act as a stirrup. Any lines over the side should be tied onto the sailboat on the opposite side from the PIW so they can help pull themselves onboard.
▶ A line over the side with a series of loops tied at intervals so the PIW can assist themselves or even climb back aboard unassisted.
▶ A paddle over the side tied in the middle so it becomes a "T" bar for the PIW to stand or sit on.
▶ A block and tackle (preferably four parts) rigged to a pre-hoisted halyard that is then used to lift the PIW from the water.

NOTE: If you are unable to retrieve the PIW, ensure that the PIW is securely attached to the sailboat, and call for help on the VHF radio ch.16 (**"MAYDAY"**), or attract the help of a passing sailboat.

AFTERCARE

Be aware that the PIW may be suffering from hypothermia or some other injury. Get the PIW back ashore as soon as possible and treat this as a serious first aid issue.

VHF COMMUNICATIONS

Your smartphone can be used for many communications on the water and can give you access to marine weather forecasts. But what if you want to communicate with a boat(s) near you and you don't know their phone numbers?

A VHF (Very High Frequency) radio provides voice communication with nearby boats or your sailing center. VHF radio range is "line of sight", so typically doesn't go around hills. The distance it reaches is limited by the power of the unit and the antenna height. Hand-held VHF radios typically have ranges of only a few miles, while "fixed-mount" radios installed on board with an antenna at the top of the mast reach further.

SKILL EVALUATION

☐ **VHF Radio Channels** - Identify two important VHF radio channels for communication and safety: VHF channel of your sailing center and VHF Channel 16 monitored by the U.S.C.G.

☐ **Monitoring Weather** - Demonstrate how to check weather conditions using VHF radio.

☐ **Radio Check** - Demonstrate how to use the VHF radio to make a radio check (key mic, call "radio check" three times, followed by your sailboat's name, release mic).

☐ **Radio Hail** - Demonstrate how to use a VHF radio to hail another boat (key mic, call other "(vessel name three times)", say "this is (vessel name three times)", say "over" and release mic).

☐ **Safety Phrases** - "MAYDAY", Used when a person or vessel is in imminent danger.

VHF RADIOS OFFER MULTIPLE CHANNELS

Beginner sailors should know at least three of those channels. Your VHF radio may also have a red emergency distress button. To activate, press and hold down until you hear a beep. When the U.S.C.G. receives your distress call, your VHF radio will automatically switch to channel 16.

1 Channel 16 is the universal hailing and distress channel.

That means if you want to call another boat, you would use this channel and hail them by their boat name. Except in an emergency, upon receiving a response, advise the other boat to switch to a non-commercial working channel (68, 69, 71, 72, and 78) to continue your conversation. Channel 16 is continuously monitored by the U.S. Coast Guard.

In the case of a life-threatening emergency, you would use channel 16 to start your broadcast by saying the word "MAYDAY" three times, followed by "This is" and "(your boat name three times)". Then you would provide your location, vessel description, and the nature of your emergency.

Emergency call on Ch. 16 Example:
"Mayday, Mayday, Mayday. This is Lead balloon, Lead balloon, Lead balloon"

This is followed by your distress message - remember the 3Ws: who you are, where you are, what is your emergency, assistance desired, and any other information to help.

You should have your VHF radio on channel 16 while you are out on the sailboat, in case someone wants to reach you, or if there is another vessel in distress.

It's a good idea to test your VHF radio regularly by asking for a "radio check" on a working channel such as that used by your sailing school, but **DO NOT** do the radio check on Channel 16.

2 If your sailing school/club or marina has a specific VHF channel that they monitor, you will want to know that channel to reach them directly.

3 VHF radios also have weather channels that can give you marine weather forecasts. On many radios, you toggle to the weather bands with a button labeled "WX".

BASIC USE OF VHF

1 For a fixed-mount VHF, ensure the electrical panel switch for the radio is 'on'.

2 Turn on the VHF radio unit.

3 Switch to the appropriate channel.

4 Adjust the volume and then the squelch control by turning it down just under the crackling sound.

5 Use the "push to talk" (PTT) button on the side of the microphone to talk.

6 When finished talking, say "Over" and release PTT button to listen.

SKILL EVALUATION

☐ **Highwires** - Always check for overhead power lines.

☐ **Lightning** - Prepare for lightning hazards, review weather forecast.

☐ **Distress** - Demonstrate a distress signal or display a distress flag on your sailboat.

Floating electronic hand flare

LIGHTNING AND DISTRESS SIGNALS

DISTRESS SIGNALS

▶ Using the VHF radio distress button.
▶ Slowly and repeatedly waving both outstretched arms.
▶ An electronic hand flare.
▶ A smoke signal giving off orange-colored smoke.
▶ A rocket parachute flare or a hand flare.
▶ Rockets or shells, throwing red stars, fired one at a time at short intervals.
▶ Flashlight or other device signaling SOS (dot-dot-dot, dash-dash-dash, dot-dot-dot) in the Morse Code.
▶ Continuous sounding of a horn.
▶ "**Mayday**" spoken over a VHF Radio, Ch 16.
▶ A signal consisting of a square flag having above or below it a ball or anything resembling a ball.
▶ A high intensity white light flashing at regular intervals from 50 to 70 times per minute.
▶ Signals transmitted by an Emergency Position-Indicating Radio Beacon (EPIRB).

USE AND REGULATIONS FOR FLARES

Pyrotechnic flares fired from a pistol or launcher are visible over the horizon day or night. Handheld flares can pinpoint your location for rescuers but should be held downwind and used with great caution. An electronic flare and flag are certified to meet the applicable U.S. Coast Guard requirements allowing them to be carried in lieu of traditional pyrotechnic flares on most recreational boats. The U.S. Coast Guard requires vessels over 16 feet to have three daylight and three night flares or three combination daylight/night devices. They should be stowed in a readily available location, and their expiration date should be checked during your pre-sail check list.

ELECTRICAL HAZARDS

While there are hazards on the water and on your boat, there's one very important hazard you need to look up to see.

Electrical power lines can be deadly! Make sure you have the proper clearance before crossing under power lines, especially when moving boats on trailers onshore. Remember to take into account higher water levels from tides, river runoff, or recent rains.

Another electrical danger in some regions is lightning. Should you be overtaken by a lightning storm, you should head immediately for port and keep your crew away from the mast and any metal or electrical components aboard your boat.

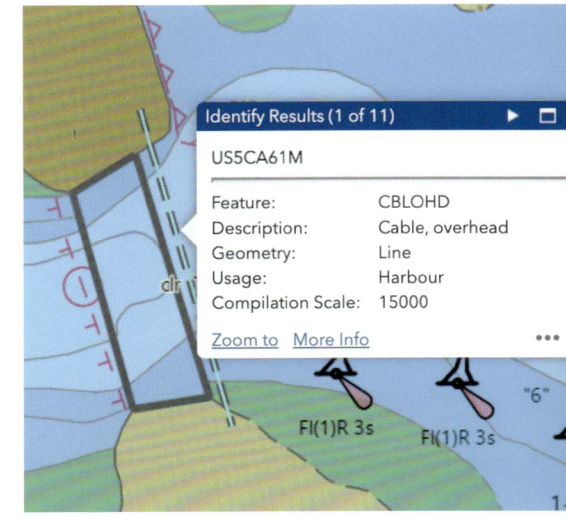

RUNNING AGROUND AND TOWING

RUNNING AGROUND

Running aground happens to almost every sailor at some time. If you run aground on a soft, muddy bottom with a rising tide, you'll float off easily with no damage to the boat.

SKILL EVALUATION

☐ **Running Aground** - Use sails and crew weight to heel sailboat.

☐ **Single Line Tow** - Explain how to accept a single-line tow.

☐ **Seamanship** - Be conscious of hazards in your sailing area and restricted zones.

Chapter 8 | Health, Safety, and Emergencies

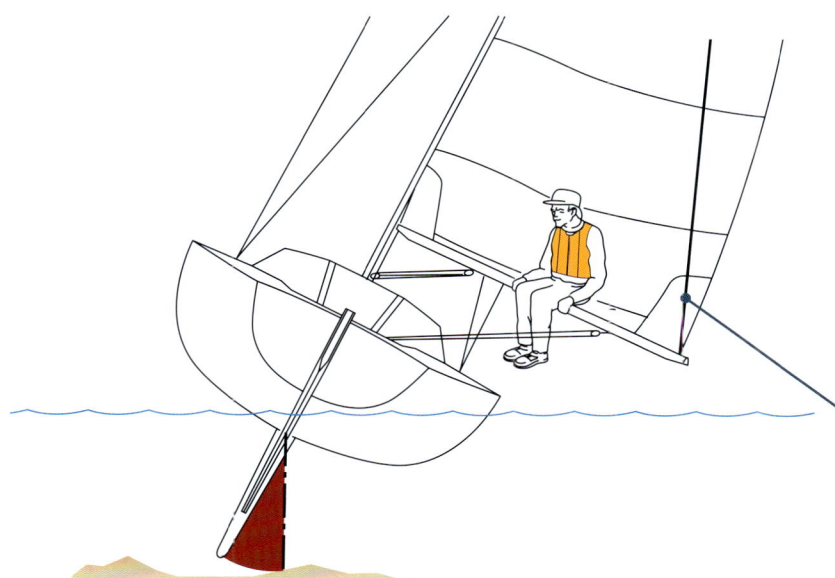

If you get stuck, use the sails and crew weight to heel the sailboat. You may have to get some crew members to sit on the boom and slowly swing it out over the side to tilt the sailboat enough to raise the keel off the bottom.

NOTE: You will need to support the end of the boom with a topping lift or spare halyard.

ACCEPTING A TOW

You may need to accept a tow from a powerboat due to lack of wind, equipment failure, weather, excessive current, etc. Sailboats may be towed either *"astern"* or *"alongside"*. Towing procedures vary by type of boat and conditions. You should agree on the towing plan with the person towing you ahead of time (perhaps by VHF or phone), including expectations about compensation.

The basic procedures for towing are as follows:

▶ Ensure all of your crew are in life jackets and briefed on the plan.

▶ Furl or lower the jib.

▶ Secure one end of a long line to the sailboat; a cleat hitch to a strong bow cleat or a round turn and two half hitches around the mast (unless it is 'deck-stepped').

▶ Feed the rest of line forward, clear of all obstuctions then aft outside the shrouds to the cockpit so that it is ready to give to the towing boat.

▶ When close enough, heave the line to the towboat.

▶ Lower and secure your mainsail as needed.

▶ Ensure everyone is seated in the cockpit before the line comes tight!

▶ Remain at the *helm* of your sailboat, steering towards the stern of the towboat.

▶ Don't let anyone stand next to or in line with the tow line, in case it breaks and snaps back.

▶ You may need to quickly release your towline.

ADDITIONAL SAILING EMERGENCY PROCEDURES

KNOCKDOWNS

A *knockdown* is when a sailboat heels over so far that one of its spreaders touches the water. This usually happens because it has been carrying too much sail for high wind conditions or because of a mistake by the driver or crew.

To recover from a knockdown:
▶ Release the sheets and the boom vang.
▶ Get the crew up to the windward rail.
▶ If the rudder responds, head up until the sails luff.

SWAMPING

A knockdown may cause the boat to fill with water if hatches are left open.

If your boat becomes swamped:
▶ Release the sheets.
▶ Lower the sails.
▶ *Bail* with buckets and *bilge* pump.

SINKING
If your boat is taking on water and is in danger of sinking:
▶ Make sure everyone is wearing a life jacket.
▶ Bail with buckets and bilge pump.
▶ If the boat has been holed, try to find the source of the leak and plug it.
▶ Try to sail to shore and run it aground before it goes down.
▶ If the boat becomes completely *swamped* with decks awash, and it looks like it will sink, DO NOT leave the boat...let it leave you by going down.
▶ Make sure you are not tangled in any lines.

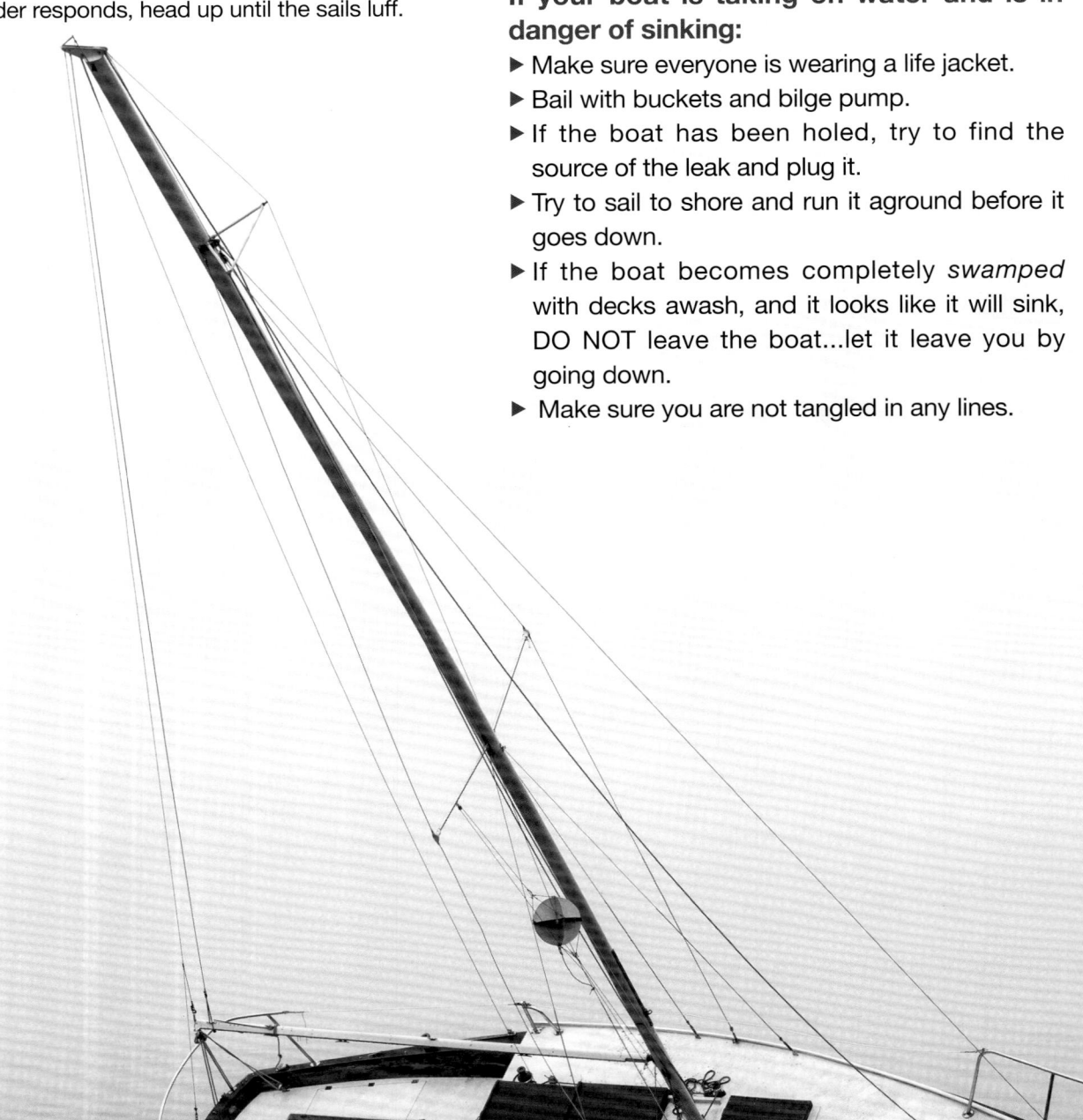

PUTTING IT ALL TOGETHER

SUMMARY

- A crew briefing promotes a safe sailing experience, covering essentials like clothing, life jackets, boat dynamics, the crew's roles, and emergency procedures.
- Promote crew comfort by anticipating weather changes, dressing appropriately, staying hydrated, and staying vigilant to emergencies and the onset of seasickness.
- React swiftly to a crew overboard; yell "Crew Overboard", provide buoyancy, maintain visual contact, return the sailboat, stop alongside, and bring them back aboard. Be prepared to mark a GPS location and make a Mayday call.

- Use VHF radios for on-water communication with nearby boats or sailing center. Note: Range is limited by power and line-of-sight.
- In a life-threatening emergency, use VHF radio channel 16, say "Mayday" three times, followed by your boat name and location, description, and the nature of the emergency.
- Be aware of overhead electrical hazards.
- When accepting a tow, don't let anyone stand next to or in range of the tow line in case it snaps or breaks.
- If the sailboat seems to be sinking, do not abandon the sailboat until it sinks.

KEY TERMS AND CONCEPTS

1. Filing a **float plan** entails informing someone on shore about your sailing plan, offering essential information for authorities or others in case of difficulties.
2. Swift rewarming from hypothermia can trigger dangerous heart rhythms.
3. **Mayday** means an imminent life-threatening situation.
4. **Channel 16** is the universal hailing and distress channel monitored by the U.S.C.G.
5. A **radio check** is an important safety measure. Do NOT do the radio check on Channel 16; use a working channel, e.g., 68, 69, 71, or 72.

CHECK YOUR UNDERSTANDING

1. What is one of the steps advised when rescuing a crew member who has fallen overboard?

   ○ a. Steer your sailboat back to shore for help.
   ○ b. Shoot flares so that your vessel can be located.
   ○ c. Assign a spotter to keep visual contact of the PIW.
   ○ d. Call your local U.S.C.G. office before heading back to the PIW.

2. What should you do after receiving a response when hailing another boat on Channel 16?

   ○ a. Continue the conversation on Channel 16.
   ○ b. Switch to a non-commercial working channel to continue communication
   ○ c. Turn your VHF radio off and back on.
   ○ d. Wait for the U.S. Coast Guard to instruct you on what to do next.

GLOSSARY OF SAILING TERMS

A

Abeam - off the side of (at right angle to) the boat.
Aboard - on the boat.
Aft - at or toward the stern or behind the boat.
Aground - a boat whose keel is touching the bottom.
Aids to Navigation (ATON) - buoys and beacons that indicate channels or show the location of submerged hazards.
Amidships - toward the center of the boat.
Apparent wind - the speed and direction of the wind felt aboard a moving boat.
Astern - behind the stern of the boat.
Athwartships - across the boat from side to side.
Auxiliary power - sailboat with either an outboard or inboard engine.

B

Backstay - the standing rigging running from the stern to the top of the mast, keeping the mast from falling forward.
Back - to stop or to propel a boat backward by holding the clew of a sail out to windward.
Bail - to empty a boat of water.
Balance - the capability of a boat to sail straight without changing the tiller position.
Ballast - weight in the keel of a boat that provides stability.
Batten - a thin slat that slides into a pocket in the leech of a sail, helping it hold its shape.
Beam - the width of a boat at its widest point.
Beam reach - (point of sail) sailing in a direction at approximately 90 degrees to the wind.
Bear away - to fall off, head away from the wind.
Bearing - the direction from one object to another expressed in compass degrees.
Beating - a course sailed upwind.
Below - the area of a boat beneath the deck.
Bend - to attach a sail to a spar or a headstay, or to attach a line to a sail.
Bight - a loop in a line.
Bilge - the lowest part of the boat's interior, where water on board will collect.
Bitter end - the end of a line.
Blanket - to use a sail or object to block the wind from filling a sail.
Block - a pulley on a boat.
Boat hook - a pole with a hook on the end used for grabbing hold of a mooring or retrieving something that has fallen overboard.
Boat speed - the speed of a boat through the water.
Bolt rope - the rope sewn into the foot and luff of some mainsails and the luff of some jibs by which the sails are attached to the boat.
Boom - the spar extending directly aft from the mast to which the foot of the mainsail is attached.
Boom vang - a block and tackle system which pulls. the boom down to assist sail control.
Bottom - 1. - the underside of the boat. 2. - the land under the water.
Bow - the forward part of the boat.
Bow line (BOW - line) - a line running from the bow of the boat to the dock or mooring.

Bowline - (BOE-lin) - a knot designed to make a loop that will not slip and can be easily untied.
Breast line - a short dockline leading off the beam of the boat directly to the dock.
Broach - an uncontrolled rounding up into the wind, usually from a downwind point of sail.
Broad reach - (point of sail) sailing in a direction with the wind at the rear corner of the boat (approximately 135 degrees from the bow).
Bulkhead - a wall that runs athwartships on a boat, usually providing structural support to the hull.
Buoy - a floating marker.
Buoyancy - the ability of an object to float.
By the lee - sailing on a run with the wind coming over the same side of the boat as the boom.

C

Cabin - the interior of a boat.
Can - an odd-numbered, green, flat-topped buoy marking the left side of a channel as you return to port.
Capsize - to tip or turn a boat over.
Cast off - to release a line when leaving a dock or mooring.
Centerline - the midline of a boat running from bow to stern.
Chafe - wear on a line caused by rubbing.
Chainplates - strong metal plates which connect the shrouds to the boat.
Channel - a (usually narrow) path in the water, marked by buoys, in which the water is deep enough to sail.
Chart - a nautical map.
Charter - to rent a boat.
Chock - a guide mounted on the deck through which docklines and anchor rode are run.
Choke - a control for starting the outboard, which changes the fuel/air ratio.
Chop - rough, short, steep waves.
Cleat - a nautical fitting that is used to secure a line.
Cleat hitch - the knot used to secure a line to a horn cleat
Clew - the lower, aft corner of a sail. The clew of the mainsail is held taut by the outhaul. The jib sheets are attached to the clew of the jib.
Close-hauled - the point of sail that is closest to the wind.
Close reach - (point of sail) sailing in a direction with the wind forward of the beam (about 70 degrees from the bow).
Clove hitch -a knot used to attach a line to a spar or other round object.
Coaming - the short protective wall surrounding the cockpit.
Cockpit - the lower area in which the steering controls and sail controls are located.
Coil - to loop a line neatly so it can be stored.
Come about - see tack.
Companionway - the steps leading from the cockpit or deck to the cabin below.
Compass - the magnetic instrument which indicates the direction in which the boat is headed.
Cooling water outlet – The place where the cooling water exits the outboard. Seeing this discharge verifies water circulation.
Course - the direction in which the boat is steered.
Crew - besides the skipper, anyone on board who helps sail the boat.

Crew Briefing - a meeting where members of a sailing crew discuss and coordinate various aspects of their roles, responsibilities, and plan for a specific sailing activity or race.

Crowning – the process of securing a coiled line.

Cunningham - a line running through a grommet about eight inches up from the tack of a mainsail that is used to tighten the luff of the sail.

Current - the horizontal movement of water caused by tides, wind and other forces.

D

Daysailer - a small sailboat.

Dead downwind - sailing in a direction straight downwind.

Deck - the mostly flat surface area on top of the boat.

Deep broad reach - sailing as far down wind as possible with both sails still full of wind.

Depower - to release the power from the sails by allowing them to luff or making them flatter. This is done to reduce heel.

Dinghy - a small sailboat or rowboat.

Displacement - the weight of a boat; therefore the amount of water it displaces.

Dock - 1. - the wooden structure where a boat ma be tied up. 2. - the act of bringing the boat to rest alongside the structure.

Dockline - a line used to secure the boat to the dock.

Downhaul - a line used to pull down on the movable gooseneck on some boats to tighten the luff of the mainsail. The Cunningham has the same function on other boats.

Downwind - away from the direction of the wind.

Draft - the depth of a boat's keel from the water's surface.

Driver - the person responsible for steering the boat.

E

Ease - to let out a line or sail.

Ebb - an outgoing current.

Engine cut-off switch - Emergency Button or switch that stops the outboard.

F

Fairlead - a fitting that guides a jib sheet or other lines back to the cockpit or along the deck.

Fairway - a channel.

Fake - to lay out a line on deck using large loops to keep it from becoming tangled.

Fall off - see Head down.

Fast - secured.

Fathom - a measurement of the depth of water. One fathom equals six feet.

Fender - a rubber bumper used to protect a boat by keeping it from hitting a dock.

Fend off - push off.

Fetch - a course on which a boat can make its destination without having to tack.

Fitting - a piece of nautical hardware.

Figure-8 knot - a knot designed to act as a stopper in the end of a line that takes the form of an eight.

Figure-8 rescue - a manuever used to return to a person or object in the water.

Float Plan - a brief description of your intended boating activity that is left with a trusted friend, family member, or sailing club office. A float should include the vessel's name and description, names of persons onboard, destination, planned time of return, and cell phone number on board.

Flood - an incoming current.

Flooding - a vessel taking on water.

Following sea - waves hitting the boat from astern.

Foot - the bottom edge of a sail.

Foredeck - the part of a boat's deck forward of the mast.

Fore - forward.

Forepeak - a storage area in the bow (below the deck).

Foresail - a jib or a genoa.

Forestay - the standing rigging running from the bow to the mast to which, the jib is hanked on.

Forward - toward the bow.

Fouled - tangled.

Foul-weather gear - water-resistant clothing.

Freeboard - the height of the hull above the water's surface.

Fuel line - tubing that carries fuel from the fuel tank to the outboard.

Full - not luffing.

Furl - to fold or roll up a sail.

Furling line - a control line led from the furling drum to the cockpit, used to turn the drum and control the size of the jib.

G

Gaff - on some boats, a spar along the top edge of a four-sided sail.

Gear - generic term for sailing equipment.

Gear lever – shift lever on an outboard used to select forward, neutral, or reverse gear.

Genoa - a large jib whose clew extends aft of the mast.

Give-way vessel - the vessel required to give way to another boat when they may be on a collision course.

Glide zone - the distance a sailboat takes to coast to a stop.

Gooseneck - the strong fitting that connects the boom to the mast.

Green Beacon - is a square, odd-numbered green sign mounted to a piling that marks the left side of a channel when returning from sea.

Grinding - the movement of the winch handle that rotates the barrel of the winch.

Grommet - a reinforcing metal ring set in a sail.

Ground tackle - the anchor and rode (chain and line).

Gudgeon - a fitting attached to the stern of a boat into which the pintles of a rudder are inserted.

Gunwale (GUN-el) - the edge of the deck where it meets the topsides.

Gust - see puff.

H

Halyard - a line used to hoist or lower a sail.

Hank - a snap hook that is used to connect the luff of a jib onto the forestay.

"Hard a-lee" - the command given to the crew just prior to tacking.

Hard over - to turn the tiller as far as possible in one direction.

Hatch - a large covered opening in the deck.

Haul in - to tighten a line.

Head - 1. - the top corner of a sail. 2. - the bathroom on a boat. 3. - the toilet on a boat.

Headboard - the reinforcing small board affixed to the head of a sail.

Header - a wind shift which makes your boat head down or sails to be sheeted in.

Heading - the direction of the boat expressed in compass degrees.

Head down - to fall off or bear away, changing course away from the wind.

Head off - see head down.

Head up - to come up, changing course toward the wind.

Headsail - a jib, genoa, or staysail.

Headstay - the standing rigging running from the bow to the mast.

Head-to-wind - the course of the boat when the bow is dead into the wind.

Headway - progress made forward.

Heave - to throw.

Heave-to - to hold one's position in the water by using the force of the sails and rudder to counter one another.

Heavy weather - strong winds and large waves.

Heel - the lean of a boat caused by the wind.

Helm - the tiller.

High side - the windward side of the boat.

Hike - to position crew members out over the windward rail to help balance the boat.

Holding ground - the bottom ground in an anchorage used to hold the anchor.

Hove-to - a boat that has completed the process of heaving-to, with its jib aback, its main loosely trimmed, and its rudder securely positioned to steer it close to the wind.

Hull - the body of the boat, excluding rig and sails.

Hull speed - the theoretical maximum speed of a sailboat determined by the length of its waterline.

I

Inboard - inside of the rail of a boat.

In irons - a boat that is head-to-wind, making no forward headway.

J

Jib - the small forward sail of a boat attached to the forestay.

Jibe - to change direction of a boat by steering the stern through the wind.

"Jibe-ho" - the command given to the crew when starting a jibe.

Jiffy reef - a quick reefing system allowing a section of the mainsail to be tied to the boom.

Jury rig - an improvised, temporary repair.

K

Kedge off - to use an anchor to pull a boat into deeper water after it has run aground.

Keel - the heavy vertical fin beneath a boat that helps keep it upright and prevents it from slipping sideways in the water.

Ketch - a two-masted boat with its mizzen (after) mast shorter than its mainmast and located forward of the rudder post.

Knockdown - a boat heeled so far that one of its spreaders touches the water.

Knot - one nautical mile per hour.

L

Land breeze - a wind that blows over land and out to sea.

Lash - to tie down.

Lay - to sail a course that will clear an obstacle without tacking.

Lazarette - a storage compartment built into the cockpit or deck.

Lazy sheet - the windward side jib sheet that is not under strain.

Lead (LEED) - to pass a line through a fitting or a block.

Lee helm - the boat's tendency to turn away from the wind.

Lee shore - land which is on the leeward side of the boat. Because the wind is blowing in that direction, a lee shore could pose a danger.

Leech - the aft edge of a sail.

Leeward (LEW-erd) - the direction away from the wind (where the wind is blowing to).

Leeward side - the side of the boat or sail that is away from the wind.

Leeway - sideways slippage of the boat in a direction away from the wind.

Lifeline - wire supported by stanchions, around the outside of the deck to help prevent crew members from falling overboard.

Life Jacket - a piece of equipment designed to assist a wearer, who may be either conscious or unconscious, to keep afloat.

Lift - 1. - the force that results from air passing by a sail, or water past a keel, that moves the boat forward and sideways. 2. - a change in wind direction which lets the boat head up.

Line - a nautical rope.

Low side - the leeward side of the boat.

Lubber's line - a small post in a compass used to help determine a course or a bearing.

Luff - 1. - the forward edge of a sail. 2. - the fluttering of a sail caused by aiming too close to the wind.

Luff groove - the slot into which the luff of a sail is inserted.

Luff tape - an attachment to the luff of a sail consisting of a small, internal boltrope inserted into the luff groove on a roller furling system.

Lull - a decrease in wind speed for a short duration.

M

Magnetic - in reference to magnetic north rather than true north.

Mainmast - the taller of two masts on a boat.

Mainsail (MAIN-sil) - the sail hoisted on the mast of a sloop or cutter or the sail hoisted on the mainmast of a ketch or yawl.

Mainsheet - the controlling line for the mainsail.

Marlinspike - a pointed tool used to loosen knots.

Mast - the large aluminum or wooden pole in the middle of a boat from which the mainsail is set.

Masthead - the top of the mast.

Masthead fly - a wind direction indicator on top of the mast.

Mast step - the structure that the bottom of the mast sits on.

MAYDAY – An internationally recognized distress signal, only used in cases of imminent danger when immediate assistance is needed to save a life.

Mizzen - the small aftermost sail on a ketch or yawl hoisted on the mizzen mast.

Mooring - a permanently anchored ball or buoy to which a boat can be tied.

N

Nautical mile - a distance of 6076 feet, equaling one minute of the earth's latitude.

Navigational charts - navigational charts are essential maps for safe sea travel, offering details on water depths, coastlines, hazards, and aids to navigation (ATONS) produced in paper or electronic formats.

Navigation Rules - laws established to prevent collisions on the water.

No-Sail (No-Go) Zone - an area into the wind in which a boat cannot produce power to sail.

Nun - a red, even-numbered, cone-shaped buoy marking the right side of a channel as you return to port. Nuns are usually paired with cans.

O

Offshore wind - wind blowing off (away from) the land.

Offshore - away from or out of sight of land.

Off the wind - sailing downwind.

On the wind - sailing upwind, close-hauled.

Outboard - 1. - outside the rail of a boat. 2. - a portable engine.

Outhaul - the controlling line attached to the clew of a mainsail used to tension the foot of the sail.

Overpowered - a boat that is heeling too far because it has too much sail up for the amount of wind.

Overtaking - a boat that is catching up to another boat and about to pass it.

P

Pay out - to ease a line.

Performance level icon – Icon located on a life jacket inside label that indicates USCG approval for specific types of use. Standardized across the U.S and Canada

Pinching - sailing too close to the wind.

Pintle - small metal extensions on a rudder that slides into a gudgeon on the transom. The gudgeon/pintle fitting allows the rudder to swing back and forth.

PIW - abbreviation for "Person in Water" in a man overboard emergency.

Point - to steer close to the wind.

Points of sail - boat directions in relation to wind direction, i.e., close-hauled, beam reaching, broad reaching, and running.

Port - 1. - the left side of a boat when facing forward. 2. - a harbor. 3. - a window in a cabin on a boat.

Port tack - sailing on any point of sail with the wind coming over the port side of the boat.

Prevailing wind - typical or consistent wind conditions.

Puff - an increase in wind speed for a short duration.

Pull-cord starter – pull-handle with cord to start an outboard.

Pulpit - a stainless steel guardrail at the bow and stern of some boats.

Push mode - with the wind coming from behind, the sail is simply pushed forward through the water.

Pushpit - a stainless steel guardrail at the stern of some boats.

Push-pull principle - the explanation of how sails generate power.

Q

Quarter - the sides of the boat near the stern.

Quick-stop rescue - a maneuver used to return to a person or object in the water.

R

Rail - the outer edges of the deck.

Rake - the angle of the mast.

Range - the alignment of two objects that indicate the middle of a channel.

Reach - one of several points of sail across the wind.

"Ready about" - the command given to the crew to prepare to tack.

"Ready to jibe" - the command given to the crew to prepare to jibe.

Red Beacon - a triangular, even-numbered, red sign mounted to a piling that marks the right side of a channel when returning from sea.

Reef - to reduce the size of a sail.

Reefing "cringle" - A metal eye in a sail through which reefing lines are run.

Reeve - to pass a line through a cringle or block.

Rhumb line - a straight course between two points.

Rig - 1. - the design of a boat's mast(s), standing rigging, and sail plan. 2. - to prepare a boat to go sailing.

Rigging - the wires and lines used to support and control sails.

Right-of-way - the right of the stand-on vessel to hold its course.

Roach - the sail area aft of a straight line running from the head to the clew of a sail.

Rode - line and chain attached from the boat to the anchor.

Roller furling - a mechanical system to roll up a headsail (jib) around the headstay.

Rudder - the underwater fin that is controlled by the tiller to deflect water and steer the boat.

Run - (point of sail) sailing with the wind coming directly behind the boat.

Running rigging - lines and hardware used to control the sails.

S

Sail cover - the protective cover used to preserve sails when they are not in use.

Sail ties - pieces of line or webbing used to tie the mainsail to the boom when reefing or storing the sail.

Sailing in the groove – the optimal sailing angle to the wind for making best progress to windward.

Schooner - a two-masted boat whose foremast is usually shorter than its mainmast.

Scope - the ratio of the amount of anchor rode deployed to the distance from the bow to the bottom.

Scull - to propel a boat by swinging the rudder back and forth.

Scupper - cockpit or deck drain.

Sea breeze - a wind that blows over the sea and onto the land.

Seacock - a valve which opens and closes a hole through the hull for saltwater needed on board or discharge.

Secure - make safe or cleat.

Set - 1. - the direction of a current. 2. - to trim the sails.

Shackle - a metal fitting at the end of a line used to attach the line to a sail or another fitting.

Shake out - to remove a reef and restore the full sail.

Sheave - the rotating wheel inside a block or fitting.

Sheet - 1. - (noun) the line which is used to control the sail by easing it out or trimming it in. 2. - (verb) to trim a sail.

Shoal - shallow water that may be dangerous.
Shroud - standing rigging at the side of the mast.
Singlehanded - sailing alone.
Skeg - a vertical fin in front of the rudder.
Skipper - the person in charge of the boat.
Slip - a parking area for a boat between two docks in a marina.
Sloop - a single-masted sailboat with mainsail and headsail.
Sole - the floor in a cockpit or cabin.
Soundings – a measurement of water depths on a nautical chart or a boat's depth sounder.
Spar - a pole used to attach a sail on a boat, for example, the mast, the boom, a gaff.
Spinnaker - a large billowing headsail used when sailing downwind.
Splice - the joining of two lines together by interweaving their strands.
Spreader - a support strut extending athwartships from the mast used to support the mast and guide the shrouds from the top of the mast to the chainplates.
Spring line - a dockline running forward or aft from the boat to the dock to keep the boat from moving forward or aft.
Squall - a short intense storm with little warning.
Square knot - knot used for sail lashings and sail ties.
Stability - a boat's ability to resist tipping (heeling).
Stanchions - stainless steel supports at the edge of the deck which hold the lifelines.
Standing rigging - the permanent rigging (usually wire) of a boat, including the forestay, backstay, and shrouds.
Stand-on vessel - the vessel or boat with the right-of-way.
Starboard - when looking from the stern toward the bow, the right side of the boat.
Starboard tack - sailing on any point of sail with the wind coming over the starboard side of the boat.
Stay - a wire support for a mast, part of the standing rigging.
Staysail (STAY-sil) - on a cutter, a second small "inner jib," attached between the bow and the mast.
Steer - to control the direction of a boat, using the tiller or wheel, in order to maintain the desired course.
Stem - the forward tip of the bow.
Step - the area in which the base of the mast fits.
Stern - the aft part of the boat.
Stow - to store properly.
Swamped - filled with water.

T

Tack - 1. - a course on which the wind comes over one side of the boat, i.e., port tack, starboard tack. 2. - to change direction by turning the bow through the wind. 3. - the lower forward corner of a sail.
Tackle - a sequence of blocks and line that provides a mechanical advantage.
Tail - to hold and pull a line from behind a winch.
Telltales - 1. - pieces of yarn or sailcloth material attached to sails which indicate when the sail is properly trimmed. 2. - wind direction indicators attached to standing rigging.
Throttle – gas outboard engine accelerator.
Tide - the rise and fall of water level due to the gravitational pull of the sun and moon.
Tiller - a long handle, extending into the cockpit, which directly controls the rudder.

Tiller extension - a handle attached to the tiller which allows the helmsperson to sit further out to the side.
Toe rail - a short aluminum or wooden rail around the outer edges of the deck.
Topping lift - a line used to hold the boom up when the mainsail is lowered or stowed.
Topsides - the sides of the boat between the waterline and the deck.
Transom - the vertical surface of the stern.
Traveler - a track or bridle that controls sideways (athwartships) movement of the mainsail.
Trim - 1. - to pull in on a sheet. 2. - how a sail is set relative to the wind.
True wind - the actual speed and direction of the wind when standing still.
Tune - to adjust a boat's standing rigging.
Turnbuckle - a mechanical fitting attached to the lower ends of stays, allowing for the standing rigging to be adjusted.

U

Underway - to be under the power of sail or engine.
Unrig - to stow sails and rigging when the boat is not in use.
Upwind - toward the direction of the wind.
USCG - abbreviation for United States Coast Guard.

V

Vang - see boom vang.
Vessel - any sailboat, powerboat or ship.

W

Wake - waves caused by a boat moving through the water.
Water intake – opening that allows water in to cool the outboard.
Waterline - the horizontal line on the hull of a boat where the water surface should be.
Wearable - a life jacket or personal floatation device (PFD) designed to be worn, as opposed to a ring or cushion intended to be thrown.
Weather helm - the boat's tendency to head up toward the wind, which occurs when a sailboat is overpowered.
Weather side - see windward side.
Westerly Wind - wind that comes out of the West and blows toward the East. Winds are named for the direction from which they come.
Whip - to bind together the strands at the end of a line.
Whisker pole - a pole, temporarily mounted between the mast and the clew of a jib, used to hold the jib out and keep it full when sailing downwind.
Winch - a deck-mounted drum with a handle offering mechanical advantage used to trim sheets. Winches may also be mounted on the mast to assist in raising sails.
Windward - toward the wind.
Windward side - the side of a boat or a sail closest to the wind.
Wing-and-wing - sailing downwind with the jib set on the opposite side of the mainsail.
Working sails - the mainsail and standard jib.
Working sheet - the leeward jib sheet that is being used to trim the jib.

INDEX

US Sailing Basic Keelboat Certification

The Basic Keelboat graduate will have successfully demonstrated the ability to responsibly skipper and crew a simple daysailing keelboat in familiar waters in light to moderate wind and sea conditions.

Recommended Equipment: It is recommended that Basic Keelboat Certification courses and examinations be conducted on 18' to 27' daysailing sloop-rigged keelboats with tiller steering and with adequate equipment inventory to complete all required certification outcomes.

Prerequisite: There is no prerequisite for the Basic Keelboat Certification.

Certification Requirements: Basic Keelboat Certification requires the successful completion of the following knowledge and skill requirements. These requirements are expected to be able to be performed safely with confident command of the boat in familiar waters with a wind range of 5 to 15 knots. Some regions may have stronger prevailing conditions, which are acceptable if the candidate can safely control the boat and be aware of his or her limitations in these conditions. The certified candidate will be able to skipper a tiller-steered keelboat up to 27 feet in length.

Practical Skills

Preparation to Sail

1. Demonstrate ability to recognize and forecast prevailing local weather conditions.
2. Demonstrate how to properly board a boat.
3. Perform a presail check for the boat's flotation integrity, safety and legally required equipment, and crew indoctrination.
4. Demonstrate the proper rigging of the sails, halyards, sheets, blocks, and winches.
5. Check all other equipment specific to your boat not indicated above.

Crew Operations and Skills

6. Demonstrate how to put on a life jacket.
7. Demonstrate tying and use of knots: stopper knot, bowline, cleat hitch and square knot.
8. Demonstrate the use of these sail controls: halyards, sheets, Cunningham/downhaul, and outhaul.

Leaving the Dock or Mooring

9. Demonstrate appropriate helmsperson and crew coordination and skills for departure suitable to the conditions: raising sails, line handling, casting off and boathandling.

Boat Control in Confined Waters

10. Demonstrate in close quarters under sail: starting, stopping, speed control, tacking, jibing, steering control, sail luffing, the No-Sail (No-Go) Zone, getting out of irons, backing the jib, and crew coordination and communication.
11. Demonstrate sailing a predetermined closed course and maneuvering around obstacles.

Navigation

12. Point out Aids to Navigation in the harbor and local waters that you are sailing, and respond accordingly.

Navigation Rules, International-Inland

13. Demonstrate use of Navigation Rules while sailing.

Boat Control in Open Water

14. Demonstrate proper sail trim with accurate sheet adjustment of the main and headsails. Make use of the sail telltales and identify points of sail.
15. Perform a heaving-to maneuver.
16. When appropriate, demonstrate sailing "by the lee" and explain the inherent dangers involved.

Heavy Weather Sailing

17. Demonstrate how to reef and/or depower sails.

Overboard Rescue Methods

18. Properly demonstrate one of the overboard rescue methods, which is most appropriate for: your sailing ability, boat type, crew experience, wind and sea conditions, and maintaining constant visual contact with the PIW.

Safety and Emergency Procedures

19. Explain the proper procedure for using an approved distress signal.

Returning to the Dock or Mooring

20. Demonstrate appropriate helmsperson and crew coordination and skills for arrival under sail and/or power suitable to the conditions: boathandling, deploying fenders, stopping, tying up and lowering sails. Explain at least two different approach plans for other conditions.

Securing the Boat Properly

21. Demonstrate stowing of sails, rigging and equipment. Thoroughly clean the boat, and install any covers.
22. Check both the electrical and bilge systems for dock operation if required.

23. Check the locks on companionway, lockers and hatches. Make a final check of docklines, spring lines and fender placement.

Knowledge

Preparation to Sail

1. Describe personal preparation such as clothing and sun protection.

Crew Operations and Skills

2. Be familiar with the nomenclature for basic parts of the boat, sails, battens, and rigging.
3. Describe the proper use of life jackets and throwable flotation devices.
4. Describe the use of sail controls.
5. Explain potential electrical hazards such as overhead electrical wires and lightning.

Sailing Theory

6. Describe basic sailboat design, sail theory, and boat dynamics.
7. Explain how to read the wind and determine all points of sail.
8. Understand what is meant by the term "sailing by the lee" and explain the inherent dangers involved.

Leaving the Dock or Mooring

9. Understand the effects of wind, tide and currents in relation to the boat and surrounding area while preparing to get underway.
10. Describe the differences and alternatives for leaving under sail and/or power in upwind, crosswind and downwind situations.

Navigation

11. Be familiar with basic chart reading specific to your local waters.
12. Describe Aids to Navigation: buoys, daymarks, regulatory markers, and other markers specific to your local waters.

Navigation Rules, International-Inland

13. Describe the Navigation Rules, International-Inland, for stand-on and give-way sailboats and powerboats for collision avoidance and understand your state and local boating regulations.

Heavy Weather Sailing

14. Describe weather warning sources.

Overboard Rescue Methods

15. Understand the Quick-Stop and Figure-8 overboard rescue methods to include: constant visual contact with the person in water, communication, rescue plan, sequence of maneuvers, boathandling, course sailed, pickup approach and coming alongside the PIW (or simulated object).
16. Describe methods of getting a PIW on deck.

Safety and Emergency Procedures

17. Be familiar with treatment of overheating, hypothermia and seasickness.
18. Describe the use and regulations for flares.
19. Be familiar with at least six different distress and emergency signals per Navigation Rule 37.
20. Be familiar with the U.S. Coast Guard requirements for safety equipment.

Anchoring Techniques

21. Be familiar with anchoring procedures for emergency situations such as loss of boat control, sudden storms, prevention from going aground, or injured crew situations.

Returning to the Dock or Mooring

22. Describe the differences and alternatives for arrival under sail and/or power in upwind, crosswind and downwind situations.

What Can US Sailing Do for You?

US Sailing is committed to helping you discover and enjoy the beauty, relaxation, challenges and friendships of sailing. As part of this commitment we offer:

KEELBOAT CERTIFICATION SYSTEM with its various levels of training and certification:

Basic Keelboat. To responsibly skipper and crew a simple daysailing keelboat in familiar waters in light to moderate wind and sea conditions.

Basic Cruising. To responsibly skipper and crew an auxiliary powered cruising sailboat during daylight hours within sight of land in moderate wind and sea conditions.

Bareboat Cruising. To responsibly skipper, crew or bareboat charter an inboard auxiliary powered cruising sailboat within sight of land to a port or an anchorage during daylight hours in moderate to strong wind and sea conditions.

Coastal Navigation. To properly use traditional navigation techniques and electronic navigation for near coastal passage making.

Coastal Passage Making. To responsibly skipper and crew an inboard auxiliary powered cruising sailboat for coastal or offshore passages in strong to heavy conditions, including zero visibility and nighttime, in unfamiliar waters out of sight of land.

Celestial Navigation. To navigate using celestial techniques and integrating celestial with traditional navigation techniques.

Cruising Catamaran Endorsement. To responsibly skipper and crew on a cruising catamaran near shore with at least 10 knots of wind.

Offshore Passage Making. To responsibly skipper and crew an inboard auxiliary powered cruising sailboat to any destination worldwide.

Performance Sailing. To analyze, adjust and shape sails for maximum speed, and backstay and jib leads for optimum performance.

SMALL BOAT CERTIFICATION SYSTEM which is available for dinghy, daysailer and multihull sailors in two wind speed ranges: light and heavy air.

US Sailing certified instructors help you achieve new skills and knowledge using up-to-date and safe methods.

PUBLICATIONS AND RESOURCES

Course materials presented in a highly visual format to help you gain competency and confidence in your sailing skills and knowledge.

The Official Logbook, recognized nationally, to document your US Sailing certifications and experience when chartering boats nationally.

Website (ussailing.org) of resources including an extensive list of accredited US Sailing schools that use both US Sailing certified instructors and US Sailing course materials.

US Sailing Safety at Sea Courses

Racing Rules & Handicap Rating Systems

US Sailing membership makes you a part of the National Governing Body for the Sport of Sailing and provides discounts on products and services that US Sailing offers.